Unsent
Love Letters

AN ANTHOLOGY
OF WORDS LEFT UNSPOKEN

Also by R. Clift

TO FEEL ANYTHING AT ALL
TO BE REMEMBERED
TOMORROW WILL BE KINDER

UNTIL WE MEET AGAIN
YOUR THOUGHTS DESERVE A DECENT PLACE TO LIVE
THE POETRY OF WILDFLOWERS: FIELD JOURNAL
BEAUTY EXISTS SO CLOSE TO AGONY

Unsent Love Letters

AN ANTHOLOGY
OF WORDS LEFT UNSPOKEN

COMPLETE COLLECTED LETTERS EDITION

With a foreword by C. Le

Curated & edited by R. Clift

2021 | 2022

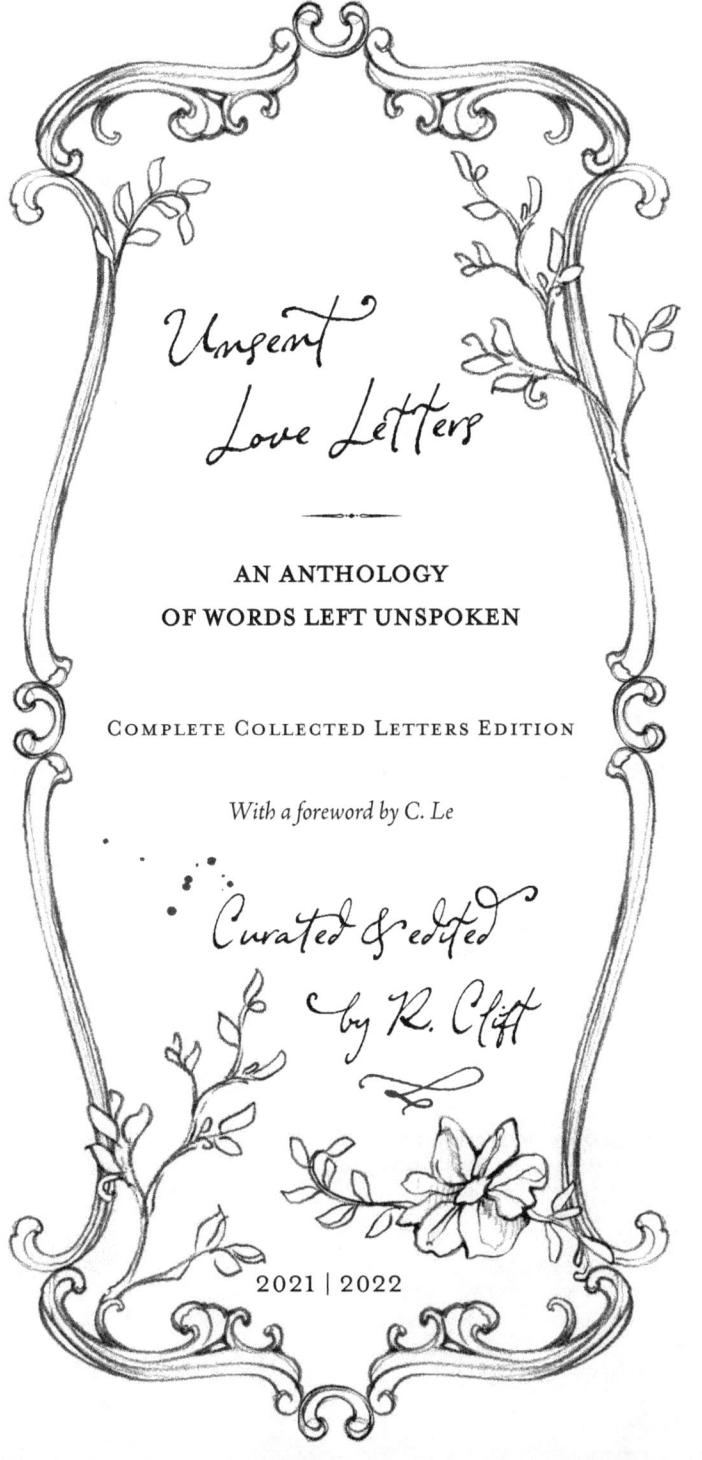

*Unsent Love Letters: An Anthology
of Words Left Unspoken*
Copyright © 2022 by Rachel Clift.
Foreword copyright © 2022 by C. Le.

All rights reserved. This book or any portion thereof may not be reproduced or used in any manner whatsoever without the express written permission of the publisher except for the use of brief quotations in a book review. For information, please contact the publisher.

ISBN: 978-1-960045-00-3 (TRADE PAPERBACK),
978-1-960045-01-0 (HARDBACK),
978-1-960045-02-7 (EBOOK).

Book cover design & interior layout by R. Clift.
Unsent love letters term concieved by C. Le.
Compiled & edited by R. Clift.
Copy edited by T.L.C. & Sarah Jeannine.

First printing edition, 2022.

R. Clift
@r.cliftpoetry
rcliftpoetry.com

To the hopeful strangers, whose letters
fill these pages with words left unspoken,
may they finally be heard.

And to you,
who is choosing to listen.

*"And so it seems I must always write you letters
that I can never send."*

SYLVIA PLATH

Contents

FOREWORD, *by C. Le*   xi
INTRODUCTION   xiii

Letters

AUTUMN   1
WINTER   69
SPRING   137
SUMMER   203

AN AFTERTHOUGHT   283
YOUR UNSENT LOVE LETTER   286
ACKNOWLEDGEMENTS   291

Foreword

*by C. Le, the author of the first unsent love letter
ever sent to R. Clift*

A few years ago, Rachel responded to one of my letters and called me a writer. At the time, and usually still— I believed that I was as far from being a writer as the sun is from the moon. So, I rolled my eyes and thought, *you might as well call me a magical fairy while you're at it.*

Yet, here I am, on a cold November evening, writing to you. Among the most popular things an average person fears more than anything is vulnerability. The fear of being vulnerable ranks even higher than shark attacks, skydiving, and death. I grew up in a quiet suburb, so I can't imagine what it would be like to share the most vulnerable parts of who I am— my inner thoughts and feelings— to a room of people, let alone in a published book, or on social media to nearly a hundred thousand people. Of course, this is just another day for my friend, Rachel Clift, having created an Instagram page dedicated to sharing her poetry with the world– her words with a soul.

It wasn't until the world shut down and I decided to write letters that I truly got to know Rachel. We began trading letters, telling one another about ourselves, our dreams, and about people who had impacted us profoundly. We began sharing words left unsaid to them, with each other. As our friendship deepened, it didn't take me long to discover what many have learned about her on social media– that she has a vibrant soul and feels deeply, that she has the innate ability to reach others with words, that she is brave and embraces her vulnerability, even when it's terrifying.

I never believed that anyone would ever read these words— my unsent love letters— they were only ever meant to be tucked away in a drawer and left to collect dust. Instead, they found their way into the hands of a poet, who saw in them something I hadn't even thought to look for. After months of correspondence, she came to me with an idea for a book— of a collection of unsent love letters— written by anonymous strangers from all over the world. We both believed there must be more people out there who needed the kind of release found with writing these letters.

I've come to realize that most of us carry around words left unspoken, to some degree. Words that were meant for someone we can no longer reach, for whatever reason. We try to ignore this, telling ourselves we tried, thinking — *oh, if only I was brave enough*, or *if only I could've had one more chance to say how I feel*, or *if the stars aligned just one more time... then I'd take that chance*. But we never feel brave enough, there's never enough chances, and the stars don't align the same way twice.

Those who have contributed letters to this book— who have shared a piece of their most vulnerable heart— know this best.

To the writers, I hope your words have freed you and that the words of other writers here may embolden you to feel again. To those who these letters are written for, wherever you are, I hope the letter that's meant for you will reach you. I hope you feel how abundantly loved you are or have been. What a gift it is, to be loved so fiercely that you are immortalized within these pages, even if you may never realize it. Whenever you look up, may the sun on your face tell you for us. May you, somehow, feel these words— this love.

And finally to you, dear reader, I'm so glad that you've picked up *Unsent Love Letters*. In these pages, you will witness the infinite ways of loving and having been loved. While reading this anthology, as you experience a small, yet profound, fraction of the kaleidoscope of souls from around the world, I can only hope that their letters help you feel a little less alone and feel a little like coming home.

I am in awe of, inspired, and encouraged by Rachel and all the contributors who were brave enough to share a piece of their soul in this anthology.

Until we meet again,

C. Le

Introduction

There's someone out there you can't talk to anymore, but there may be words left unspoken. If you could write a letter to them— that someone you love, have loved, or want to love— what would you say? In the summer of 2021, I had an idea— for a book of letters. A book of unsent love letters. I was inspired by a series of letters sent to me from a dear friend in the year prior— she's the reason this idea began.

Her name is C. Le, and in May 2020, she wrote the very first unsent love letter. At the time, we were strangers to each other. She knew only of my poetry and one day, decided to send a letter to my P.O. Box open for the purpose of readers being able to correspond with me. Within her letter to me, though, was a letter for someone else too. Someone she had lost. She had words left unspoken, and didn't quite know what to do with them. She couldn't send her letter to that someone she lost, so instead, she sent it to me.

She wrote in that first letter to me, *"Your words inspired me to write a letter though never sent, & I thought I would share that with you here…"*. What followed was her unsent love letter. Her first of six unsent love letters, sent to me over the course of several months. You may turn the pages and find her letters here, in this collection. I remember feeling inspired by her words and absolutely honored to have been trusted with such a vulnerable part of someone's heart. I sent my own unsent love letter back to her, completely enchanted by the concept. What I didn't expect was the kind of release that came with writing an unsent love letter and sending it to someone, even if it wasn't to who the letter was originally written.

This got me thinking. As a poet who's published a handful of books, I know the intention behind sharing my words. Most of the time, I put a poem out into the world, hoping it will somehow reach that one person I wrote it for. It's that hope that keeps me sharing, keeps me writing, keeps me going. I don't need to know if they read it, I just need to hope that they will.

Surely, someone else out there might do the same if they had the opportunity. Too many people walk around in this world with regrets, with things they wish they had said— and if I could offer a place for them to be heard, a reason for them to have hope— even for just one person— then I had to find a way to do so.

So, with help from C. Le and my twin sister, Laura— the concept of this anthology was brought to light. I knew this was going to be quite the endeavor, and I could only hope that maybe a few people would submit letters to be featured in these pages. What I didn't see coming, was the sheer amount of submissions I would receive— nor the absolute heartfelt beauty and diversity of the letters themselves.

We collected letters for an entire calendar year. I wanted to know if the seasons affected people's writing, and they do. I noticed patterns through the letters, the use of certain imagery, and people even submitted letters on certain dates that corresponded to events in their life. You will even read from a few writers who submitted letters to each of the four chapters, you will follow along with their story and recognize pen names and initials like old friends. You will find parts of yourself reflected in the words of strangers and it is my hope that this may help you feel a little less alone.

Without even meaning to, this anthology became an intricate and nuanced showcase of the human experience, our many kinds of relationships, all types of love, and our shared emotions. In a way, it can illustrate the idea that maybe we aren't so different after all. I'd like to think, if anything, this book can bring us closer together.

This collection contains over 280 letters written by strangers from more than 35 countries around the world. I ask you to treat these letters with respect and kindness, for it took a great deal of bravery for these writers to send them in. May you listen with an open mind, a compassionate heart, and cherish each one— as I do.

So here we are, with the first book of unsent love letters, in chapters of seasons to inspire you again and again— autumn, winter, spring, summer, written by all kinds of people, out there together— hoping with all hope that their words might make it to that one person.

Who knows— maybe one of these letters was written for you…

Rachel Clift
November 2022

May 2020

To the first person I've ever truly loved,

If you ever find yourself dreaming about the lake & finding rocks, sand between your toes, moonlight so bright it might even be sunshine in your eyes, & rain in your hair, spirits burning your throat & running through your veins, stars when you look up above, and grass way down below your feet hanging over the edge, know that you are not alone. Think back to the first time you knew, and know that I felt it too.

The ghosted city will be brought back to life with your whispers. Our veins will bleed from the seeds our hands planted pressed together, filling the crevices of our hearts that will never love the same way again. You are deserving of all the light, love, and laughter in the world.

We'll meet again in another universe where the sky would always be pink so we would take pictures when it turns blue. And again in another one where trees would grow downwards with their roots in the air, & we would bleed flowers because even the most painful parts of life can be beautiful.

And in another life, I would be patient and you would be happy, and we would meet at the age of 6, chasing the same butterfly down the street. With a whole new beginning and the ending we deserved;

when the sun sinks to where the ocean meets the sky, we won't have to wish we had time on our side.

We will meet again & again & again. After all, we are fashioned from the same star that went supernova.

The fear of losing you was keeping me here, but the truth is— I lost you long ago. Life gave me a chance to see you again, you gave me the chance to feel you again, & after so many hands, I let you feel me again too. It was as if the past two— maybe even three years had never happened. All these years and I love you still. In fact, I love you more, but the only way we fit together are the pieces of our broken hearts.

So here we are, my love; my old soul. What is left of us is the shell of a universe that no longer exists. We are silenced whispers that will never wake the vacant city. We are shattered pieces of a whole heart that will never fill to revive the veins that fulfilled our love.

Wherever you are on this lonely planet, I hope you're looking up at the stars right now. I hope you remember that we are fashioned from the same one, and that you are brilliant and bright and beautiful as the sun. As mundane as the world is without you, there's a certain comfort in knowing we're under the same sky.

To a million more supernovas, brilliant universes, intertwined lives & moments of infinite freedom.

I love you more.

C. Le

Letters

"This is my letter to the world that never wrote to me."

EMILY DICKINSON

Hamza,

With every passing day of September, I realize that soon the days won't be hot anymore. That this summer will end soon, and with this summer, my love for you will end too. I remember clearly, it was five years ago, in September of 2015, by the corner of the street. You smiled at me, and I gave my heart to it, your smile — the one that shines brighter than the daylight itself. I fell madly in love with you. I loved you persistently. For such a long time, you started to feel like a drug I couldn't live without — but more than a drug — you became a curse. My heart was sealed to you and you alone.

I have to break this curse now. I have to unlove you because, in order to love you, I had to forget how to love myself. In order to make you smile… it's been ages since I've smiled myself. So, I'll let my feelings for you burn in the last warmth of this year. September.

From now on, I'll only think about you in Septembers. How they bonded us and how they tore us apart.

Hadia
Pakistan

Dear Dad,

The leaves are falling again.

Sometimes, I sit by the window and watch them, leaf by leaf, dance through the air and kiss the earth.

How does she do it? How does Autumn make dying look so graceful? I wonder this because I've kissed death's forehead and it wasn't graceful. It was slow. Slow, like the changing colors of Autumn's hair. And I think maybe I mistook her slowness for gracefulness. Like how I often mistook your smile for happiness, and I believe had I truly given my full attention to both of those things, I'd have noticed sooner.

Autumn used to be my favorite season. I loved watching the trees change colors; loved the short days and long nights; loved feeling the breathless summer heat tiptoe into crisp moonlit evenings. But then I watched you change colors; watched your days grow shorter; felt the warmth drip from your body. You became Autumn and suddenly, it wasn't so beautiful anymore.

I sit every day watching, waiting—waiting for that last leaf to fall, like how I watched and waited for your last breath, because when you know that Winter is near, you get this innate urge to prepare. You, making me write down the songs you wanted to be played at your memorial; how you wanted your ashes scattered over water, but not the ocean because oceans had sharks and you were scared of sharks. Then there was me, making arrangements with the crematorium; calling the pastor; calling my sisters. No matter how much you try to prepare, nothing readies you for that final day of Autumn, the moment that last leaf falls and Winter steps in. And though we live in seasons as the earth does, you won't return in the Spring, but your memory will hold strong in my heart forever.

>   Most sincerely
>   your daughter,
>   Frostie
>   *United States*

M.,

Time parted us once. Decades of adolescence, breaking hearts and breaking hands, you stood alone in shadows, silence, and frustration.

Behind umber eyes, hearts hang heavy like punching bags. Your sweaty hands at a middle school dance echoing the songs stitched throughout time, hanging onto every line. Standing on the night's edge, ready to embrace the fall, time lent extended hands as two souls found their way to one another once again.

Oddly enough, trapped within those same school halls we once ran from.

The sight of your smile as it reaches up to meet your eyes, fine lines seal fates as the warmth of that smile is the light my soul chases. Your whispers reaffirm there is no one who can hurt me as the ashes inside our hearts part ways with where they were once bound.

I dream of days spent together, I in a green dress and you in a grey suit, chasing the morning sunrise until phosphorescent moon meets twilight. Sundown brings visions of sparklers against black sky as we slow dance together. You whisper in my ear, "I just get lost with you." I listen intently as you sing to me slowly, talk to me softly, teaching me the lyrics to this track. When we sing it together, it doesn't sound so bad. It doesn't feel as sad.

This is the time for one more try at a happy life. For it is within your beautiful heart I find a reflection of mine and within your arms where I feel at home. It is anywhere that you are, I will be also.

>   A.
>   *United States*

P.S. Letter to a broken soul finding love within darkness.

Dearest Kal,

Although the endless golden fields took you away from me that morning— that soft kiss lingers on my lips and I have yet to truly say farewell. Your name is still on the curve of my neck, your fingertips still trail down my back when I close my eyes. The way the moonlight wrapped around you made me wonder of the mysteries I am missing out upon. It is in this moment of reverence where butterflies had made a home in my core; an aching heart beating against the soft rise and fall of your chest.

Our time may have been but a brief moment, yet the red strings still gleam in the starlight when I look out upon this city of blue; time will tell if this story is worth the warmth that has settled into my body. However, hope waters the flowers that always seem to bloom when things feel right. Summer's end may have brought a stop to the vices of the sun, but perhaps it brought us together in a way that the world retains its colour in this cruel, cruel existence.

Insephriel
Canada

P.S. A letter to the boy who stole my heart; who left the next morning at 6 am to drive far, far away from where our story began.

Dear E.,

There are times when the world spins so quickly on its axis and the dizzying of my soul transports me to another time. When the flowers in the field bloomed just for us and the magic of the rain washed away all our sins. I held onto you so tightly that night when I fell in love and I go back to that spot often to remember the smell of your hair in the warm summer night's breeze.

Life moves on by, this I know. I see it every day while the world moves around me, the trains zoom by, the clouds blow in and out again, and the days come to a close. But my heart is still stuck in place. Frozen in the moment when our souls were bare between the pines and I laid myself on the line. The night when your soul tried to meet mine in the middle but got caught in the wind and never returned again.

My words are mostly blank now, and autumn has set in, begging of me to change with her but I cannot go. So I lay down on the pine needle blanket and let the stars cover over me as I die again with you each night.

ELLE R.
United States

P.S. An autumn letter to my heavenly daughter.

J.H.,

I left attached. I kept going and coming back— knowing I should leave but not wanting to disappoint you. I then realized that not wanting to leave in fear of disappointing you was the root issue. Your overconfidence manipulated me, till the last hour. Even though I know you may not have been aware of it. I forgot what I forgot. I forgot that I had forgotten about all my weaknesses and brokenness when I was with you. I forgot the times I have broken myself to fit into you and your values and how I left mine and myself in the corner. It's true— there were times I hadn't spoken my truth. It's true— I agreed to participate in what didn't match my core self and values. But the overconfidence, the boldness of your words. That stopped me from saying my words. How I agreed to pain. How I agreed to be part of humiliation, not to me— but to my soul. Because on the outside, it didn't look like humiliation. We were seen as youthful, with a deep emotional connection. But it was only emotions of what I thought love was. It was a humiliation to my soul for what it accepted to encounter: a love that fed my constant expectations of affection from you— rather than focusing on growing together and growing nearer to Love, to the ultimate source of love, God. How I was always afraid to choose. To choose myself. My values that I was afraid to embrace. I forgot who I am. Who I was. I only focused on how I felt with you. I lost a lot of me. I lost God on the way.

Now it's okay. I've learned that I can miss you, but I also learned the reasons why. Partly because I miss you as a person. Mostly because I loved my broken self in refuge to you. Now I am aware. Aware of what it means to love and be loved. I will not be going back to you to love you better— because the broken me has now turned into a healed me— and this healed me cannot resonate with what it got away from.

All the values, I have returned to my core, to remind me how to love myself.

This letter isn't about your flaws. It isn't about our mistakes. This is a letter to my past self that was afraid to be who she truly was and should've left from the start— from the moment she didn't feel herself around you.

Your road is different, and I need to choose mine. Your love can stay still, but my heart will live on to find what it was always meant to connect with celestially from the beginning.

And now I tell myself, only stay where you can grow.

>   J.H.
>   *Lebanon*

P.S. I'm choosing to send this letter to myself.

R.B.,
>   I have not lived in the land
>   of stars and stripes.
>   But I have travelled there,
>   over a treacherous pool of water.
>   Although unknowingly, but to
>   breathe the air of the same
>   continent, as you do.
>   I haven't seen west coast sunsets,
>   tinting the skies
>   in breathtaking hues
>   of pink, purple, and red.
>   But I have watched suns set and rise
>   from my window, transforming
>   the large canvas of blue
>   into dreamy pastels.
>   Yes, they unfailingly
>   make me think of you.
>   I have not held your hand
>   while strolling along the streets
>   with no place to go or be, enjoying
>   the shared moment; you and me.
>   But I have imagined, in fulsome detail,
>   what it would be like
>   and somehow
>   it left me with feelings of love,
>   contentment, and hope. Enough
>   to keep me going another day
>   on my own, yet your presence
>   an obvious knowing of mine.
>   I have not heard the sound of your

euphonious voice speaking my name.
But I have heard you talk and laugh
merely from recordings — but on repeat.
And I guess the familiarity in that sound
and the way your eyes glisten into the camera,
to pick up what others are blind to see,
not blinded by your acts and roles,
sensing
there's more behind this facade,
these are all signs
for me to trust, and still I'd like to know—
that feeling of certainty, I mean.

    K.J.
    Germany

P.S. A letter to someone with whom I once believed to have shared a deep bond. Words that never were spoken out loud.

O.S.,

I promised myself that I was never going to write this letter. Not out of fear that I'd get no response or that your mother would pick faults with my language. But more, I wouldn't know whether to fill it with love or hate. Whether to send you all of my best days, posted straight through your letterbox where you could feel good in knowing that we shared those smiles and held hands on nights we couldn't feel our toes. Or whether to send you the bitter pain that still lies deep in my chest, the hurt and embarrassment that you caused me in an attempt to cure your own. The years of mourning I've only just come out of, the nights that you'll never get to see.

Still, now, I don't know which version of the letter I want to own. I have forgiven you for the dirt you've thrown. I have overcome those hurdles you made sure stuck to the ground. I have watched my face change in the mirror as I have grown into the strongest woman I have ever been. I have turned my life into one I thought I'd never get to see. And for that, I should truly thank you. Tell your mother I say hello, though I am sure she's currently hovering over your shoulder. As always.

    L.G.
    United Kingdom

Dear Sebastian,

I have carried the memories of you in the deep corners of my heart. The memories lay in the foundation of my soul, preserved in the embers of my heart. A place remaining only for you, even though I will never see you again.

I look for you everywhere, always knowing I will never find you, yet I always look. The person I strive to be, the kind, deeply caring, respectful and empathic person is because that's who you believed me to be.

When I met you I was a shell, a shell of the person I used to be. My internal embers had gone out and I was existing as a body with automated reactions, not as a heart with a soul. Within the hour that I met you, I remember feeling I had found a home I had never had, a place of belonging I had been yearning for all my life. We laughed and talked about our lives, and for once, I let it be and allowed myself one simple and great act — I fell in love. You filled me up with your warm heart, your laughter, love and goodness and thus relit my internal embers. Even now, years gone past, I can feel my warm internal hearth with all those embers that you lit.

I was so fragile when we met, and maybe you knew this… Maybe this is why you filled me with such love, so much love so I could go on and flourish in the world, even though it would be without you.

I remember the day I sat on the window ledge that overlooked a courtyard garden. It was a dark night, all the lights were out and I could see the stars so brightly. As we talked over the phone, I said to you no matter where in the world you are, the stars are the stars, and everyone you love is somewhere underneath them. The world isn't such a big place after all.

I live now in the far North, and sometimes late at night when the world is asleep, I go out and sit in the dark and gaze at the bright stars and Milky Way. I always think of you and our time together when I sit beneath them. I like to imagine you sitting and smoking your cigarette on your deck overlooking the lake, while you gaze at the stars too. I wonder if you ever look at the stars and night sky and think of me. In these quiet moments with the stars, I ask them for a chance - if not in this lifetime then the next.

In our next life, we will be young when we meet, before life has carved and made something of us. When we see each other for the first time, even though we have long forgotten our memories together, our souls will light up and will know that we knew each other once before. We will live a lifetime together, laughing, making memories, having children, raising a family, and watching them grow. We will travel together far and wide, eating foreign foods, embarking on long road trips, and fulfilling the many dreams we talked about. When our souls leave our bodies, we will depart no more than a day apart as we cannot exist in the world without each other. A lifetime together sounds nice right? I think it would be nice.

I love you. I still do and always, always... will love you through this life and all the rest. So I will not worry about seeing you again in this lifetime, we will have the next one together.

That's how I would like to imagine it, anyway.

>   ANNIE
>   *Canada*

MY DEAR,

I've been wondering what it would be like to kiss you for one thousand three hundred and forty seven days. From the minute we met I have been drawn to you as the tide reaches for the moon and from the way you look for me in a crowded room, I want to believe you feel the same way too.

Or felt, at least, so long ago, for we keep saying goodbye more than anything else. I want to belong with you, but I don't. I never truly have and never truly will and maybe that's the saddest part of all. We can never find the words to say *I wish it could be you. I wish it were as simple as you.* So maybe that's why I avoid those sinking blue iceberg eyes— they draw me in, all too quickly, all too completely— and I'm afraid that if I look too long I'll drown in all of the what-ifs that wade in your gaze.

Maybe that's why I do my best to keep a little more distance than I would like. Why I close the door and sleep alone instead of walking across the hall to arms that would hold me. Why I pretend I don't know how to dance when you hold out your hand. Why I stay sitting down, eyes to the ground, when I should have twirled under those lights with you. Maybe I'm protecting myself from breaking again, from aching for someone who will never be able to choose me completely.

This mind can separate plenty, but this silly heart of mine doesn't know the difference between all these kinds of love, and any one of them could shatter me in an instant.

Maybe I should swallow my pride and tell you all of this, but I don't know where to start.

>   BIRDSONG
>   *United States*

P.S. To the sweetest blue-eyed boy I've ever known. I wish I had kissed him when I had the chance.

R.M.,

In the moment I met you— my breathing stopped with the strength of your presence. My heart danced with the sounds of your words and found its refuge in the stillness of your silence. My mind lost control of my thoughts. Meaning abandoned my words. Happiness found her home inside of me. All my eyes wanted to see was you. My biggest temptation was to have my nose on the back of your neck, under your blond hair. My fingers started to tingle, because all I wanted was to feel the warmth of your skin against my own. Every cell in me screamed that I should run non-stop to get closer to you. I realized all I really wanted was to make you feel, anything and everything.

In that moment was when you stole my heart and in that moment was when you left me.

MAYARA K.
Brazil & Japan

P.S. A love letter to someone who stopped talking to me soon after I fell in love.

TO THE BOY I HOPE TO SIT BY THE FIRE WITH,

I didn't know I'd be the one to put the peace in your backyard, my perfume making the woodsmoke taste sweet on your tongue. When the stars failed to sparkle you looked to my eyes and the cat watched us from the window.

I hoped tomorrow wouldn't exist and you wished to never hang up from the phone as the moon wondered when we would be together again.

YOUR FUTURE FRIEND,
M. C. FLORA
United States

P.S. I experienced a newfound love for the fact of the thought I'd one day have those autumn bonfires again, sitting with friends, lovers, company, family....it has such a romance to it. I thought I'd have a piece for such a feeling, and a letter to whom I'll experience it with!

October 2022

Dear Reader,

Start by leaving your European lover on a train platform. Watch him stare through the glass, wait out the 25-minute delay so he can wave goodbye. Grasp the final memory of you in his gaze until you lurch forward and glide out of sight. Forever. You will never see him again. And he probably already knows it. Yes, he knows. You've already warned him.

Every two years you disintegrate into a pile of ash and arise in a new city. A new country. Begin again and rewrite the strength of your own name. His mother called you a vagabond. Said she meant it in the best way possible and honestly you agree. Though you prefer terms like phoenix. Free spirit. Odysseus. Because the truth is there's someone, somewhere you've spent your whole life trying to get back to.

Meanwhile, you kept trying on new lives like hats and sweaters just to see how they fit, how they cushioned the ache of the arrow in your heart, how they numbered the stars and numbed the pain. But these garments are only temporary. For their many sparkling threads are so easily hung on doorknobs and fence posts and quickly unravel with every step forward. And before you know it, you are left naked and shaking, ashamed of the shape of your body after you look down and find it altered. Conformed to clothes you never much liked and were never really meant to wear.

Stripped of such costumes, you crawl under the covers, seeking warmth. Instead, you have a dream the man of your dreams is killed. Then you wake up on Valentine's day right before the whole world shuts itself down. You believe for a few hours that you are too late. That he is dead, along with the hope you've held all this time that one day, the love that felt so inexplicably forbidden and familiar will finally be yours.

So this time, you shed more layers than you ever believed you could. Hair. Nails. Teeth. Skin. Peel it all back and let yourself bleed out. Lie in a pool of yourself until you have no choice but to die or be born again out of the puddle of primordial muck and mire you have been reduced to. You regain consciousness and the landscape of your mind becomes frighteningly apocalyptic. You buy a ticket.

Pack your bags. Leave half your clothes behind to make room for your library to fly over the ocean one last time. Enlist your European lover to help you make your escape. Let him drag your fifty pounds of books through the city streets at 4am, drunken partygoers shouting as you carry the final remnants of your identity to the station. Board the train. And then the plane. Put pen to paper and divine the truth you always wished to live.

What I mean is, decide to write your own story. And wait until it eclipses reality before you cut through the dense forest of your memory and name the strange pathways that led you here. Here, to the magic mountain. To the castle in which you were fated to dwell. To the arms that pulled you in – again – after such a long voyage and so many years away. To the lips that kissed your forehead and whispered the words you had always longed to hear. *Welcome home.*

>Ever yours,
>Cheyanne
>*United States*

My dearest sweetheart,
    I am sentimental
so I walk in the rain,
to feel something,
as the drops brush
against my face.
Feelings arise and I think
of you and I at the movies,
holding hands and laughing
as the credits roll by.
I am sentimental
so I walk in the rain,
to reminisce on
times by the bay
where we kissed as the
sky turned to gold.
I am sentimental
so I walk in the rain,
to feel how much I miss you
and to make sure no one sees my pain.
— These memories of you will never be enough
to stop the pain that you scattered over me when you left,
like discarded pieces of broken pottery.

>Yours forever… or should I say no longer,
>Magic & Musings
>*England*

P.S. A lost love in Positano.

October 17th, 2021

J.R.,

I'm writing you to say that I forgive you. I forgive you for what you did to me, even though if you had the chance today I know you'd probably deny it.

I was 18 when we met, and in such a dark hole I didn't think I would ever be able to crawl my way out. And when it was all said and done you single-handedly pushed me back into that hole. You tossed me in and walked away, threw away the key, and kept the ladder. I don't forgive you for cheating on me, for lying, for breaking my trust, for making me think I was crazy. I don't forgive you for that because I don't have to, it's all so far behind us now it doesn't matter whether I forgive you or not.

What I forgive you for is what came next. For leaving me stranded in the cold on the side of the road, waiting to be picked up by our friends, the police, my family? Anyone but you. No, that is not a metaphor, that is a memory of a day so dark in my story, when not you, but your friend grabbed me in his arms and scooped me up, running across the street to drive me to the hospital, as blood ran down my arms and stained his backseat.

I couldn't stop crying, I didn't want the hospital I wanted my mom. I wanted to go home. But the problem was I didn't have a home, not any more not since you left me. But Jeremiah listened to me, he decided I probably didn't need stitches, and our friend Hannah drove us to my parent's place where I wailed and cried and stomped my feet demanding to see you. I just wanted a chance. I just wanted to talk I wanted an explanation. I wanted anything. I wanted you to give me anything, but you wouldn't, not even my dignity.

Do you remember when I left work in the middle of the day and came home to surprise you in the shower, because I had just found out about her? Do you remember sitting on the floor in our hallway crying in a towel, and when I asked you to choose her or me you said you didn't know.

Do you remember taking me to the mountains, to our favorite spot on the cliff to overlook the entire valley? We put up the hammock and talked about life, except not really. You were so cryptic. You still wouldn't tell me what you meant or what you wanted. I understand now that you just didn't know. You were just a stupid little boy who didn't understand what it meant to say "I love you" who didn't understand what it was like to break someone's heart.

Do you remember the night a few weeks before the shower, a month before the night on the side of the road, days before the mountain when you were staying at your friend Alex's house because you needed space and

I didn't know what that meant. Do you remember that night when I left to stay with my parents because I didn't want to sleep in an empty house, but you came home. You came home to a freshly made bed, with photos of us scattered all around and 100 slips of paper, written on them all the reasons I loved you. Do you remember calling me and telling me you wanted me to come home. Telling me you wanted to work this out, you wanted me and our relationship and our future. Do you remember giving me hope weeks before you would tear my life away from me?

When I talk about you now I say you are my ex-fiance. You probably think that's stupid. You never proposed. You never got down on one knee and professed your love in front of all our friends and asked me to be yours forever. You never did that, did you? But still. There was a ring. But still, there was a binder full of guest lists and color schemes. But still, we looked at venues and still, we bickered about dates, and flowers, and seating arrangements. Still, your mom and I talked about dresses and invitation ideas.

You never proposed, but still, you said your heart was for me and foolishly I handed you mine in return. I say ex-fiance because how else am I supposed to convey the devastation of you leaving.

You started dating her 12 days after we broke up. Did you know that? The girl I was told not to worry about. I remember Alex telling me not to worry, that you'd wise up eventually. "You don't marry the rebound," he said. And still, you did. It hurt at first, seeing her with you. Her snide comments in her instagram posts make me wonder what on earth you said to her about me.

It hurt. I used to like her pictures out of spite. So she knew I saw them. When I found out you were engaged, I was hurt. But so much less. I figured it would never last, and maybe I was wrong but the earth still turns, there is still time left yet.

It hurt less with another guy's tongue on my lips and his hands dancing around my hips where yours once were. It hurt way less when I saw the wedding photos.

You should know this now before I go on that by this point I harbored no ill feelings towards you. By the time you and she tied that knot I was so far moved on I was 2 years deep in another relationship that wouldn't last. But when I saw those photos...I mean come on. A church basement? She wore a tutu for gods sakes. And then crashing her family reunion cruise in place of a honeymoon?

I felt insulted. I spent months carefully crafting the perfect wedding it would have hurt less had you used the one I created! But maybe when you're truly happy you don't care. Though you always said you did. You used to dream about weddings with me, I was the one who would pull your head out of the clouds, and in the end you settled on poor lighting, too much tule, and a church freaking basement-not even the sanctuary.

Though I'm not writing to bash your wedding or hate on your relationship. I do hope you're happy. Though I wouldn't really care if you weren't. You have once again become a stranger to me, and though I may wish them well I don't think about them after they have left. Their happiness is not tied to mine, any more than yours is.

Does it hurt to know I don't think about you often? Or is it a comforting thought? I think, if you told me that you thought about me, I would feel very uncomfortable.

You leaving me the way you did. Cutting me off completely, moving out and refusing to speak to me, cuddling up with someone else after three years was exactly what I needed. The cleanest break it could have been I think. I think if it hadn't ended that way, with me cursing your name for months. Even after the heartache of the relationship was gone I cursed you for leaving me alone. I put all of myself into you so when you left I was no one. I had no future, no career, no sense of self, I was a clean slate and I hated it.

But without it, I would have never become the person I became next. Or the one after that. Or the one I am now. All the people I have been since you were important. I had to be broken down over and over again so that I could build myself up stronger and better and kinder each time. And that never would have happened if you hadn't left me in the cold. So not only do I forgive you I thank you.

I love who I am now. I love my life. I love the adventures I get to go on and I love that I don't have a life with you. I would have hated it. Everything I thought I always wanted with you could never compare to what I've had without you. So thank you.

Thank you for the freedom, I never would have chosen it myself, not back then. But now. It's all I choose.

Thank you and know that my heart at 19 will always be yours. But my life is mine.

>   With warmest regards and no regrets,
>   M.
>   *United States*

Dear K.,

They say the chances of meeting someone you like (and even someone you get along with in the first conversation) get fewer and fewer as you grow older. People you've known and befriended as a child all seem like strangers after just a few years apart. What were the odds of me finding you that day or our paths meeting at some other point in this lifetime? I'd say one in a million. How lucky I felt for the time I knew you. Compared to all the men I'd known before, you truly came to me like a breath of fresh air. I was a moth drawn to your flame, and maybe somehow I knew our time together would be short-lived but oh! How I wished you were mine until infinity.

Life happened thereafter— we moved cities, and we grew older. Something felt like it was missing, and my heart knew the something— the someone was you.

We reunited for a short spell, way after stormy seasons and grueling reality checks for both of us, yet it felt like we had never been apart.

I had you, and for the shortest time, I felt like myself again. How I wish I could go back and tell you to never go away, to keep me in your warm embrace and say you loved me as I loved you. Alas, sometimes dreams are better than reality because you vanished the same way, never to be found again. I keep hoping and wishing I could meet you again. You were the first and only one I truly fell in love with, and like all love stories, ours had an ending. A sudden and unfinished one.

I write this letter in the hope that even if not the words, at least my feelings could reach you. I give away all my love to the wind, hoping you are safe and warm wherever you are. I hope the wind finds you and caresses your cheek the way I did. I hope it calls out your name, and just for a fleeting moment, I hope you think of me.

I want you to know, whenever and if ever we are destined to meet, I'm right here where you last saw me— hoping your wave meets my shore...

Love always.

Yours,
B.B.
India

P.S. A letter to the one who got away, my first and only love.

Marcello,

When I met you, it was the first time I understood how much could be shared simply by sharing a look. I had watched my friends fall in love and had wondered if it would ever happen to me. My list of ex-boyfriends, a very short one at that, consisted of boys who I thought I had the potential to love. But I've learned not to base a relationship on potential. In you, I saw a man who was sensitive, passionate, someone who cared about dignity and loved deeply. We never shared a kiss or had any intimate relations, but you never knew how much I wanted to. When you wrapped your arms around me, it was the first time I realized that even a hug has the ability to mean "something more." I really thought you felt the same way about me. You flirted, you stayed up into the night talking, and you showed me your poetry… your poetry that I was stupid enough to think might actually be about me. All my friends said you were showing clear signs that you had feelings for me… so the night of your birthday dinner, I planned to talk to you about "us." Remember your birthday dinner? That was two years ago this week. You hadn't lived in the city long and didn't have a lot of people to celebrate with, so I invited a group of my friends to come with you and me to dinner. I paid for your meal and bought you chocolates, a warm winter scarf— because you weren't used to the cold winters, and an Uber gift card— because you didn't have a car and told me you had spent $800 on Uber rides in the past month. It wasn't perfect, but it was pretty damn close. I remember walking out to the car and feeling the air. It was cold… a couple more days, and it would be my birthday, and I thought I would surely be with you. I drove you home, and a little while later, you called me to thank me for the wonderful night. We were talking when all of the sudden, you said something that changed my life. You said, "Well, I better get going because my fiancé wants to video call."

I don't know how long I sat there staring at the wall, going through different emotions. I was confused, I was angry, I was sad… Then I took 5 shots of vodka and cried myself to sleep. Did you know how many tears I cried for you? Did you know it was the first time I got drunk? Did you know that in the past two years, I've only told two people about what happened? How you broke my heart? And you weren't even mine… After your dinner, we saw each other at the university about a week later, and then not again for another year— when you texted me to tell me that your fiancé had married another man. I wasn't sure why you told me that, but I drove to you, and we sat in the car and talked until 3 in the morning. You were so upset, and I was just sitting there thinking, "He had feelings for me. If he didn't, I wouldn't be the person sitting in the car with him in the middle of the night listening to how his heart got broken." Part of me wanted to tell you how I had felt about you. You were single now… but something had changed. I realized that no matter how attracted to you I was, I would never be able to trust you. You used me, you deceived me, and no, it wasn't in the form of sex, but you still led me on, and I would never be able to forget how pathetic I felt that night. I don't love you anymore, but I still think of you from time to time. Because there was something there… there was electricity between us that people only read about in romance novels. And I wonder what you're up to, or if you graduated and are an engineer now, or if you've found someone else. I wonder if you ever think of me.

> VALENTINA
> *Ohio, United States*

P.S. A letter to my first love.

DEAR SELF,
Don't lose hope,
have a little faith.
Not on others,
but on yourself.
You are like that star you gaze at every night,
that star is looking at you to see your light,
and shine with you for life.
Don't lose hope,
have a little faith.
We are all stars,
meant only to shine,
even during our most shattering times.

> ROMA
> *India*

P.S. A poem from my present self to my past self.

TO MY FIRST KISS,
It was silly, wasn't it? To think I was more than a passing romance. Now I see how silly it all was— but in the moment— you were the handsome prince in my fairytale. I spent years, you know, so worried about my first kiss. Wanting it to be perfect— afraid I'd mess up— terrified of whoever would come along, wondering, for far too long, if I was even worth kissing. I remember when I was 10 or 11, I read in a Tiger Beat magazine that most people have their first kiss by age 13 or 14 and that terrified me. And then after 13, 14, 15, 16 passed— I felt embarrassed and I felt like I was falling behind. But mainly, still terrified. When I was 17, I was told "you're not the kind of girl people fall in love with." And when you're 17— you believe

something like that. I carried it with me every day after, darker than my shadow.

You were the first person to make me question if it was true— and I really I needed that. God— I was 20 at the time— and you were 26. You never knew you were my first kiss. I never told you. I know it probably should have happened long before and I'd be lying if I said it didn't make me feel insecure, but I must admit, you were worth the wait. You were exhilarating.

Now I'm 26 and we haven't seen each other since the day you left town six years ago. It was raining— I remember watching you run out onto the sidewalk and jump into a taxi to take you to the airport. I remember knowing in my bones, I'd never see you again. I was right.

I guess I'll always wonder what you thought of me in the short time we knew each other— although— I'm pretty sure I know the answer. I was a small-town young thing that was cute and intriguing— but you didn't want to get too attached. You were a big New York City actor auditioning for Broadway shows and living in Brooklyn and walking around with a confident air about you that was intoxicating. You didn't want to get too attached because you knew you'd be leaving. I could feel you putting walls up, I should've done the same, but the day you left broke my heart anyway.

At least— now— I have a damn good first kiss story— even though no one really asks for those stories anymore. It's amazing how little people in their late 20's care— about anything. Now I understand how it was so easy for you to leave with an absent-minded goodbye. The thing is— now— I bet I'd do the same. Running out into the rain, never looking back, forgetting his name with every step forward.

Maybe that's why I can't even be mad about you leaving and never speaking another word to me— I can't find a part of me to care enough to get mad. I don't know what that says about me, and I don't know if it's any good.

Dia
United States

Dear Stranger,

It was one of the first crisp days of fall. The wind was blowing wild and more and more leaves were falling on the streets.

As much as I usually enjoy stormy weather, it really annoyed me on this particular Thursday afternoon while I was in this giant, unknown city, trying to find my way to Central Station. I was stressed and a little late. My soft coat was wet and heavy from the rain and my suitcase stopped me from moving quickly, as I kind of needed to do. When I finally arrived in the halls of Central Station, I took the beanie off my head and surveyed the next train arrivals, looking for mine.

Right in this moment, you were suddenly there, by my side. I didn´t notice you at all until you spoke to me. You didn´t speak the language of our country, although I understood the language you spoke— I just wasn't prepared to hear it. By the time my gaze followed your voice, you were nearly finished with your question.

I saw sorrow in your eyes and disappointment.

And then you left.

You left before your words made any sense in my preoccupied brain, processing too slowly. Before it was able to understand your words and build an answer. Maybe you didn't stick around because you had asked this question already so many times and heard too many nos. You were just gone. Lost in a place full of rushed people with wet umbrellas and concentrated faces. I can´t quite remember your face. Could only catch a small glimpse of it. But I remember your dark hair and brown eyes in a pale face. A face which was younger than mine. You were long gone, but your words stuck around in these great halls and even more in my heart.

"Please, can you buy me some food?"

I never had the chance to give you my answer. Which haunts me till today. But my answer would have been yes! Of course, I would have bought you some food. And maybe a scarf that keeps you warm or a little candle that shines just for you through the dark nights.

For weeks, I carry these words in my heart, never able to let them go. You were just a girl, our meeting was just a heartbeat long, but you've kept me company since then. Because I am so sorry! I am sorry, I wasn't faster. I am sorry, I didn´t buy you some food. And I am sorry, that I am just another stranger to you, who didn´t help you.

I am thinking of you every day.

>   Lots of love,
>   Vanessa
>   *Germany*

X.D.V.,
   Flattering.
   Charming.
   You are always such a smooth talker.
   Texter.

Words on screen,
cannot truly sate my needs.
I've got a taste of you.
I crave you often, badly.
I yearn for you in the physical.
For actions as strong as the words you send.
But when will you be ready?
Oh, I shouldn't rush.
Patience has been my friend thus far.
You're unraveling it seems.
Like a flower blooming after an unforgiving storm.
You will come to me in time,
if you choose to do so.

> A.J.X.
> *United States*

Dear former lover,

I know it's been a while since it ended, and I won't pretend I miss you— because I don't.

But this time of year, as living things die, I can't help but remember the oceans of tears you made me cry. And when leaves, dried up and fallen crunch beneath my feet, I think of yours, with my heart underneath. I thought of you as glowing— how naive I was not to realize you kept your darkest side from showing. What I thought were my insecurities before, now I know, were actually yours— and you needed me more than I ever needed you.

So, my former lover,

deep in my bones, I have something to say— thank you. I'm braver now and know my worth, and after you buried me beneath the cold earth— I found him. And he showed me a warmth, covered in gold, and what I deserved, so much more than you taking off my clothes. I hear that now you have a baby girl, and what you made my former nightmares, now will haunt you as yours. But perhaps now you'll realize what you did to me was to somebody's daughter. sister. friend. And your heart will soften, and you won't use other women again. Thank you.

For like these autumn leaves, letting me fall.

I let go of your branches once and for all.

For now, my heart has re-blossomed in vibrant colors. Because now, I know how it actually feels to be loved by another.

Never more yours,
Your former, the other (woman)
United States

P.S. This is perhaps an anti-love letter. The darker side of a love letter's reflection to a former lover who, unbeknownst to me at the time, made me into the other woman. Writing this helped remind me that despite this time being one of the darkest and most isolating periods of my life, I deserved and ultimately received— my happy ending. Only light can overcome darkness.

Paree,

Can I still call you that? I hope so. I don't even know where to begin, but let's go with— how have you been? I heard you moved. How's the new city treating you? I am doing well, better even. Not that you would want to know. You know, I spent weeks pondering where it all went wrong and what I did wrong. Until I came to the realization that maybe our time just might be over. I mean, our relationship was doomed from the beginning, wasn't it? A student dating her teacher. It only works in stories, not in real life. Everyone said it'd never work, but we never believed them.

It was bitter coming to terms with the fact that you were no longer a part of my life. It was never really said that we were over until you stopped answering and I stopped texting. Now, all that is left is a stack of "what ifs". We really sucked at goodbyes, huh? I mean, how do you even do that? So you're just supposed to stand back and watch people walk away from you slowly? I had a feeling a long time ago— I'd feel you slipping away through my fingers like grains of sand. I tried to close my hand tight, so tight that it gave me a burn but you just kept going. It was devastating— watching you go on and have a life with me standing outside of it. Watching you smile with people that I'd never met stung because I wasn't standing by you anymore to meet those same new people.

I used to think about you a lot, but these days you are more of a distant memory that comes by once in a while and leaves a bittersweet taste on my tongue. I wanted to forget all about you. I tried to hate you— but hate and you never felt right in the same sentence. And forgetting you was a punishment. Everything I remember about you now resides in a box tucked away in my brain. Your phone number, address, favorite color, ice cream flavor, song, movie, fears, pet peeves, guilty pleasures, favorite place, your sibling's birthday, and where your birthmark is. All of this is now stored in that box, the box that refused to be thrown out or burned. That sacred box with your name embossed on the top of it. At one time, it was a name that rolled carelessly off my tongue, and now I can't say it without exposing all the sentiments attached to each letter.

I still have everything you gave me, the ache, the love, the laughter, the joy, the hurt, the happiness. It is dusty and slightly rotten and I guard it without thinking. Tell me, did you find a new person to call yours? One who would eat Chinese with you? Share your daily ritual of evening ice cream? Go on bike rides in the middle of the night? To sit on the kitchen counter talking to you while you make coffee? To have you stand between their legs and kiss your mouth? Recommend books? Someone to share new songs with? Play ludo with you? Steal your shirts? Write you poetry? To watch movies with you while your head lays in their lap, their fingers fiddling your hair? I hope that you do, if you still haven't. Sometimes I think that maybe I should text you and talk to you and maybe we could fix things— but my fingers tremble whenever I open your contact. I hover over your name when there are things I want to tell someone, but I can't because you are not here anymore. All of this shouldn't feel right, should it? All of it feels the same sometimes, but sometimes not. I try to make sense of it and understand it, but I fail every time. It feels so known. But it doesn't feel okay. Maybe I did see it coming, maybe it is entirely my fault, and this is my punishment. I believed I was under the right lamp post in the right street. I now look at the moon and the stars and hope that you are watching them too— with me— even if we are miles apart. I wished I loved you a little less so I would be able to talk about you to other people, but that's not the case. Those five sacred letters of your name are too heavy to be said these days. I have so many things to say to you, so many things to ask, but I know for a fact that my voice will break and my fingers will tremble, so I won't. I will let them be, just as they are. Maybe in some other life where you and I are meant to be.

I know these words will never reach you, but I will still say this— that no matter what, no matter where I am— my love will always be there for you. I will love you more than I love myself, more than I will ever love anything. Ever. Only when my heart stops beating will you be free of my love. Only then and not a second before that.

All my love,
Motu
India

P.S. A letter from a student who fell in love with her teacher and was lucky enough to be loved back, but couldn't hold on to it.

Dear TSI25,

The legendary poet who still managed to linger in the shadows - you're the one who started all of this, you know. You had to comment on my talent and my imagination. Then you were just so inclined to know whether or not I was okay. If maybe I wasn't actually making anything up. You're the one who was so interested in teaching me your code - your secrets and tricks of both trades. You're the one who said those words first - the reason they've now become nothing more than yet another glass of watered-down soda.

And yet, I'm the one plagued by the person I became. Haunted by the person you were. Abandoned by us both, without any sort of warning or goodbye, or even the excess of lame excuses you always seemed to have for everyone else.

Hun: that's what you always called me, 'cause you swore I was too young for *babe* or *baby* and too old for *sweetheart* or *darling* — what a strange limbo to be in. Well, Hun, if that was the case, you should have kept me at nickname's length instead of so explicitly purposefully naming me.

It's funny - only a handful of people from our old community remember you. But the ones who do swear you were a legend. They tell me that being so close to you is why I was so prolific. Why every piece was exponentially better than the one just before it. They insist on reminding me of the way you just vanished. They laugh in agreement that you are the reason "ghosting" is even a term. They mock the way I write of cinnamon and orange juice and the original "Charmed" haunting me.

I hate that you had to be a poet and a few years older. Everyone thinks you're the reason I developed my voice, my style - even my penmanship. I detest being able to see how they might think that - how they might even be right. I'm burdened by the name of a phantom - that's just so incredibly cruel. Even "Wednesday" cannot change my perspective. Nor can "The Middle". That's all your fault too, you know.

I've written books - gone through the work of self-publishing and everything. I moved out of that ridiculous town and left nearly everyone from then behind too. Or I've been left behind, by a few. Just following in your footsteps, I suppose. Oh - and I work in a coffee shop - every time they play the songs you introduced me to my heart flutters and I wonder if maybe, just maybe, this will be the day we accidentally meet again. Maybe some small part of ourselves will be able to sense it even if our minds can't recognize voices or faces or coffee orders anymore.

I like to think you'd be proud and disappointed in the person I've become. And I'm strangely alright with that. Even if I can say with certainty that I have not moved on. That I continue to live haunted despite every move, change, or other various attempts at evicting this ghost of you. Hun, I have to admit, you did a pretty decent job of securing immortality in a way.

Something far beyond even the words you're so famous for writing. Beyond your craft or talents or hobbies. Beyond anything, you've ever actually done.

Congratulations, Hun.

A Dreamer
United States

P.S. For a love that simply could not last.

Dear Bee,

I am writing this letter to let you know how I feel. I know that people change and are busy. I know you are busy with life. Your family and work. And what you love. I know you have new friends and I am happy for you but I also feel upset. Sad.

I mean, once upon a time, we were best friends. You would call me and text me. Also, message me and like and comment on my posts. And I would do the same back to you. You said no matter what, we'd always be best friends. That you would always have time for me. But then things changed, and we didn't spend as much time together (even though we still tried to have time for each other and hung out when we could). But then, one day, something happened and you changed. You no longer bothered with me. You didn't call me, message me, or text me like you used to. You didn't bother with me online at all like you used to. I had to bother with you and message you first, and sometimes you bothered back, but even then, you didn't bother with me much. I feel like I am the only one trying here to keep this friendship alive. You say you miss me, and we need to hang out, but when I give you my days off, they never work for you. And now, when you say they do, you don't even follow through with the plans. Is it just air, empty words? Are you just saying it to make yourself look good, or because you think it's what I want to hear? Why do you say these things and not follow through with them? Why don't you seem to care? You've really changed. Not just by ignoring me, but by caring so much about what you look like and, in a way that is bragging about your looks. Caring only for vanity. Wanting tattoos. The way you are acting, it's like you are a stranger, and I don't even know you anymore.

I am done trying to keep this friendship alive by myself. I have not bothered with you in almost a month. Have you even noticed that my name doesn't show up in your notifications anymore? Do you even care? It seems like you don't. That makes me sad.

I could go on but don't want this letter to be too long, and besides— I won't ever really send this letter to you.

>Sincerely,
>Me
>*United States*

Lake Shine,

There are days when I am so filled with your rivers that my veins tremble. Your eyes have drowned me, my heart and my thoughts. I never knew eyes could have such force, waves of gentle tranquility, this strange magic that possesses the smallest parts of me. They replaced everyone else`s gaze and made it dull like dying embers compared to the flame yours stored. Their color changed with the seasons, bronze like the crowned gold of autumn`s trees, then suddenly green and brown like the hazel depths of a clear, sun warmed forest creek. If who you chose over me gets to gaze into those eyes of marble, it is with great agony that I wish she would know how wonderful that privilege is.

I don't know if I can ever tell you this, but I love you more than you`ll ever know, especially in that summer afterglow.

I fell in love with you three times, and three times over. The first three are:

1. The first day we met, and how summer sunlight and your hazel eyes altered my very existence.

2. The night I taught you to dance, and woke up remembering how your hands had curled perfectly around my waist.

3. The one perfect July evening when we swam in the river, the one I look in today and still see the bronze depths of your gaze in their gentle waves.

The second three:

1. Was when you listened, truly listened, and kept quiet when my words choked me.

2. When I realized I was always left with an ache to see you again, as if my soul was left in tatters when you would leave and needed your thread to sew it back up, your eyes being the needle.

3. When I couldn't stop remembering how perfectly your hand was accustomed to the shape of mine.

But I also have three fears:

I fear you never saw my eyes in the clouds or the storms or the blue sky.

I fear you will never wake up and see them, how moonstruck they are for wanting to shed their glow upon the pools of your eyes` surface.

I fear you will find someone who will love differently, who will love better than me - who is better.

I am afraid that has already happened.

Lake Shine, I wish to tell you that when I dated the boy from Britain it felt wrong, I couldn't go through with the romance, because you were always in the back of my head. That when I hugged you for the first time after two years something inside me came together, all those threads of our friendship bound together in a pleasantly constricting knot. That when I am with you I feel complete, like you were the final lock to secure the door inside my heart that felt so open and incomplete for years without me ever noticing until I met you.

I don't know how I even breathed without you in my life - I finally was breathing when you came into it. I wonder if you loved someone as much, if you felt the weight I've carried of loving you, it would crush you. You're a friend I needed, and a lover who I didn't think I would need. But now I do, and if you leave my life I fear I will grow as wild as vines in desperation just for your company or to look into your lake-shine eyes. Guns N' Roses ballads echo in different meanings now.

There is a lot unspoken that I can never say, words I am putting here in the vain hope you will read this. That`s called Soul Speak, I think, where certain feelings that have no words come out as silent and brooding, deeper than velvet nights and river depths. Ones where all you can do is write their feeble interpretations and hope they come across as accurate. I hope you see this, Lake Shine, and wake up.

If there was a way to make you realize who is writing this, I want to give you three clues. You put white stripes in your hair because you wanted to be Joe Perry, you gave me your leather jacket that smelled so good I wore it on every walk I took before the scent wore out, you bought me tickets to a concert that I never thought would be possible for me to go to.

But there is a fourth clue. I want you to know that that clue is my name.

> Forever to never be yours,
> McCartney
> *United States*

P.S. This is to a friend who gave me so much more than I asked for. I didn't know his eyes would drown me in such poetic illusion, or how much his presence was needed. Since I can't express my love for him in spoken words I am doing so through this letter, and I hope with all the hope that's left in the world that he will find it when the time is right.

To the ones that are still here,

I hope you all outlive me so I have a few less things to mourn. These are words I don't know how to speak out loud.

I think of death every day— like a clock is always ticking behind every conversation. 'It's only a matter of time.'

I see my last remaining grandmother sip her second cup of decaf coffee and I wonder if this is the last time I'll see her— or will it be a year, or five, or ten. I always hug her when she says goodbye and if I have to get up out of my chair to do so she says, "Oh, you don't have to."

But yes I do. Yes I do.

I wonder— does everyone think about death this much? I was sitting at a family Christmas dinner when I realized that for the rest of my life, I'll be burying those I love. I keep thinking about how being in my late twenties is such a dichotomy of living and dying. This is the season of weddings and funerals. Baby showers and wakes. Engagement parties and burials.

I think about losing my parents and it rips me in half. I can't imagine a world without the few people I have left and I know one day I will have to live in that world and it terrifies me more than anything. Does anyone else feel this way? Are you scared, too?

Adrastea
United States

Dear M.,

I wish I had gotten to say it one last time. I love you. I love you, and it's my own burden to bear. Sometimes I dream about you calling me and breathing all heavy on the line like you always do. And I sit there listening to you breathe, loud and clear. You don't cough or sneeze. You breathe. I listen, and when you are about to put the phone down, I whisper, "I love you," and you inhale, and then your phone dies. Because I wouldn't know what else to say. I love you and that's all there is to it.

But I wake up, and no miracle, no amount of waiting, no amount of apologies can make it a reality. You are a dream now, perhaps because my friends say that they see you lingering on the underside of my eyelids. I would never call you a ghost, even as you haunt my being. It feels terribly ironic to call you my life nowadays. I wish I could say I miss you too much, but darling, you haven't left me yet. You sit snug in the melodies of that song you mumbled into my ear that night, drunk and dreamy (I still don't know what it means, but as with everything about you, I believe it's love). You hold me from somewhere between the lines of the poetry books you annotated for my benefit. You coyly smuggle yourself in these words I write because I had promised you a letter and a love but failed to give you either. You seek me out in the smiles of sweet strangers and serenade me in each sarcastic quip my friends hope will cure me of you. So I say to them what you never heard. I love you. I love you and you won't ever know. I love you and nothing takes away from that. I love you and you are nothing but ashes scattered in the air of a city I have never been to. I love you and you are everywhere. I love you and you are dead and it's time I let you die. It's time you become just another love that couldn't last a lifetime, just another journey meant to end, just another gorgeous city that isn't home. But nothing about you could be reduced to a simple "just another." I love you, and I'll learn to live with it. I love you and I'll learn to let you die.

Till then, I will love you as I love you still.

STILL YOURS,
SUR
India

P.S. A love and a letter a little too late.

To Our Lifelines - Mamma and Dedaa,

So gentle yet strong was that hold, we still remember. How you took us through the joyous and the challenging phases of time, since that very day we were born, with so much love and comfort that we never wanted to be gone.

Ever since, you've kept us warm and safe. Making us who we are today, sometimes with rains of admonishments, sometimes with everlasting chapters of life lessons, sometimes with never ending laughs and sometimes with nothing but your eternal, incomparable love. Making us cherish the treasure boxes of memories, values and all that love you embedded in us.

You're the light leading us through every dark tunnel. You're the sun paving the way, shining courage in every difficult struggle. Your sweet voice is the only lullaby that brings a peaceful sleep to our ever curious eyes. If it wasn't for you, our days and nights wouldn't be as nice. You're the answer to all our prayers. You complete us wholesome in layers.

Thank you would be an understatement to appreciate you both. Yet, whatever is left unsaid is gratitude, which we this time can't hold. Our hearts are yours. You're our home. We love you to the stars and beyond.

AMIRAH AND AAMILAH

Sri Lanka
P.S. A letter from daughters to their parents.

To: The Mad Hatter,

Do you believe in twin flames? That there is that one person you are magnetically drawn to and destined to be with? No? Well neither did I until I met you. You were so easy to talk to. I remember the first time we talked on the phone, what seemed peculiar at first within seconds became so natural. Minutes became hours and before I knew it, it was time to end our call. Funny, it felt like I knew you. Like we had known each other for years. There was nothing I couldn't say or speak to you about. Your voice sweet and patient. Your touch wanting, but yet hesitant to make the first move. You gave me love, compassion, and companionship. The things I needed and had been longing for.

Do you believe in soulmates? Someone you just feel mentally, physically, and spiritually connected to? That's how I felt about you. When we connected, you took my body to a higher plane. But our ascension could never last because you belonged to another and so did I. Maybe we will meet again and circumstances will twist our fate. Until then, time will pass and new memories will be made while most of the old ones will be forgotten, but you will forever be engraved in my heart.

The Dreamer
United States

P.S. I wanted to share this in hopes someone else can relate to it and know they're not alone.

The one who disappeared,

I recently found screenshots of our video calls. It's 5 in the morning, and just a minute ago, I was holding that screenshot to my face. Staring at your eyes. And for a split second between those still minutes, when my eyes were filling with water— I felt the picture moving. I felt your eyes feeling, watching. I felt that you were right there. I swear, just for a split second.

I am so glad I had you— so infinitely glad. You know that one feeling in a heart— a feeling so big and so beautiful and so unexplainable that it hurts? You're that feeling for me.

I'm cold while writing this. I'm glad I'm out of the phase where I denied, where I waited. Some part of me still waits. It will always wait. Like, right now, I'm thinking– do you remember my birthday? I don't think you would.

So, yes, I have accepted you're not here and that acceptance somehow lessened the ache in my heart. The void– I still feel it, but not as much as I thought I would. I always believed– if I accepted your absence, I'd break. Or maybe I couldn't, I just couldn't do it. But then, in a single brave moment, I said to myself– *you are gone*. And there was no tear, no ache, I didn't feel anything. Is this, somehow, similar to how you felt?

Still, I love you, even if you're gone. Even if you were never going to be mine. Truthfully, I don't know what I would do if I saw you with somebody else. Do you sometimes think the same? I mean, ah, I just hope that I don't see you with somebody. I hope I never find out if you get married or have a girlfriend… or fall in love with somebody else. Of course, I want you to be happy, I want you to be able to move on– but, you see, you're a part of me now– in my subconscious. You are somehow mine, even as just an idea.

I really hope these letters come and find you– someday after I'm gone. I can't stop imagining how pathetic it would be to confess to you after being dead. Or to put you through that pain. My love for you went from selfish to selfless– so I'm really not sure what to do.

If you're thinking that I'm dumb to believe that I'm over you, since I'm still writing to you, then yes– you'd be right. Maybe, I'm over the idea that you're ever going to come back, or be mine, or have a happy ending with me. Maybe, I'm over the idea that I'll find you again, but I'm not over *you*. I'm still head over heels in love with you. I still love your stupid face and I still think it's the prettiest thing in the world. I still hear your voice saying, "Oh, bhaee," in a way that made me want to say it just as you did.

Ah, my imperfect love. Before you, I loved perfection, but you— I found a perfectness in your every imperfection. I miss your voice singing to me. I miss hearing you say things like *I wanna play with your hair*. So, yes. I'm not over you– and I'm never going to be! I don't want to be! I will always love you, Ely.

Even if I stop writing letters– because at some point, I will— and now it's making me cry. (I think these letters are also a form of closure that I'm trying to give myself.) Even when I stop writing letters and I grow up and that 27-year-old me forgets that their was once a boy– know that I'll still be in there loving you. I'll be buried inside every future me as this 17-year-old Zahru– your Zahru– loving you. Even if I make it to 55, know that somewhere inside her, a little girl– that little me– will still be in love with you. After all that time, this moment has frozen. Even if we're forgotten, it'll still be there. Always. Your memory may be a little to time, but you will still be my home. God, I love you. I wish I could run to you and hug you so tightly– and kiss you so madly. I wish that we would never have to let go– that we'd forget the rest of the world existed— but, you're gone. You're forever gone.

> ZAHRU
> *Pakistan*

TO HER,
> I have written
> wedding vows
> to you
> for a ceremony
> that will
> never occur,
> those words
> instead
> to be intoned
> alone
> when my ashes
> fall
> upon your land.

Bryllupsløfter
Wedding Vows

> LOST TREASURE LOVE
> *United States*

P.S. This is the most honest and raw thing that I have every written. It is for the most special person, best friend, lover, soulmate, that I have ever known or will ever know. Separated by thousands of kilometers, an ocean, and years— the time that we spent together, while but a blink in the universe— will live eternally in every version of my being.

MY LOVELY LATE GRANDMOTHER,
Countless things have been happening all around since you've been gone from our lives. First of all, our family has been growing— expecting additional kith and kin. Not for me, at least, although— in the past years, I underestimated myself at being able to accomplish achievements beyond my capabilities. You may be proud of my achievements, if you were here.

We got married, went on to live our imperfect life as well as we possibly could. Along with being content and blessed with my significant other, I hold onto hope when going through hardships as the almighty is watching over me. Lavender and cotton flowers instilling a sense of peace within me, no matter how chaotic the world gets— it will not change who I am.

I am focusing on the positive changes in myself towards others and the constant shifts in life, especially in this new normal. I needed a bit of adjusting myself, even though it has been going on for more than a year. An everlasting thought, I wish you could have seen how I turned out to be after that final goodbye I had with you.

Reminiscing about the past with my favourite memory of you— a charm-sized teddy bear you gave me on my birthday that I have kept ever since. Reminding me of the blissful moment at every glance, whenever it caught my sight. The time we spent our summer surrounding ourselves in nature or sitting by the beach engulfed in that vast landscape of the never ending sea. The forgotten taste of your delicacies. The sight of your sweet smile that will always be remembered. Here, leaving my heart and soul in writing, leaving me feeling so emotional like never before. Thinking of you on the other side, offering prayers when the absence of you crosses my mind, trusting that you will never be completely erased from my memory. Knowing you will forever remain in my heart, for as long as I live.

S.I.
Singapore

P.S. A dedication letter for my late grandmother who passed away, and whom I have been missing ever since. It has been 10 years since the passing of my grandmother. Over the years her memories still carry deep within my heart. During the time she was alive, she may not have been able to read what I wrote, but I will keep on living as she watches over me.

Mrs. Edna,

There is always one life-altering moment that makes you a before-and-after person, and there have been many such moments I've encountered in my short life, but the one I remember the most is when my teacher saved my life.

Dear ma'am, to a trusting naive young six-year-old, a bully can come in many forms, an older sibling, a friend, a neighbour, but never had I imagined the first bully I would face would be my teacher. Although I don't remember much of the details, I do know that I changed from the outgoing noisy chatterbox of the class into a scared timid frightened child, scared because I was afraid of being punished, frightened of the constant shouting in class— I think even my parents saw a change in their daughter so long ago.

Of course, parents like mine retaliated, and soon you walked into our lives. On that day I knew something had changed.

You were patient, kind, and loving, especially to us— the lost ones— who feared you as much as your predecessor, but how wrong we were. You made me love going to school again, I never got tired of getting the praise from you, and over the years you've been an inspiration to someone like me as an example of how, not only just children but, our world would heal with more kindness.

The day you walked into 1-D, that very day, you changed my life for the better. I'm forever grateful for your ever-present guidance and love to this day, I will always always be indebted to you.

WITH APPRECIATION AND THE HIGHEST REGARDS,
ESHA
India

P.S. To a teacher whom I regard in the highest esteem for being the first one to believe in me.

J.,
My first love,
I wanted to be your last love.
The one you hold at night.
The one you kiss before going to work,
but you had other plans.
You saw me as an object,
a toy you can play with
a prize that you won
and once you got what you wanted
you left me brokenhearted
picking up the scattered pieces.
My heart will never be the same.
To me, you were my first love.
To you, I was your first victim.

F. WOLF
United States

P.S. This letter is for an ex-boyfriend of mine that I haven't been able to let go of. He moved on right away while I waited. I did end up falling in love with someone else, and now, I can finally let go of my past.

MY LOVE,

I hope that one day, it doesn't hurt like this. I hope one day I wake up from a dream of you and smile softly instead of tears filling my eyes. I hope one day your dreams and ambitions are all your own again, studying the ancient languages you love, instead of the broken runes in my eyes. Someday, when your arms, my war-torn homeland, are free— you'll walk through Jerusalem and it will be your promised land again, not my human heart. When you arrive in Mecca at the end of your pilgrimage, your ribcage will expand and open up the doors of this cage to let me go.

YOURS, IN MEMORY
Canada

P.S. He was supposed to be the one who buries me. That's an Arabic saying. My best friend and lover. I broke his heart and mine, for religious beliefs.

TO THE GUY I ONCE CALLED MINE,

Hey! I hope you are doing well in your life. I heard you are in a relationship now. Well, good for you. I hope the new girl in your life makes you happy and you are satisfied and content.

I know I took nearly two years to write to you, but it wasn't because I held any grudge against you or anything. It's just that I wanted to take my own time to come face to face with reality. But now that I am finally ready, here I am, with a pen in my hand, pouring out words on a paper.

I know, now that we're exes, people think that we are hunting for each other's flesh and bones. But I'm so glad that we still defend each other fiercely keeping the other's dignity. I am so glad that we aren't the usual kind of exes that try to belittle each other. But I think that it was bound to happen as we were never the usual kind of couple. My best friends still don't ill speak of you or hate you, and that, I think, speaks volumes of how great you are.

I know we both thought that it would last forever, that we were soulmates and it was meant to be. But I think we both made some mistakes down the road, we both took each other for granted and that's why we fell apart. But relationship or no relationship, I'll love you and wish the best for you, always.

From,
Someone you once called yours
India

To the girl he'll date after me,

I know it seems weird for me to write to you because I am supposed to hate you and you are supposed to hate me. We both are supposed to feel that unwavering insecurity and jealousy for each other. But let me tell you that life is more than this jealousy and insecurity. It comes in its packages of love and heartbreaks. Just because my package of heartbreak became the exact same package of love for you doesn't mean we should be at war with each other.

I am writing this to you to tell you that you are up for the most exciting roller coaster ride of your life. So never keep your seat belt unfastened.

He is the kind of guy who takes care of everyone but himself. He might be weathering the darkest and strongest storms alone, and you'll never know about it. All he knows is how to give. He'll never tell all of this to you himself, but his face, eyes, and actions will give away his soul. So pay attention to them.

He has a bad habit of hurting himself while making everyone else happy. But when it's the end of the day and the night is singing her lullaby to him, he will shut the tune off and instead ask you to sing for him. Know that he is his most vulnerable at this point. Sing him his favourite song and embrace him like a little kid.

If you are dating him, you aren't just supposed to be his girlfriend. You'll have to play every single role in his life. Sometimes, you may have to become his mother, sometimes father, sometimes best friend and sometimes his wife too. I know it sounds frustrating, and trust me, sometimes it does get frustrating, but when you see the cascade of peace all over his face, you'll forget about all the hardships you have to go through.

Please try to understand all the metaphorical language he speaks in because you'll have to decipher it a lot of times. He has faced so much life to become what he is right now. Always protect him like you'd protect a blooming flower and he'll make your life smell like heaven with his salubrious fragrance.

Lastly, love him with all you have, and he'll make even Romeo and Juliet jealous of how unconditionally and unfathomably he can love.

LOVE,
THE GIRL WHO HAD TO LEARN ALL OF THIS ON HER OWN
India

JAMES,

11.11 - I know that you don't think of me.

I know that I'm this small little memory of a dear friend, a warm heart, a light that you admired from afar. So perhaps today means nothing to you. A symbol of this real, distant truth.

But today still means the day you chose.

You chose to kiss me, erasing the insecurities.

You chose to love me with an unknown future ahead. You chose to hold me in every effort to never forget.

But now it's nothing. No dream or hope. You chose to let me go. So I'm not a thought, or a memory. I'm not even a name you wish to read. I'm barely a voice in the world you brightly lead. I'm a little ghost to wish you well. A guardian angel who's silent cheers you still can't quell.

I know today I will live as half. Half to make a wish they won't trespass. And half to see if it's me you'll come to need. I'll hear you in the voices and feel you in the air. I'll see you in the screens I pass pretending to be unaware. I'll cry, I'll scream, and maybe swear. But today I'll only wish to tell you "I'm here."

Please don't be mad, forgive me for speaking louder than the ghost you made. The one you are leaving. I'll be ok; you can keep moving. The night will end and tomorrow is new. Maybe I'll wake up and have finally moved on from you.

CAS
United States

P.S. 11.11 make a wish. 11:11 was this little hope and wish my ex-best friend and I would share growing up. After we met, we would share the time with each other over the long distance. This little minute as a thought to one another and a wish for a bright day. 11.11.2018 he asked me to be his girlfriend. The week before he confessed his love for me over dinner and a week later we began dating. He was my choice. My best friend. My person. Eventually, he decided to break it up for various reasons. Perhaps ones I'll never fully know the absolute truth. It's been several years now. I'm still healing, but I find that process results in constant letters to him. Most of it expressing how proud I am of his successes. Oh how I wish I could be visible in his corner to bolster and support him. This unrequited love may be unhealthy, but he was the one I would give anything for. A very pure unconditional love I've never understood until him. So every 11.11 I catch, he still gets a minute. Maybe he always will, or maybe his presence will finally feel silent. Either way, if he is happier far away and soaring in life where he wishes to go and my distance helps that, I will give it to him every single time. Just like I will sit and listen if he needs me then too.

Y.P.,

Your child,
somewhere within me,
is still weeping for you.
I hope you still hear her.
Through the pain and unaccepted anger,
my heart begs for you to hug it.
Through the hollowness of hurt—
I miss watching tv with you.

A.P.
Ireland

P.S. My mom threw me out when I turned eighteen, said my mental health was too much for her. I'm now trying to heal so many emotions left behind from her. And trying to accept that I still love her.

Dear Sagittarius,

This is not a letter of lost love, although a love indeed, it is. It is a letter I will probably never send to you. Unless by some high unlikelihood you read it here, it may have to be one for the books and the gods to witness. As such, you may never fully know what I think of you. The past lives I have seen us share. The words I do not dare to whisper echo through the night for leaves to fold into morning.

Sometimes when I look into your eyes; how they dance with laughter, I catch glimpses of how we used to be. Our bodies naked, supple and free. The days we swam naked by the docks when Napoli was younger and we were younger still. Our bodies' hard and browned from the ocean — salt and sun on our skin. How thoroughly we lived then, how fully, how intensely. Without holding back — the tears, the lust, the love and blood — all shone from our faces as the mud on our bronzed cheekbones.

It is a game, they said. It is all a game, we thought. And part of me still believes it.

Maybe we knew more then than we do now. Like how to hold each other freely. In this city of pleasure and blood, grapes, wine, nectarines and dirty, sculpted bodies. Of men and women alike. But I like you — and everyone knows it. And in this time — of Cesar and Marcus Aurelius — when we were boys and boys were allowed to love one another free. Death was common and we were not afraid of it. Or at least we dared to dance with our fears. And love flowed as freely as wine.

I would always come and visit you down by the docks in the morning. And we would swim naked, wrestle and carve our bodies through the water and onto each other. The juice from the apricots we stole from the orchards that dribbled down your face — I can still taste it — mixed with salt water from the sea — your saliva in me. I smile at the memory; giggling and throwing and moving into you. On your chest, where I would rest and feel at home. A familiar place it seems I have always known.

I can still smell your sweat before entering the baths. And feel your hand squeeze my shoulder hard when I sit bare bottomed on the warm flagstones. I grin because your touch always makes me feel quivering and alive. Ready— for the world, ready— to run along the walls, balancing and holding — just in time to catch ourselves from falling. And we run farther, towards the blazing sunset that caresses down on our Napoli.

I like to think we knew of Sappho. That we read her poetry amongst ourselves. Although maybe we were too busy playing, wrestling with each other and ourselves, chasing across the docks and helping our fathers carry the weight they wanted us to bear. The weight we shook off as droplets of salted water and others opinions of us. And when I watched our legs dangle over the sea and our laughter echo across the water, I smile, knowing that these are the moments I have felt most alive. The moments that, in their gentleness and fervor, are burned into memory beyond space and time. Hence why I carry you always, deep inside.

What a contrast to how we live now. Where I love you and no one in my life knows your name. Is it shame I hold, or fear that the worlds we inhabit are too different? The impossibility of our lives ever merging fully. This is my head talking. Luckily, love does not live there, but in Heart. And I have always preferred Heartspace.

And essentially, all that is irrelevant, because when you lean towards me we move into a different world. A space where we are both raptors — eagles that soar above what everyone else can see — and our identities lie far beneath, scattered to the sea. Because this flame that dances between us remains alive. And our connection stretches far beyond space and time.

Sagittarius, I will meet you again in another life.

Love,
Zerzura
Sweden & Kenya

J.,

January 10th, a moment frozen in time. The day your life ended, and I buried a piece of my soul forever.

In vain, I try connecting with that moment as heavy Autumn leaves fall. I am buried within the final hours of the beauty that begins to shed before barren landscapes reveal themselves and the emptiness which accompanies them.

A metallic bird falling from the sky as muffled thunder crashed through ethereal stratospheres. Hospital walls dinged in the beige everyday drab nothingness of ordinary. The fragile eggshell of my mind shattered as marigold memories poured out, running down, away from me.

I could not save them, or you. You are the black box of my soul I can no longer recover. Locked away behind wrought iron gates, forged of pain, drowning in sadness.

I have lost you forever and in return, I am forever lost.

Yours forever,
A.
United States

P.S. Final words to my husband.

Dear Lost Girl,

I remember the time when you thought you were high above the clouds, looking at your reflection in the mirror, thinking to yourself, it wasn't as pretty as you imagined. It was the sin and drugs that tasted like sour honey, pain, and little white lies that made you into who you were looking at. I remembered the way you carried yourself, a little too well. You had straggly hair with a t-shirt that had been stretched out from days of worn, eyes with bags under them, and weight loss from poor nutrition. I was there, watching as you tried to point blame somewhere else, but it was you that needed to be held accountable for staying when it was time to go.

I watched as you sold a part of your soul to the devil and tried fearlessly to get that innocence in you back, but deep down— you knew it would forever be gone. I've seen the sun set behind your eyes, not knowing if you would live to see another day. Like a ferris wheel, you always found yourself looking down in fear, shouting for someone to let you off, but you were the only one at that carnival in your mind. You controlled the ride.

I was there as you searched for clarity, hoping it would rise above the weeds, just beyond the fog. I should've tried harder to let you know I was there, to let you know that you weren't by yourself. I should've held you tighter until the sun broke through. I could feel the shadows in you getting darker and I could feel your heart beating out of your chest. It consumed you and you struggled to move. Life got confusing, trying to find a peace of mind, not knowing if your memories would ever quit haunting you and if the fear of deception would ever fade away. I listened as the voices pulled you in slowly, over and over again, and watched as you re-lit the flame within you each day.

I knew your desperation to swallow it all, even if that meant choking on the smoke. It's because of you that I now stop to admire the flowers blooming around me. It's because of you that I breathe in the midnight sky as the moonlight dances between the strands of my hair. The only reason why I am alive today is because in my silence, you were louder with your strength and ability to carry more than you ever had too. I hope you will stay with me, lost girl, for the days that I, too, am lost.

J.
United States

P.S. As much as I would love to have written an unsent love letter to an old flame, I know it is me that needs love the most. I'm always giving my words and love to others, but I struggle with knowing that I, too, need love.

R.M.,

Suddenly love songs are about you. Suddenly I'm dancing alone with you on my mind. Suddenly I'm imagining that we are dancing together. Suddenly everything's changed. Suddenly you took my whole heart in your hands. And I gave it freely to you. I wanted you to have it. That's the most precious gift I could ever give to you.

My heart chose you, and I chose to let it choose you.

Suddenly I'm smiling, suddenly you have a permanent place in my mind, everything I do, everywhere I go, you are with me. My heart wants you near. It can't let you go, not even for a second.

My heart chose you, and I chose to let it choose you.

I wake up every morning and I know I've been thinking about you all through the night, because my mind is restless and my heart full of longing. I lay down again so I can fast forward the time. So the day that we'll be together again will be closer. And I dream about you. I wake up and I look at my phone. Waiting for your message. The message that still hasn't come.

My heart chose you.
And I chose to let it choose you!

MAYARA K.
Brazil & Japan

P.S. My heart was still very hopeful that she'd come back after having ghosted me.

B.J.L.R.,

I was the stolen moments, only when the stars were awake, chanting with the moon. Tiny kisses tracing and imprinting promises that will never be filled. I was the 2 am call. A midnight text.

I was the girl wrapped in you arms, but could never call it home. I was a constant, not permanent. And it just hit me, I was never really your girl. Every girl could, but never me.

For comfort, I was too safe for you to settle for.

L.M.
Namibia

P.S. A letter to my best friend.

DEAR YOU,

I don't think you're aware of the things I'm going through, I don't think you ever will be. No matter what I feel, I wouldn't have been able to express it to you in person. It's crazy how you changed my life so much in mere 3-4 months, I'm talking about the worst here. I've gone through the waiting-for-your-text-all-day phase, disappointment-and-feeling-unworthy phase, the stress-and-trauma phase, and most intensely, the anxiety phase (this phase hurt me a lot). You shattered me, and it didn't bother you one percent. Of course, there was never anything from your side. You played me, knowingly— unknowingly— I don't want to know. It's important to address this because you were the first person ever to make me understand how love actually feels, which eventually, of course, transformed into heartbreak. Look, there's no hate, and there never will be, but I know it is going to take me a hell lot of time to completely heal from this phase.

Also, if I'm done addressing the worst points, I can now focus on the learnings. There's so much to learn, to rebuild my self esteem, to be happy again, to feel alive, to work on myself, to build a life I have always wished for. But to get there I need to first get out of this mess that I've created for myself. And to get out of this, you will have to go away from my life forever. It was my ignorance and stubbornness that cost me my mental health, and now you feel toxic to me. I'm only looking for good vibes in life from here on. But also, I want you to know that you're the greatest driving force in my life. Because of you and everything you've put me through, I'll change for good. I'm looking forward to some great adventures in my life, to be able to explore myself, and build a meaningful life for myself. No matter how much I feel for you, I know we can never be together. You'll be in my memories forever as my first love, but I have to accept a life without you.

You're free to go…

RUPANSHI
India

P.S. A letter to someone special who touched my heart in the most magical way possible, and who's been in my memory since then. A letter to my first love.

SAMY,
Don't be scared of your own reflection.
The shadow you see is yours.
It's:
The girl who feels too much.
The girl who thinks too much.
The girl who feels the bursting consciousness of everything;
she's a deep feeler.
She absorbs the positivity into her salty bones
and creates room for more internal strength.
This is what defines her,
she holds the world in her hands
and walks as she unfolds her life.
Let no one stop you from loving yourself,

allow beautiful things to happen to you.

NARGIS
Dar-es-salaam, Tanzania

P.S. I wrote this for my sister. I want to bring her attention towards self-love. So she could forgive, embrace & heal herself. She doesn't love herself and it is painful to see her self loathing.

DEAR TALEN,

I couldn't find my words for some time, dwelling in this void, this place of constant overwhelm, as I ponder the predetermined ending I seem to find myself at the brink of. Tonight, I stared out at a luminous waning crescent, golden in her aura, and from that moment, a poem came to me. And so here I am, my heart evidently trembling as I begin to unpack every motion I have been going through for some time.

I held on to the wrong person, unseemly through their actions, bearing a mismatched face of perfect illusions and mystery among intrigue. I suppose that's what held me unfazed by low-level expectations. In these nights, unguarded, in vulnerability and waiting. Laborious in my private efforts to conceal every dream and aspiration away, as grimace consumed the everyday awakening I was met with, as the sun took up residence — preserving the only light I would ever need. For I could not be trusted with such control as I fell hands first to my knees to his every request — an ill-spoken submission, enervating my soul as I came closer to the ground.

I wish I could call this an idiom to mask my foolish standpoint, focusing on grander possibilities and excelling where I stand, as opposed to seeking reasons for comfort in my collapse. Lessening the fire with the decline that demands and the hands that wish to nurture another. My basal body discovered within itself elements that spark when struck against the cobblestones when running fierce with intentions. I found in the depths of my despair that it was only I who ever had the ability to source my tools.

But when I met you, I was once again reminded of the wish I had set out to make. I cannot retrieve the pieces of my heart from his life, but I can place mine in a metal case preserved until we once again find our way back to each other.

Until the stars align in our favour, yours forever.

S. WALLACE XX
Australia

P.S. This is a personal poem I wrote to my significant other over the span of his 2 years in jail. It was a lengthy, unforeseen journey for the two of us including our infant daughter whom I often replace with the "moon" and "sun" in all of my poems. She is the light of my life but his love kept me strong for the 3 of us.

Dear S.M.,

It's been about 3 years. You probably don't ask yourself if I remember it all, but I do. All this time I've tried to convince myself that I've forgotten about you, but the truth is, I haven't. I spend every second of my life thinking about you and I'm afraid that will never change.

Each November, I can't help but relive all the memories, even the painful ones. This month is a reminder that the leaves in the autumn trees aren't the only things that fall. I can't forget all the times you'd fix my glasses or that time we met in the parking lot just for a hug. I could only hope all the songs you sang were about me. None of these things might mean anything to you, but they do to me.

You might not know this, but I was ready to confess how I really felt— but it didn't take long for me to realize it wasn't worth it and I deserved better. I had created a version of you in my mind that was "perfect" but you were far from that. The words that hurt the most were all the ones you didn't say.

I'm not sure if I can say that I loved you, but I did care about you. You'll never escape from my mind and I guess it'll probably be like this for the rest of my life. If you choose to love someone else, I'll try not to think about how I wasn't the one you chose. I will allow myself to feel your happiness and only hope this will heal the broken parts of my heart.

My only hope is that these words will serve as remembrance of our time together.

> Sincerely,
> Ashley
> *United States*

P.S. A letter to someone who was never mine.

Dear fellow athlete,

We met in 4th grade. My first memories of you include a basketball incident and a lucky seating arrangement. We became fast friends, but I guess like all things rushed— it ended too soon.

I remember the days when we were happy. When you cared enough to help me in a certain Physical Education activity— because who knew shooting a ball was so hard? When you laughed at my comments on your slanted handwriting. When we shared sour gumballs in the classroom.

I wish we could go back to being that way, instead of me being the naive girl that I was. Too impulsive and too reckless with something that I should have kept hidden. Instead, my words were misunderstood, and you became aloof.

You left me there, embarrassed and taking in the mockery of everyone. You joined them, saving yourself and leaving me to fall. Such a contrast to the beautiful season of autumn, where though leaves change color, they still remain beautiful.

Not so with us.

Years pass, and I thought maybe we could go back to becoming friends.

How wrong I was.

Again, I felt betrayed. I thought the fall season had passed, and with so many days after, I thought winter had given way to spring.

Alas, like leaves forever separated from the tree, we were never meant to be.

I write to you wishing you well— for I do not have the heart to mean you harm. I write to you to let you know that I think I am better than I was then. It is not out of pride but of grace that came from the only perfect Father. He made me grow into who I am now, and I'm still growing. I guess, finally, I write to you to know how you are. And maybe, just maybe, we could settle how we fell apart.

Your fellow athlete,
Glasses-and-birthmark
Philippines

P.S. A letter reaching out to an elementary friend I lost due to a misunderstanding.

To the stranger at the bar,

It was at that place years ago, when I saw you at my favorite bar. I was with my friends and you sat two tables away from us. The first thing about you that caught my eye were your hands. Hands like an artist would have, covered in tattoos and playing with your silver lighter.

I looked over to you a couple of times and fell into a deep shock when your eyes suddenly locked on mine. So bright. So blue. So confident.

Shy, I looked down to my glass. Never have I been confident or looked beautiful in someone's eyes or even in mine. Next to my pretty friends, I always thought I could not compete. In my mind I thought you were looking at one of my friends, but when I looked up, you were looking right at me! And I was looking at you! Longer than before. My heart began to race a little and I had to look down again.

The beating of my heart got faster and with that— my insecurities rolled up my back, they invaded my thoughts and made me crouch down.

"No one looks at you, when you are with your friends!" The mantra repeated countless times in my mind. After only a couple of looks, shared with a stranger, I found I was beating myself up emotionally. Caught up in my toxic insecurities, I did not see you walking out with your friends. I just felt your jacket touching my back as when you put it on. I glanced over my shoulder and saw the wink you gave to me, followed by a cheeky smile.

The beating of my heart got killed by that mantra that was screaming in my head!

"No one looks at you, when you are with your friends."

I really wanted to talk to you, but I was so convinced that the only outcome would be a hurtful rejection. So while you smoked a cigarette outside, I got up and left.

On my way home, the voices in my head went silent. They won the battle, why would they have to talk to me now? The autumn breeze was cold this night, and I took a couple of deep breaths before I crawled into bed and cried silently.

When I woke up the next morning, I thought about the night before. I wished I could have returned to that moment, though I knew— I still would not be brave enough to talk to you. My sadness faded a little, because when time passed I saw something in this situation I did not see before. I saw what was standing in my way. It was myself.

In this moment I got a small vision of who could see and love me, if I was only able to see and love myself.

We only shared a couple of moments, no words or even names. But in some way, the fact that you looked at me and not at the others, changed something inside of me.

So when I let go of the chance to meet you, I felt that it's time to meet myself! I wanted this night to be the last battle that my insecurities won over my choice of happiness! Of course it was not, but I am in a much better place now. If we ever meet again, I would say hi to you! Maybe I'd never tell you the things I write about in this letter, but I would just say thank you a million times in my head!

Even after all these years, I still think about the beautiful stranger at the bar. You probably never thought about me again. And that's okay.

You showed me that a simple gesture in the right moment can shake the world for others. Thank you so much, for shaking mine!

MELROSE
Deutschland

P.S. The night I write about in my letter was a couple of months after my first boyfriend broke up with me. He left me, saying that in my life I would never have a choice in a partner and that I would have to take whoever sacrifices himself to be with me. I really loved him at that time, so these words destroyed every piece of confidence within myself. This is also a reason I could not talk to strangers back then. Today, I am free from his toxic beliefs, but still I would like to go back to the night at the bar. Just to know, what could have happened.

X.D.V.,
    Yes, it was beautiful.
    I see a stunning image of the past all around me.
    Yes, it was beautiful.
    You've added to the life in me.
    Started a new wave of looking within.
    And I thank you, but I do not owe you.
    Yes, it was beautiful.
    What was at the start is withering away.
    The impact remains and I acknowledge it.
    But please understand,
    I do not owe you.
    The way my heart beats for you,
    it's slowly getting tired.
    No one has ownership of my emotions, except for myself.
    You had a chance.
    Maybe neither of us were ready.
    Maybe not for a while.
    The space I held is closing.
    Because, I do not owe you.
    I can feel like that again with others.
    Recently I have, and then some.
    So what is it about you that I crave?
    I believe the way you look, the physical.
    It all would be perfect if you could just pull yourself together.

Come back, only correctly.
Because I do not owe you.
Your inaction speaks louder than the charm.
I require more than that.

    A.J.X.
    United States

TO THE ONES I LEFT BEHIND,

I'm unbearable. I think I was designed to break your heart. Each of you. Slowly. And there you are, never knowing you weren't the first– or the last. I broke my own heart, you see, at the age of eight– and from then onwards, I was only ever destined to break again. It was only me, for a long time, who shattered. Then I grew up, I got angry, I got hungry, I got desperate, much like a wild thing– that's when I started to do the breaking.

I hid it from myself, my destruction. I was clever, convinced myself it was you that left, it was you that ran scared the moment things became real. But if it was you– why was it always me packing a bag? Why was it always me that said things like," I have to go, I have a train to catch." It was always me who stepped on that train and looked out the window to an empty platform. It was me who kissed you goodbye in the airport at 4AM. It was me who jumped into that taxi and didn't look back. It was me who said 'until we meet again' – fully aware that it was a lie.

I had to become this wrecking ball of a girl in order to break down the cement walls that encased my fragile heart. I had been building those walls for over a decade. They made leaving so terribly easy.

But they also stifled my heart, suffocated it. It was never able to get stronger. To learn how to endure the trials of love instead of just running from them. But now the walls are down and I'm a brand new kind of terrified. The kind of terrified that has me unkissed, unloved, unwanted by another. It has me avoiding eye contact– it has me pushing people away– especially strangers– especially the beautiful ones– especially him. My heart is vulnerable, exposed– it has nowhere left to hide. I don't know if it can handle being loved longer than a moment. I fear I will never love anyone enough to stay.

    THE GIRL WHO RUNS AWAY
    United States

SAMIR,
   You're lucky both your feet are firm on the ground,
   otherwise, I would steal you away
   just like you stole my heart and my innocence
   and we would travel to foreign countries
   where nobody knows us
   we could make up a new story every day
   be whoever we want to — and always stay true to ourselves.
   I don't have to mask myself from you
   and I don't have to tell you how ridiculous this proposition is
   and how it wouldn't work anyways
   even if the circumstances were different.
   Actually — reality isn't that dark
   just bittersweet
   and that still tastes better than getting burnt.

   LUMINA
   Switzerland

P.S. The letter is from one soulmate to another. Sadly they were never allowed to be together, yet never stopped dreaming.

J.,
   I don't know how to write this.
   To bare my soul and show the scars you left, the ones still healing: and the wounds that are so fresh they have yet to make their mark.
   We shared a love that only two souls similar in flame can share. A bond that I thought would never break. Somehow it was torn in bloody two. I'm left: shattered. We crossed mountains for each other; we took planes and trains for each other. I thought that meant something. That we were always going to be there in step with one another.
   We are separated by space but never the time that we shared.
   These bones feel so heavy: Full of memories, full of doubt.
   I still wonder if I should reach out over oceans to grab hold, to grasp at more than memories and try to mend the break, but I feel the ice holding my heart in place, keeping it from crushing from the weight of our time together.
   You: spilling tears, as I explained death's embrace was too close. So easy

to relax into. That his darkness was inching closer than I'd felt before and it was beckoning me to shut my eyes and take the plunge. You always pulled me back; your voice kept me awake and rebellious. Singing songs to keep the demons at bay.

Ghosts fill my peripheral now. Dancing in the side view. Haunting my existence, as they resemble you so vividly and their movements reminiscent of our playground days.

I write this letter to release myself of hurt, of everything I thought we were. To remind myself you are not that person anymore. The love is gone. That path cannot be taken. If you haunt me, let me dance with the apparitions. Let me cherish the time I remember, but not hope for more. You are my past, nothing more.

KELLY LYNN
United States

My dear friend,
I don't want to drift apart
but life obstructs us
and leads us to different paths.
But just once before you're gone,
can we walk down memory lane?
It has been years now
and even if we break our hearts,
we'll warm our souls with its love
with the recollection of our pasts.
~ my dear friend

I'd like to share a musing of a person
in my life. Or should I say,
a person who is no longer a part of my life.
I wonder if after we parted ways,
she even thought of me.
I remember the day like it was yesterday,
that she came up to me and told me
she would be my friend.
I spent a lot of time with her in my childhood,
those times meant everything to me.
It was always difficult to make friends.
But when we talked for hours and hours,

those times meant everything to me.
I loved finding and learning about people
by asking questions. But she never asked me back.
Maybe, I should have known that deep inside,
she never really cared.
But in the end, having asked so many questions,
I guess didn't get to know her at all, did I?
~ An ex-best friend

SAMYUKTA
India

TO THE ONE THAT WAS A MONSTER— IN THEIR TRUEST FORM,

I often wonder why the world gave you such a friendly face with your kind eyes, and an almost perfect smile. I ask myself why they couldn't have given you just one thing that would have given me a signal — a chance to save myself. Why did your voice have to be so calm and collected? As if you were the most natural being of them all. You were the most intriguing stranger I'd ever come across — still yet, and I couldn't allow myself to let that go. No matter how much of a beast you turned into. No matter how much danger I saw. You were the one I would sacrifice myself for, not that you cared enough to see it.

I walked into your traps dazed with grace, and I walked out convinced I had gone insane. No way could you have done that to me, treated me like that. That wasn't in your nature, or in all the promises of change you would repeat nightly. I was held in your captivity, unaware of your grip around my throat growing tighter. I trusted you. With everything I ever had. And in return, you broke me. And I froze.

L.G.
United Kingdom

PHYLLIS,
    When the air turns cold
    and smells of campfire
    When hot chocolate
    travels down my throat
    When the sky goes dark

and naps are taken
When dew freezes
 on morning grass
When clouds are gray
and no birds sing
When meals are heavy
but made with love
When colors fade
and trees are toothpicks
When stacks of books
are on the table
When scarves are tied
and boots are worn
When decorations
appear from storage
When I grab the flour
and use my red mixer
When mason jar lids
are being popped
When the first snow falls
and we stay home
When cheesy movies
play in the background all day
That is when
I miss you most.

STEPHY NICOLE
West Virginia, United States

P.S. A letter from granddaughter to grandmother.

December 13th, 2021

DEAR D.,

It has been 9 years, 7 months, and 1 day since I last saw you. Even after all this time, I still haven't been able to reclaim the part of my heart that you made yours many moons ago. Sometimes, the love that this part holds is just a single drop, sometimes, it is an entire ocean. Most days I go though the motions of life with joy, but some days my longing for you catches up to me. Those days are few and far between, but when they come, they come like a tsunami. Waves of grief crash over me relentlessly, over and over, and

I let myself drown in what we could have been.

    I sift through our yesterdays, searching for just one moment where you might have loved me, but I find none. When I asked you— without even a single pause— you told me that you never loved me. You didn't even give me a pause I could hold on to. I came empty handed from my search. But emptiness is all that I have of you. I wrap myself in it and weave dreams of us.

    I wonder, "What could we have been?" I can't forget how your gaze was like the setting sun, coloring the skies of my cheeks crimson. The memory of that gaze like the sun still radiates warmth to every fiber of my being, setting me ablaze in your longing. I wish that my lips had the courage to embrace yours and answer the question your gaze had asked them. Now when I have the courage, our chance has long gone. I am acutely aware that the season where we could have been anything has passed. If only healing and acceptance could come with awareness. My heart does not want to accept what I already know. I don't know how to make it stop waiting for a tomorrow. But,

> If there is a tomorrow for us,
> End the war I have been waging
> With my heart;
> My every fiber aches
> From tethering it
> Against your gravity.
>
> Let me surrender to you
> And as I fall,
> Catch me with kisses.
>
> Let's swim in the tide of passion
> As it bursts forth
> Dispersing our clothes.
>
> Cradle me in our arms
> And snow on me,
> Gently,
> Flake by flake,
> Over my valleys and hills.
>
> Wield your sword
> And silence my demons,
> Let that silence
> Be filled with our moans,

As you lap against my shores.

Thus, reign over me,
For now, and forever,
If there is a tomorrow for us.

We may never have a tomorrow and I am still learning to live with that.

I know now, that loving you was never a choice. As long as you are you and I am me, I will always fall for you every single time. If you were to appear before me today, I'd fall for you again. The decade that has passed, and the people in our lives would not matter. Such is your gravity. Like the moon orbits around the earth, my heart orbits around you. Just as I don't have a choice in loving you, perhaps you never had a choice in not loving me. I don't resent you for that. If there is anyone I resent, it is the one who made me yours and who didn't make you mine. Isn't it possible that in the billions of galaxies out there, there might be one where you wake up next to me and call me, "Mine."?

After a decade, it still matters to me that you are happy and healthy. I can't even wish you ill— for if your heart were to hurt, mine would too. It is as if a piece of my heart is meshed into yours, and whatever you feel, I feel. Thus, I wish you love, all the love that I couldn't give you and more. There are volumes of things I haven't said to you, yet all of them could be condensed into three words: I love you.

>   Forever yours,
>   A.
>   *United States*

D.,

All I need in this moment is the simple touch of your hands rubbing circles on my back. The intimacy of your hand cupping my face. The tenderness as you move my hair out of my face. And I long for these things as though there will never be another tomorrow in which I get them from elsewhere. I don't want to remember the fights and the miscommunications and hurt, the way that, in every way possible, we are the worst for each other. Just the love. Because you are who I, and I know I'm who you, have loved the most, despite in the worst way.

>   S.E.
>   *United States*

P.S. When the holding on is worse than the letting go.

Dear lost love,

I loved you from the time when I didn't even know what love was. Just a thought of you brought me joy and happiness. My heart was beating for you all the time. I loved the feeling of "being in love". I made life decisions that could bring me closer to you. You were in my heart day and night. I never accepted any other relationship and rejected so many who claimed to be in love with me. My heart was ready to be with you forever, even when you were not even aware of it. Even when we were not together. Like a good friend, you told me everything— including your relationships, and I was happy to accept everything as it was. My love was different, it was like devotion.

In the end we got together. I was happy, but something didn't feel right. I was too much in love with you to see anything but light. I still don't know why I fell for you, why I loved you and only you. And more than that, what did I do to lose you in such a miserable way that my very faith in love was lost? When I try to make sense of anything and everything that has happened between us, I realize, you were never emotionally available to me. It was all visible from the start, but I didn't want to see. Maybe that's what is called Blind Love. We choose not to see. My heart sometimes cries loudly when it realizes, nobody changed, it was just me who was blind and then just me who refused to close her eyes. You were exactly the way you had been. When someone asks me what went wrong, I can't even say you changed. Because you didn't— but, my heart couldn't take the pain anymore.

I don't know how to forget and forgive you when every inch of my skin still feels the pain caused by the humiliation in those last few months. When I was dealing with the unknown swings of being a new mother, learning how to feed without griping about the pain, learning how to sit when those stitches hurt the most, learning to say I am enjoying motherhood when it was killing me inside. And when I thought you were there to support, you told me that you knew I didn't have enough strength to be a mother. Just because my body and heart were unable to endure the pain, I was told I wasn't capable of being a mother. I can't express the pain that my heart still feels when it recalls these words from someone whom it has loved. That day, when you told me "f*ck off", my heart lost it all. I cried the loudest cry of my life and something inside me simply left in a breath. You tell me that you wonder what has gone wrong? You even say that you never said anything of the sort and that I am hallucinating.

Dear lost love, it was all wrong from the start. I chose to choose you over everything I had. I chose to be and do everything your way without making a fuss about it. I was manipulated because I was too weak to see the reality and accept my fate. The more I gave, the more you took away from me. I almost lost myself, but couldn't bear to lose my motherhood in the name of love. Finally, I decided to break free. Life has its own way to teach you what you need to learn. When you ignore what you need to see, life uses bolder tactics to show you the way. I have learned my lessons (the hard way) and have moved on. Just like you, this pain also has a special place in my heart. I tried to release it, but it wanted to stay. I have stopped fighting it. It is the result of my purity and it will go when it's time.

Dear lost love, if you still wonder what this is all about, please don't force yourself to understand— for only hearts who can love can understand the pain and the hurt. I wish you the realization of what you have done, so that you don't do the same to anyone else. I wish you the strength to see the real you and to be who you truly are. I wish you to become a human who knows the value of all your relationships and not just few. I wish to meet you in some other lifetime where we are free from all past bondages, so that you can see the real me and I can meet the real you. I wish to discover that there was just something wrong with your circumstances— and that all along you were the man, the one, my heart was in love with.

And if you wonder who have I become now, here I am in few verses:
Her innocence died a torturous death,
In the name of love.
She accepted that togetherness for her doesn't exist.
Now, her heart is broken,
letting the universe send light in.
For she can never again love the way she once loved.

> YOUR SO-CALLED LOVE,
> ROMA
> *India*

P.S. Unsaid words to the only love of my life, my husband for whom I was once his wife.

Dear R.,

Do you remember that party when I first met our crew? I have such vivid, good memories of meeting everyone, dancing, and laughing. Getting to know the people who would eventually start to revolve in my universe, and I, in theirs. It wasn't until much later that I realized — was told, actually — that there was one person I was intentionally kept from meeting. There was a plan, probably not elaborate but effective nonetheless, to keep this person out of my view, and I out of his.

That person was you.

I laughed about it at the time, to think that these people who didn't even know me yet thought they knew what was best for me. What a strangely profound control to take over someone else's life, even with the best intentions. I must admit that I do wonder, probably more than I should: what would have happened if we had met that night? Would anything be different? Would I be thinking about it still, a decade later? I'll never know.

What I do know is that I have felt every emotion from annoyed to grateful about the whole thing. Annoyed because it felt like fate was tricked, or at least postponed. Grateful because, had I met you that night, I would have fallen in love with you then. Head-over-heels. Free fall without a net. And you, undoubtedly, would have broken my young, naive heart. Not through any fault of your own, but because my heart was so fragile back then, and we both had so much growing up to do.

So, here we are. Nearly a decade, a lifetime, later. My heart has profoundly changed since that night. It is no longer young, or so easily broken. But one thing that remains — as constant as the tides that roll out each day and back in each night — is that my heart is so deeply in love with you. I fell, even with outside forces at play to keep me upright. It didn't matter when we met; the entire universe conspired for my soul to inexplicably be drawn to yours.

I know we can't change the past, and our circumstances these days are particularly complicated. I am grateful that, although we're creating two separate lives on opposite sides of the world, our stories are still intertwined in the tiniest of ways. I am content to spend my days merely in your orbit, supporting you from a distance and witnessing the incredible human you continue to become.

This letter isn't an attempt to change the course of history, and it comes without expectation. I am telling you this now for the simplest reason: it's nice to hear people tell you they love you.

Maybe one day, down the road, a twinge of doubt will creep into your mind that makes you question whether any other soul in this great big universe loves you. That twinge finds us all, at some point. My hope is that you remember this letter, and know that you are, you have been, and you always will be loved, by me. You always have someone in your corner. No matter what happens, no matter how far apart our lives take us or how much time passes until we talk again; that fact will never change.

You are loved. Forever and always.

>   xo,
>   J.
>   *United States*

P.S. I wrote this letter in an empty hotel room the weekend of my 32nd birthday. I had just spent a few days pouring my heart into a handful of poems about this same person, but there was so much pain still inside that I decided to write this letter I assumed would never see anyone else's eyes. It is written to a friend who I have loved as more than a friend for over 6 years. We are still friends; I am married and he has a serious partner; and these are the words I could never ever say out loud but that play on repeat in my mind at night while I cannot sleep.

To my bestfriend & roommate,
  You told me,
  I always leave
  I'm a terrible friend
  I can't stay in contact

  It went from,
  Let's get a drink, I need to vent,
  To Wednesday Criminal Minds episodes,
  Making sure we had overlapping days off.
  Texting all day, everyday,
  Getting our nails done together,
  Gym sessions
  Helping you move into your first apartment,
  & calling out of work together,
  The time we had job interviews together - only to change our minds
  to go to Knotts Berry Farm last minute.
  Concerts, so many concerts.
  Can't forget the festivals either,
  San Francisco to see our favorite comedian.
  Vegas two times only a week apart.
  So many drunken laughs and conversations,

just as many drunken tears and vent sessions.
Before we knew it we were roommates,
my love for butterflies clashing with your love of R2D2.
Somehow they worked together.
Best friends.
A sister I always wanted
2.5 years at a job that equated to hell but we took it on together.
We went through school together,
Helping you get that AA degree - a chore!
We went through relationships, heartbreaks, hook-ups, betrayals
Injuries, car accidents, surgeries together.
New jobs.
The ups and down of life.
Trials and triumphs.
A whirlwind.
For 3 years,
We kept each other going.

And just like that,
It ended with,
"I left the key and garage clicker on the table"
You know —
It hurt.
They say the ending of a friendship
is worse than romantic break ups —
It is true.

But,
I can't blame you,
I knew,
You told me.

>Love,
>DeAndra
>*United States*

P.S. Friend endings tend to hurt the heart in a unique way. These are words that needed to be written.

R.M.,

You showed up, took all my breath away, and whispered your love to my heart— fulfilled me with your own life. I had more words than ever running through my mind. How could I decide on what to say if all I wanted was for you to tell me that everything was okay? You were here to stay.

So many times, during the day, I'd have to stop whatever it was that I was doing to catch my breath— because I was so caught up on smiling that I'd forget I had to breathe. And at night I would wake myself up a thousand times just to know that I wasn't dreaming. You were real and I was living. I couldn't breathe, and yet I was full of life.

And when you left me you tore my world apart. All my words were lost— but still, writing to you and about you was the only way to be near you. I didn't have words to explain what I was feeling, and yet that was when I needed them the most. For a girl who always has a name for everything she feels— I felt empty, lost, and so, crying did its job. My tears became my words— words of pain, words of love.

MAYARA K.
Brazil & Japan

P.S. The beauty of falling in love and the pain of being left behind.

Every street here screams your name—

every road,
every cobblestone path,
or worn walkway in the grass.

It's all I hear on the fjord's breath.

And I want to run.
I want to follow them to you.
But I fight every instinct,
every thrum my heart sends
out in return
like a love letter kissed
with lipstick as postage.

I want to kiss you.
I want to wake up in your arms

after being lulled to sleep
by rainstorms in June
as the shadows of the mountains
blanket us through the open
latticework windows.
But I stay still,
and look out over the bluffs,
and purposefully get lost
with every step.

Because I am terrified to fall in love with you.

Because you might love me too.
And that would make our ending so much harder.

FREYDIS LOVA
United States

P.S. Honestly, I've been having dreams about Norway for years now. There's always been a pull, and after every dream, I feel as though I'm waking up from memories- so I thought I would write about it. Love letters to a place I haven't been to yet (in this lifetime).

SAL,

With time, broken pieces of the heart exist as a dull ache— which only hurts when you focus on it. For me, it is when I allow myself to dwell on the grief I felt after losing what was never mine. It was such a strange time when we met for the first time. I still remember. We were in college and you were seated two rows away, but you made every student tap the one beside them until they reached me. It was just so that I could look at you and for you to shy away and blame your friend. I knew it then, just like I know it now. It was you.

I say 'was' because what we had was something fleeting, obstructed by time and our honour towards ourselves. We had dreams to accomplish, places to go. Yet when I see your face now, I see sadness, tell me my love, are you not happy?

I remember how in every step of the way, we were put in the same group together — always. You probably didn't know but I believed (I still do) in destiny. We were united from what we learned from each other. After all these years, my parents still ask me— how did their introvert girl became more open and social? I don't tell them, but it was you who taught me not to care about other's judgements and to just laugh it off. And I pray I have helped you be kinder to yourself.

When we went on a vacation together with our friends and you were infatuated with a local girl, I wondered if it was to make me jealous. My best friends laughed at me when I told them I had a crush on you. They said I could do better and that you weren't good enough for me. But we used to talk late into the night, you told me secrets which no one knew. You showed me a side of your heart that was raw and honest. So, why did destiny choose to make us walk separate paths? I suppose I never told you that with you, I felt the safest compared to all the boys out there.

I bet people thought there was something going on with us, especially the day when you chose to sit next to me even though there were several other benches to choose from. Everyone turned and whispered amongst themselves. We were laughing at your jokes until the professor yelled at us and still, we exchanged glances and tried not to laugh again. Everyone could see the sparks between us. I hope you felt it too. Did you? Then why are we now the kind of strangers we never were before? From the first time I saw you, you had a magnetic pull that drew me in and I felt I knew you right in that moment. I sensed you carried the same burden that I was familiar with, but you hid yours behind jokes— we were never strangers before.

I remember a day before you left to study abroad, we all said our goodbyes after that final exam. I went to the mall alone to drink coffee, hoping it would ease the ache in my heart that you left me with. Little did I know, you and your boys would show up there. That is when I lost all the restraint I held around my heart and I hugged you tight. In that moment, in the middle of the mall, surrounded by people, I hugged you and left a piece of my heart in your safekeeping. I knew this was goodbye.

After a couple of years, we met again at a party with our friends, and as expected, things changed. We were left with a fragment of the memories we created because the awkwardness took place of the emotions we once felt. We had stopped talking within days after you left, I still want to know— why? The one thing I will remember is that you never stopped praising my Starbucks hot chocolate order. It's silly, I know, but that was the one time I got to hear you call out my name in front of others, adorning a smile that I will always remember. The same smile that described those unsaid, unnamed feelings we once shared— our secret.

I ask you now, in the comfort of anonymity, did you ever love me too?

LUNA
India

P.S. The one who got away. Still not sure if I want to call it love or be safe and label it a two year long crush. Whatever it was, he will always have a piece of my heart.

Dear you,

I miss you. I miss the laughter and the tears. I miss having you here.

So much has changed since you went away. I'm not a child anymore, I've grown up. How I wish I could stop by and get coffee with you. How I wish I could hug you once more. There's so much I want to ask, so much I want to tell you. Time has flown by, yet you are still an integral part of my life and the way I live it. If only I could find a way to visit you, wherever you are. If I could find a way, I'd swing by in a heartbeat.

There's so many people I would want you to meet. There are so many memories we've made. There are so many questions left unanswered.

I wish I could bring you back, even if just for one day.

Hope still remains that someday in another realm, our souls will find each other again and know without a doubt there's a history between us. Maybe, in another realm, I get to hug you once more. Maybe, in another realm, you get to meet your great-grandchildren and the love of my life. If only...

One thing is sure, a dreamer I will always be.

Just like you will always be a part of me.

Ever yours,
L.W.
Belgium

P.S. She was my nan who died in 2006 at age 59.

J.,

It's the end of autumn again. Almost all the leaves are on the ground now. They don't crunch anymore when I walk over them. The weather in Oklahoma is weird. It's warm one day and freezing the next. December doesn't feel like December should. It's nothing like Washington. There's little green here. I miss the green. There's more sky here, more wind, more sun. The sun is brutal. Even as winter approaches, it blinds. I try not to miss. I try to be in the present, to find the beauty here; a teal door inlaid in red brick, the grackles gabbing in the Walmart parking lot, the crimson clay cracked along the shores of the Cimarron River and how it looks like cinnamon. My favorite view is from inside the Devon Energy Tower, the tallest skyscraper in downtown OKC. When you stand in the center and look up and see the blue, it feels like being inside a massive kaleidoscope, with triangular cut glass. There's a sky bar on the 49th floor. I wish that you and Cyndie and I could have a drink up there. The sky is endless.

I've never seen someone miss anyone as much as my sister misses you. She is the strongest person I know. The love you two share is raw and real and rare. The type of love that inspired ancient sonnets. Eros and Psyche carved from marble. It's a love I don't quite understand but I admire it. Not all of us get to experience this type of devotion. It is both a blessing and a curse for grief is the price of love. I try not to think about that April night, about the man that shot you, about how cold that truck bed must have been, about how so many lives can be forever shattered in less than 60 seconds and the pieces we pick up are the sharpest slivers of silver.

Yesterday, I saw a man inside Lowes wearing tan work coveralls, identical to the ones you last wore. He had a beard and sunglasses and for a moment he was you and that day came rushing back. That's the terrible thing about grief, it ebbs and flows and we construct motes and walls to entrap the hurt, but it always comes back, floods the levees, forces us to rebuild.

I wish that I could tell you that living with you and Cyndie saved me. The kindness you two extended toward me by opening up your home altered the course of my life in a deeply profound way. Moving to Washington instilled strength in me, reinforcing that I have the power to go anywhere I want. I wish I could tell you that my favorite part was waking up and smelling coffee, that your home was the first time I ever felt warmth inside a home. You taught me patience and play and that I can literally do anything as long as I put fear in the backseat, seatbelt it in and keep driving; through snow, ice, and ash.

I love you.

Always,
Amethyst
United States

When I told you I'd love you forever,

it came with the weight of the universe, and it was then that I knew it would take a lifetime to get over you.

We were made up of stolen glances, drowning in each other's eyes because they say "I love you" at the same time. Our snippets of silence meant more than anything that might've been said in a moment of truth. Let's get lost in the dreams that flood our minds when looking into each other's souls.

Your love was as big as the sky. Bright, magnificent, & beautiful. But it was also cold & more lonely than the Earth we walked on together. All I wanted was to keep you warm, always. In that moment & in every moment I knew I would've burned for you. I would engulf myself in flames to keep you warm. And I did.

For the first time I believed in love. In reckless abandon. In lawless devotion. Maybe I believed too hard and burned too strong. Because those flames turned into smoke, & it blackened your sky as I watched the sun set in your eyes.

I thought that was it. A love that burned so fast it suffocated and died just as it had begun. But I didn't know love could exist in the dark. Your night sky shattered, revealing the constellations of stars that you are made of. Your soul is a kaleidoscope of colours I could marvel at forever.

My mind constantly replays the nights where the magic of Old Europe had us under its spell. Between cobblestones & constellations, it was your soul, my eyes, & our night sky that became one. In that moment I believed we would last forever, but maybe a moment is all we were ever meant for.

Because in the morning we would have to forget. Last night was when I believed in magic and forever, but now I'm not so sure. I was deceived in thinking the brilliant light I saw in you was all you, but it only exists when we combine. Whatever I see in you is a reflection of the fire in me.

Now all that's left is just me, the sea, and the morning light that looks so much like your soul, but not quite. Even still, my irrational heart fully believes that something inside us has always, and something inside us will always know that love is real and forevers exists.

When our souls return to the universe, we will dance along the infinite constellations of lovers who lived. No longer looking up at the sky wondering how we could ever be one again, because we will be the sky. Although we may be apart, day & night, we will be what makes the next world turn. Bright, magnificent, & beautiful. Dark, mysterious, & yet full of light— for the lovers & the lonely who know where to look. Up. Because the stars belong to the sky & we belong to each other. In a moment of truth, burning in love, I knew you would be the kind of person it takes more than a lifetime to get over.

C. Le

P.S. It's so fitting that you sent me a picture of your piece, "For a moment I believed / we would last forever / and maybe that's all / we were ever meant for." because these words inspired another one of my unsent letters…

Winter

Dear Elias,

We said all we had to say. Now things between us are silent. Hardly anything echoes in the well between our thoughts. And thus, it feels slightly futile writing this letter. But it seems, with you, there are always more words to say.

I don't really miss you. Not daily. You were a total pain in the end. A three-year tornado. So no, I do not want you back.

But every now and then, I think of you and what we shared. The glimmering moments of magic that so often drifted between. Opening portals beyond what we could see, far into the night.

The adventures we unravelled through mind — dreamscape & the subconscious. I know a soul agreement when I see one. And thank our higher selves for bringing us together. And for pulling us apart.

I liked the way you smelt, the way your skin felt against mine. The way you were always curious. And how you blew my mind, with your intellect & conversations that stretched far into the night.

I liked watching you paint walls, and lose yourself in it. The hues & the colour. Dragged along the shorelines of waking and sleep.

You taught me to love the winter. In the beginning, when you told me winter was your favourite season, I never understood it. But how — when I walked with you through November and all her snowy days — that too made sense. For she made the whole world clear again. She made the world transparent.

And even though that was years ago. Your memories are planted like smooth stones in my pocket. The ones I left at home. And every now and then I catch a glimmer of winter sun on snow. I see what you saw, standing there looking out of the window. At birds dancing on fallen snow.

Love always,
Zerzura
Sweden & Kenya

P.S. What a relief it has fallen. To the ground, it rests. How beautiful our winter was. A season I will never forget.

My dear,

Although time has clouded my view of you, there are still instances etched into eternity. One was the first time I saw you.

This morning I woke up early to the crickets chirping faintly in the distance. Occasionally a car whistles by in the distance. I sit in complete silence, thinking back to the first time we met. It was a warm fall day at that cafe, my emotions flew despite the silence our initial connection made as we collided simply through that silent line of people. Though the sound was quaint, my heart pounded loudly like crescendoing drums.

Moments before, I remember noticing the ways you fiddled with your hair when you were lost in conversation. You kept swooping your hair behind your ear with your left hand, yet you wrote with your right. You primarily sat idle in your friend's conversation, but your eyes lit up at the possibility of sharing some brushed-aside wonder. You had a shy fascination with those you were with and somehow held all their joys in the depths of your gaze. Though I had come to this cafe numerous times before, when we collided, I never knew how deep your eyes resembled the coffee I sought for. I tried to play off the nervous tension with simple opening chatter that later ended with a "see you later." Your gaze held a storm, golden, strong, and beautiful, yet somehow calm.

Another storm brewing within the palms of my hand in a ceramic frame merely moments later, made me think of the calm to any storm. The white swells crashing, against the deep dark colors of freshly poured coffee, made me believe that somehow even here, not all storms were bad. That day somehow I knew, that I would do anything to weather your storm, if it meant stillness in you. But then you were gone. With that, the exit cafe bell chime transforms into my snoozed alarm.

And all of a sudden, the memory is gone and the sunlight begins to dance on the blinds reflecting over my eyes. Sleepily, I yawn as I start my day.

B.E.
United States

P.S. This is the only person I ever believed in love at first sight for, the features I often desired gained deeper meaning. She didn't just have beautiful eyes, but ones that nurtured, loved, included, and gave power to others. She didn't just smile with her mouth, or eyes, but with her entire being.

M. & H.,

I don't know which is colder— this December, or your heart. Truths are unraveling, and I can't question you, yell at you, or even begin to understand you. How could you hurt so many people you've claimed to love— so easily, so selfishly, so recklessly, leaving so much damage in your wake? This cold is captivating— it feels as if we may never escape it and the web of lies you've entangled us in, without choice or reason.

Part of me believes you don't deserve these words on these pages. But I deserve freedom— from the binds of my mind, the memories, the trauma, the questions, the anger, the resentment, the sorrow, the love, the hatred, and the confusion. I deserve to be set free from the answers that I do have, and from the ones I'll never know.

Unlike you, this cold spell will change. This season will pass. The clouds will clear. Things will once again change— they will start anew, and I will keep moving forward, leaving you behind.

DESIREE M.
United States

P.S. A letter to an ex-stepmother with issues of her own, but swore she wouldn't leave and then did without batting an eye and we were super close. This is also for an unofficial stepfather who had many demons as well who passed away leaving many things to come to light, adding to previous issues. These are the things that come to mind when thinking of them and the wreck left behind by them both.

DEAR YOU,

I've spent my last years as a teen and my first years in the twenty-somethings wondering how you feel about me. Wondering why it is that you've never wanted to go out with me or wanted to introduce me to your friends. Wanting you to want me in the same way that I crave you. I'm desperate for your touch and desperate for your attention.

I think I might be obsessed with you.

Wondering whether you've ever thought about me and pictured vivid pictures of me as I do of you. Your picture is spread through my mind, found embedded deep in memories of occurrences that haven't occurred yet. I have memories of your laugh and your voice that are splattered all throughout visions of the future in which I want to live in; a future with you.

I wonder if you ever sit and compare her and me, and internally wish it was her who had you in her mouth; her, who, with her slim waist and long silky hair, is probably ten times better than me at this. Me, with my 50 pounds of excess weight and nonexistent self-esteem, who could never possibly compare. I apologize internally, for not being the girl you deserve. I understand why it is that you keep me a secret, truly, I do; for I would probably keep myself a secret, too, if I could. I also apologize for all the reassurance I make you supply. I know it can be annoying.

I'm sorry. I'm a fixer-upper. In a big way.

All my windows are broken. My floorboards whine every time new steps land upon them. My kitchen sink no longer has running water, and dust flows freely through every walkway in me. The restoration process for this house called ME will take years to complete. It will be an arduous, daunting task.

But– complete it correctly. Take your time with it. Make the flowers on the patio blossom and I will feed you forever. Make my water run again and I will become a pool of incessant love for you to drown yourself in. Fix my floorboards and you will be able to walk alongside and inside of me for as long as my walls remain standing.

Love me, and I will give my all to you.

J.
The Dominican Republic

MY PRECIOUS,

I wonder how many words I need to borrow to put this together for you. For, everything is unknown and yet, nothing is not known to you. My heart is warm in this semi-evergreen land; as I proceed to pour it all out…

It's been a long time since we talked, love. It feels dumb wanting to hear your voice, feels dumb not to… and it has always been this way, yet never been this way.

My apologies… I do tend to go on in an endless jigsaw pattern, you see.

You left around mid 2020, and haven't returned since. What else have you left to hold on to? What remains, that is to hope for?

My eyes are witnessing a 'not so bright' summer, but my heart is stuck in the forever frozen Narnia. I am in a dark place right now, wrapped inside a cocoon, but I hope your homecoming can give me the courage to fly. And it better be as well with our world healing from years worth of pain, loss, and sufferings.

The cacophony might be getting louder now, but I like to believe— at the end of this agonizing traffic, there's a free highway waiting for a long drive. Where I can leave the wheel to you and bask in the glory of my first summer in a long while.

The world turned into a giant hell hole, my darling… it was just as they said, "The hell is here!" The same burning, suffering and shattering into new pieces every day. I wish I could pick up the pieces and put it back the way it was– never broken. I wish I did not exist to cease in a moment like this.

But then, I probably wouldn't be writing this letter either. I haven't written poetry in months, you know? No matter how hard I've tried, I just can't gather enough wings to carry everything that's inside me. It's like a swelling wave with no land to crash on. I am not the type to give up on hope, though. I long for a rainbow sky spilling confetti over the horizon and the softest snow to fall on when Santa comes to town.

I know one day we will get there, although it seems impossible for the time being…

For now you may wonder, what made me write this? At this point, does it even matter? Perhaps not, but I haven't been this vulnerable and uncertain since I was 13. You knew it. All of it. And you chose to fly. I might not have been the bravest or strongest in that time, but I always remembered to choose my wings.

I know you will come back and when you do, I will keep this letter to commemorate the journey we wayfared through… not necessarily together, but always to get back to each other.

Oh dearie past, I hope you are in a better place in the future… forgive me as I leave this intense present for you. You might be no one anymore, but will always be 'the one' for me.

Woven from burning heartstrings ~

Your ghost from the future,
Arani
United States

The month of December,

It's sad days for me. It reminds me of what I've lost— a very important companion to my heart. All month, I find myself only thinking of the memories we made together. Hero was a very kind and gentle soul, he made everyone feel better. Feel happy. He, himself, was made of the best ingredients: sunshine, hugs, love, happy days, and bright beautiful nights.

I miss my Hero so much, but it brings me comfort to know he's always watching and protecting me, even though I can't see him.

I can feel it— there's an invisible soul string that will always connect our hearts to each other. Forever.

Kristal
United States

P.S. Thank you, my Hero, for the unconditional love, happiness, and wonderful memories. Hero was the best dog and companion I could've ever asked for.

To my loving dad,

Time stops for no one, yet the night I was told you were gone has probably been the slowest of my life. To watch my healthy, happy, full-of-life father wither away like the last leaf of winter still brings ice over my healing heart.

So much has happened since you left, Dad. I could write pages and it still would never be enough. I moved cities, Mom has grown more reserved, and your younger daughter is so much more independent— you would have been very proud of her. Mom still misses you, Dad. We still miss you. You never left the dinner table conversations we'd have at the end of every day. I still keep your glasses folded away in my box of favourites, though over time, they look withered, perhaps wishing their owner would come back.

I've grown, Dad, from always having you as my backup in any problem, I've had to fall many times, but I've learnt to pick myself up. I can fix a tyre on my own; I manage my finances all thanks to your planning. I've lived in two new cities and have so many stories in my box— the wonderful people I've met, the adventures I've had, the pictures taken to reminisce— and yet, the very person I wish to tell all of that to is not here.

Remember the day you told me how you felt when you lost your Dad, the way you felt the earth move beneath your feet? I never thought I would have a day like that, but losing you felt like that and more.

I still see you in your favourite chair on the balcony. I remember you when I eat your favourite raspberry ice cream. I miss your warm hugs and your pats on the back, but most of all I miss the entirety of you. You were my rock and I still feel like I'm making my way to the shore, still swimming, still trying to find sunshine on gloomy days.

If I never told you before, I wish to tell you now, I love you Dad. And I miss you so. so. much.

I wish I could go back in time and have just a few minutes with you, or for just a couple seconds, be held in that hug from my favourite person in the whole world.

But like I said before, time doesn't stop for anyone,— life continues moving until it becomes legacy— mine now moving as yours.

My favourite physicist says that matter always remains the same, it just changes its form.

So you have only changed from a person to the wind around me. You are still here, and you will always be next to me.

Until I find you again.

All my love,
Your little girl
India

P.S. A letter from a daughter who never got to say I love you to her dad.

The Man of the Winter Moon,
   I'm in that winter of my mind again
where snow falls across the picture of your eye watching me
and ice crosses over my heart.
It's where the color blue has weight to it over my shoulders,
reminding me of your gaze in the stretching shadows.
I don't know who you are in winter's blue:
starlight, ice under moonlight, or evening's golden hue,
but there's always a hand that takes me out of my warm house
and into your cold embrace.
Without thought or reason, just a gentle pull
to tell me what I already knew, that the color blue has weight to it.
A weight telling me that though summer has my heart
I will always love you.

M. C. Flora
United States

P.S. This is to the man of the winter moon, who shone his light for me on my walks under ombre blue and pink skies. Who followed me while I went, and somehow always got me outside in the cold winter. He never failed to show up and make my night worthwhile as he shone over homes and woods.

That one person who changed my life forever,
   I am soaking in the warmth of the winter sun, the winds gushing over my face and the leaves rattling over the rooftop. There's beauty everywhere and every single detail reminds me of you. Every road leads to you as my destination, unaware of the fact that I won't find you waiting for me. I know you're not a part of my life anymore, but I still have overwhelming moments of pain in my chest— knowing I no longer have you around. At times, I thank the Universe for letting you out of my life. Then immediately, it seems, I'm reminded of the question: how could I be thankful when my

soul is adhered to yours? I've tried hard to let go, but there's still this hope that you're going to return. That the laughter that was gone with you, shall return too. I am waiting for the moment to arrive when I won't have to chase happiness anymore, when things will be the same with you again, when the glance of my eyes will meet yours and our hearts will smile, knowing how important it was for us to part ways, so that we could reunite. Knowing that we will no longer have to chase happiness, to come to terms with the magic of present moments. I am waiting for us to get back together. ♥

RUPANSHI
India

P.S. The stories and poetry I wrote during the departure phase are the closest to my heart. I felt so deeply for someone that my soul drifted away when they left. It was painful. Ever since, I've been coping with the grief, hoping for the day to come when they become a part of my life again...

December 2021

DOM,
Death of Me.

Last night, I read your old letters.

A nocturnal loneliness had crept inside. It made me nostalgic for what I had severed— I'm sorry I never replied. Like sifting for gold through your handwriting, I found it wasn't as bad as you said. Once, you compared me to an eagle in flight: *Graceful and beautiful to have beheld.* Now, after a year of non-correspondence, I wonder if I'm even worth your free thoughts. Or if you, too, revisit the days when all that mattered was if we were caught. As I brushed off the old emotions, a postcard and travel stickers fell from the envelope. I read *Take me to the Natchez Trace* and stared at Sabin snapshots of bald cypress lying pleadingly on the floor.

I fumbled over the sweet souvenirs and your letters, tucking them back inside.

Seven months of heaven, scribbled on paper, still sitting in an envelope on the bookshelf of a girl who tried.

CLEANTHA
United States

P.S. A letter to a right someone who came into my life at the absolute wrong time.

Why do these tears come at night?
To warm the snow before the morning,
and welcome spring with a kiss
after all the sadness of winter.

    FREYDIS LOVA
    United States

December 20th, 2021

DEAR GRANDPA,

It isn't only one day or a week without you. It is again another birthday, another fall, another whole year. Christmas is just around the corner. My favorite holiday of the year, even though it is a little less bright and beautiful than a couple years ago. But I'm still holding on to our traditions. That´s why I´d like to bake cookies today.

The recipe with coffee. The one that you always wanted Grandmother to make each year, because they were your favorite of all. This year, I´ll bake them all by myself. Grandmother doesn´t bake anymore. Actually, not at all since you´re gone. I gather all the ingredients, mix them together and maybe add a tear or two– because this time of the year it's so loud– how much I´m missing you.

Christmas is just around the corner. My favorite holiday of the year. Maybe it is a little less beautiful and a little less bright, but my heart still warms, because I will forever have all our beautiful memories, deep inside. I miss you!

    VANESSA
    Germany

P.S. This is a letter to remind myself of the beautiful memories I have– and not the ones we weren't able to make.

WITHOUT YOU,
    I'm lost in the maze of my path
    penned words written to express myself

I try to unscramble me
a weary sigh, reflected in the mirror

the ground feels heavier when you are not here
I feel my empty hands and know you are not here
grimacing at our empty bed
and a hallow voice that sounds like mine
I wish you were here

I have to let go
I need to let you go
my heart falls apart
I'm not ready to let go

picturing my life without you
a colorless daydream without you
my mind steers to you
what are you up to?
what are you thinking?
are you happy?

I'm too tangled in our memories
in the 'what if' and 'what could've been'
too hard to say goodbye
I'm lost in the maze of this path I'm on
what do I do without you?

BONNIE FAY
United States

DEAR E.,

The sky cried with me again last night with howls and thunder clapping through the skies. My soul held onto strings that keep me connected to you through memories in my head. My whole life I waited for this one moment, and my one moment with you was shattered. Too many pieces now on the ground to pick up again. And the haunting voices of the future, the "what could have been" and the "what should have been" scream loudly in my mind but no one else can hear them. Tell me, how am I to move forward now, when every moment is scarred with your face but you won't ever be here.

You don't realize how quiet the world can be in winter, until the world is born again in the spring. I didn't realize how quiet my soul could be, until I felt your life spark inside of me, and then blown out like a winter wind.

I am left in awe of how time can slow in moments like these when I'm used to the world spinning so quickly, dizzyingly. But in moments like these, time stops and I can only feel your cold hands and hear the soft hum of my heart and I wish I could give you every piece of it.

The cold months bring a stagnant energy in the air, similar to the one in my heart. Like broken trees dead before spring's air, or like this crunchy grass under me, dormant from winter's cool breath. I lay here breathless and begging; pleading for you to be here with me, because I can't accept you're already home.

Elle R.
United States

P.S. A winter letter to my heavenly daughter.

December 22nd, 2021

Letter to L.,

I really thought that after six years, we were safe.

Six years. Camp and youth group trips. Game nights and dessert dinner theatres. I thought we were safe after I fell for you, confessed my feelings for you, moved on from you. We went into our own separate relationships; she broke up with you, he married me. Life went on. Somehow we were still good friends.

But damn, when she broke up with you, I had your back. My phone rang as I was settled in our apartment for a relaxing bath; you were driving back from BC in the same vehicle as the girl who'd just broken your heart.

We talked for over an hour.

In the months that followed, I did my best to console you. I invited you in on the summer of adventure with my husband and I; he and I agreed you needed some decent humans in your life.

We celebrated your birthday; it was the night you finally said "I love you," no joking strings attached to the words. I looked into your eyes.

I love you I love you I loved you.

You came for game nights, drinking nights, overnights. We went for a walk in the snow that one morning, that crazy mutt in tow. And I looked at you and I knew that a part of me would always love you.

We went back inside and you left and I curled up next to my husband, content with how the lines had fallen.

Time passed and things got worse and finally I was whispering to you, is this okay is this okay is this okay? as I described the actions of the man I had sworn till death do us part.

You said, no it's not.

I said, I know, now what?

I remembered your summer of grieving, the way you told me that she was the one person that truly broke your heart. I remembered jealousy and wishing that I had left such an indelible mark.

My own summer of hell came and went. I was so relieved to know that even though man had failed me, curtailed me, scared me... at least I still had you.

My best friend.

Six years.

And yet, it would seem I did not.

It's not even the ghosting that wrecks my heart. It's the empty promises that begin to choke that part of my being that swore I would never allow such shallow hu(man)ity to sink me again. It was the enthusiastic words - oh how I've always loved our words - that put a chokehold on the way I thought we had formed.

I'm coming to you. I'm phoning you. I'm investing in you.

You matter you matter you matter.

I guess... not?

Six years and a part of me wants to symbolically delete your number. The other part wants to call you up and scream your name and ask how you could be the further cause of my wrecking?? I've been bulldozed and torched and yet somehow, still I rise! Why couldn't you have been one of the rungs in my rescue ladder who allowed me to lean on them? You said you would. You said I could!

Such a vacuous vacuum of promise, all your empty words! They used to be the choicest gold I kept close to my heart. Have they been pennies all along? Or did they just become a useless currency when you decided to string this friendship up by its neck?

Perhaps I started this mess by swimming in your gentle eyes and flinging my honest heart at you through them. And yet... I remember you invited me in.

I cry for you and I would've died for you! Many a night a part of my soul has withered like a rose. There will always be that love inside me, but I cannot afford to keep holding out my palms for you. My heart has bled and bruised enough.

Six years and the lines have fallen in different places. I don't know who I am without that part of me that lives for the connection with you.

This is my goodbye to my expectation from you. I have lost so much this

year, I suppose my heart can afford to lose one, two, three, four...
Six years, and this is the line in the sand: there will be no more.
Even as my heart still whispers in the depths of the navy night sky,
I love you.

DABRIA K.
Canada

P.S. I fell in love with my best friend when I was 18 years old. Over the course of six years, multiple girlfriends on his part, and an abusive marriage on mine, somehow we retained our connection and the love that had grown out of unspoken feelings. When my marriage ended, my best friend ended up ending our friendship because of the girlfriend he's currently with. This is my heart's cry to him, my last love letter, my release.

GRANDMA,

I'm making your trifle recipe.

It's just started snowing, too— I know you're looking out for me, I hope I'm making you proud.

I let my nails grow now, so they can be as long and as beautiful as yours used to be (I remember you telling me I shouldn't bite them). I often reminisce on the days we would walk to get fish and chips during the school holidays and when you'd make me fish finger sandwiches for tea...

When I take our dog for a walk in the winter (you'd love her by the way), I look over at the trees and think back to you catching frosted spider webs with twigs. They always looked like tiny, magical dreamcatchers.

There isn't a day that goes by that I don't wish you were here to see me walk down the aisle. My big day simply won't be the same without you. But I am just glad that you got to meet B, he's wonderful and makes me laugh every single day. I sure do hope that our marriage is even half as happy as yours and Grandad's.

Anyway, back to the trifles.

I LOVE YOU, ALWAYS X
MAGIC & MUSINGS
United Kingdom

P.S. For my late Grandma, who I miss everyday. x

R.A.J.,

In my world, you're the most certain thing.

R.J.Z.
Philippines

P.S. You are the most certain thing in my life, and one day I will open up to you. Please be patient with me. You're a very special person in my life, and I know I want to spend the rest of my life loving you.

To the one who's good to all,

Before I let you go… It's raining, the clouds are playing their notes, while I play the songs in my playlist. The lightning keeps penetrating my dark room with its glow through the windows. I have covered the glass with paper, but no matter how much I lock myself in, the light will find a way to enter. It's raining, I hear the drops falling on every surface, it makes me long to see you, to feel the gaze of your eyes on me, and to be a part of the land that you are a part of. I don't want to write this letter to you that I have already started piecing together. I'm tired of the entire process of writing letters, of not being able to send them, of safekeeping them with the hope that they will reach you someday. I'm tired of finally submitting to the realization that I won't be inhabited by you, so I delete all that I wrote to you. I regret it, I want to relive what I felt, but I can't.

It was 2:14 AM and I woke up shivering again, from a beautiful dream that turned tragic. You were leaving me, again. You never actually left and it was me who kept standing there with my hands stretched out to hold yours, to help you stand as you were hurt. And thinking all the while that you are letting me in your life by making me a part of your joys and grief. Being the biggest fool in this huge bed of flowers blooming for you with love dripping like honey from my fingers, all for you. I still remember every line from the only poem I wrote for you and the rest about the loss that I felt at your lies. It's been years and years yet to spend but things are better now, as it always is. One can never change the lines of one's palm, but can only choose to walk through its course, changing paths, a change for the better. You know, I forgot to wish you on your birthday and I felt so proud, having forgotten a day that was star marked in the calendar of my head. I screamed with joy, patted my back, and said, *I am proud of you.*

Today went well, I ticked off everything from my to-do list and I'm exhausted in a happy kind of way, satisfyingly. But I want my heart to feel again, it seems that these feelings have left me with numbness of a numb practical world. I want to feel, I want to take your name. But I also realized that I cannot be both, I cannot love and not be loved. But please, come break my heart again, come say those words that kept giving me hope, that made me believe, *you are good the way you are, you are enough.*

So right now, I'm in the practical world but I don't want to let go of how I feel about everything, so I keep writing. What was reality is becoming fiction with a belief that someday I will get to feel everything, and so I cling to these emotions by writing them. It will get better, as everything eventually does. I won't let your lies strip away the love that I have. I said, remembering everything, *I am love, I am love.* A little drop fell from my eyes, invisible in the dead of night, only to be felt on the skin, and I went back to sleep. I hope that you are okay and I hope that you're at peace with yourself. Please have a good tight sleep. Be happy.

Yours,
Muskan
India

"Love you, see you later.",

It was last year, 2020, in December. A few days before Christmas— the darkest day of my entire life.

I remember it like it was yesterday. It was a nice cool early morning, and your eyes had no life in them. It's like the brightness of your soul had left. I had never seen you look so lifeless. The nurse came to tell me that your condition… she said it wasn't good. She said you weren't going to make it.

I still had hope that you were going to be okay. I never expected the nurse to tell me that you were going to die.

I couldn't stop crying— the salty tears kept running down my face like an endless waterfall. I was in shock. I didn't want to believe her. I didn't want it to be true.

I asked the universe or whoever was listening, "Why did this have to happen to him? Why did have to happen to me? Why?!"

And in the next minute or two, you were gone. Forever.

I never got to see you later that day, but you knew how much I loved you. I miss you every day. The hardest part was because of the pandemic, the hospital wouldn't let anyone go into the rooms to be with loved ones. I tried to go into your room anyway— I tried. I didn't get to be by your side to hold your hand. But you knew I was there. You knew how much I loved you.

> Kristal
> *Puerto Rico & United States*

My granny's last words to me the year before she died:
April 16, 2017
   It looks like an awful dark night.
   Bye baby, I love you.
   Take it easy.
   Y'all be careful.
May 27th, 2017
   Bye darling, I love you.
   They're about to grow up on me.
   See you all later.
   Bye bye.
December 10th, 2017
   Is Carl here? Oh no. No.
   I must have been dreaming.
   I had two girls and one boy.
   My boy died when
   he was 10.
   Take care, honey.
   Have a good time.
December 24th, 2017
   This is better than I thought it would be.
   This is the best Christmas.

- I wish I wrote it all down. Every story. Every word.

   I barely saw you the next year, after moving away. I don't remember my last conversation with you. I don't remember your last words to me. I don't know if I said I love you, I don't know if we said goodbye, or if we just said *see you later* and believed it.

> Leda
> *United States*

P.S. I need these words to be read and remembered. By someone other than just me. Please remember her.

Hello again, love,

You really make a fool of me when I'm not paying attention. I'm almost embarrassed of loving, love, so much. I'm not embarrassed of loving who I want or the way I want to, but I'm embarrassed about the way you make me feel. You turn me into your slave, doing whatever is needed to keep you, even if that means losing myself. I'm always waiting for you. Sitting in love, basking in the hope of it every day, with or without the presence of a lover, because even if they're not physically here, mentally, I know my love for eternity is coming. Love has driven me crazy. A one-way road to mad love, as I like to call it, and it doesn't matter how I get it or where I get it from, I want it. I've accepted that nothing in my life about love has been traditional, and I used to be sad about that, but I'm not anymore. Traditional love doesn't matter to me anymore. I'm finding out that what I really wanted all along, was a love that lasted and a love that was just mine.

Every love I've ever known has humbled me because I knew I was blessed to have it, even if it was a fleeting feeling. I gave every ounce of love I had with you watching from a distance, knowing I would make a deal with the devil to have each love lift me up, and of course, you knew I was promised that I would soar above the streets of the brokenhearted and those looking for love— but you never tried to tell me that the expense of soaring was too high for some, regardless of how fast or hard I loved. You didn't warn me that they would clip my wings so that they could look elsewhere for a love that they thought was better than mine. Tossing me to the side with no regard for my feelings, only looking for the next semi-best thing.

Love, you left me weak and alone in so many ways, walking the streets of those I once looked down on, struggling with whether I could be loved through the pain and if not, what could I do to invite love back in? How could I align myself with a new healthy love instead of letting the old toxic love, that you sent me, consume me? It was in my weakness, though, that I found out only strong people know how to love, even if they feel like there is no reason to be loved or to love at all. It is within my weakness that my pain was transforming into something much more beautiful than I could have ever imagined.

People who now soar above me criticize me for not dating or rushing into relationships, but day after day, I try not to pay them any mind and I try not to feel embarrassed to be alone anymore. Ironically, the one thing from someone, emotionally, that I longed for, for so long— some days— I find within myself and from family and friends. I wish I could tell those that worry about me not to because there is a peace that I have found beyond the love of a potential lover, even if it comes and goes. Most days, I feel loved and powerful— more than I ever thought humanly possible, and it is a love and power that is mine. Love and power that can't be taken away from me, regardless of who I let in.

Today, love, there is no fear in not being loved tomorrow, because I know today and if only for today, I am loved for all that I am, regardless of if a stranger sees it or not, and I will strive to live my life proving my love for everything to the faithless.

>   Sincerely,
>   A Hopeless Romantic
>   *United States*

P.S. I have always loved the idea of love and for so long, I thought that I needed it from someone else. Truth is, I still love the idea of having love from someone else, but I know there is a love for myself that I need, also. Without a love for myself, there is no love for anyone else.

Rob,

Do you remember when you told me that in the world there are people who are zirconias and diamonds? How when you look at both of these, they look the same to the naked eye. It's only when you get a little closer that you are able to tell the difference. You said, with a world full of zirconias, the trick in life is to find the diamonds.

I think I knew the moment I first saw you in the bar years ago, that you'd be special to me. You came over to me on the dance floor and kissed me in front of everyone. We laughed and danced, two carefree young people. I am glad you knew that girl, I think I was a lot fuller back then, more innocent, less carved by life. You cared about me when I was no one, long before I became a someone. You arrived in my life at the end of an era, and at the start of a new one. I didn't know at the time you'd become a pillar I could lean against when I wasn't strong enough and a lighthouse so I could find my way back home. Through friends leaving, heartbreak, many tears, travels, new jobs, and moving away - you were there for all of it. A pillar and a lighthouse.

I read a story long ago that spoke of a phenomenon that happens only in the far north. On very cold windy, sunny days below -20, ice crystals will form in the air and when the light from the sun hits them, they sparkle like diamonds. When you try to catch those little pieces with your hands, they disappear - yet they still float all around you. For the many moments and people in life you cannot keep, you appreciate and love them for the time that you have. They call this phenomenon "diamond dust".

Thank you for years of dancing, lovely chaos and for the wonderful times we spent together.. I will never forget them. For during my worst times, you always pulled me back into the light and reminded me I wasn't alone. You constantly prove to me that people can be good, loyal, kind and gentle. You've never judged me for the suitcases I hide from the rest of the world, rather you're especially caring and gentle to them. To have known you has been the biggest privilege of my life.

If you fall in love one day, and we don't talk for years and you find yourself in a place where you feel alone, hurt or in need of someone who loves you, I will always, always, be there. I hope you know no matter where in the world I am, you will always have a place in my life and in my heart.

I imagine one day - a long time from now - someone picks up this book and reads this letter, and they will wonder whatever happened with us beyond the time this was written. My wish is for you to be remembered long after I am gone as the diamond you were to the world... and to me.

The last thing I would like for you to know is I love you and I see you. It will remain like this for however long I have.

Just like diamond dust.

ANNIE
Yukon, Canada

AUSTIN,

His kisses were like snowflakes, soft to the lips and gently melted into my warmth.

BEN
United States

P.S. To the one who keeps me warm, even on the coldest nights.

J.,
It's been nearly ten years, and sometimes I still think of you, even when I shouldn't. I remember the way you smelled and the taste of your collarbone.

The chapstick you used on the cold days — the berry tobacco from your pipe. You were such an old soul, your eyes ancient and a bit sad — like you'd lived a thousand lives and seen a thousand loves before you ever looked my way. Sometimes I think about the stack of books by your bed, well-read with cracked spines and worn pages. I remember you most on cold nights, and maybe that's why winter lives in my bones as it does: we met in the summer, and in the winter, we parted ways. Our time was very short, but you taught me many things. I was seventeen and naive, and hopelessly in love. For the first time in my life, I felt seen.

You cried the night you broke my heart, and I wiped your tears away — even though I was the one who was shattering to pieces. You held on to me so tightly as though you didn't really want me to walk through the door, but you couldn't ask me to stay or say this was just some cruel misunderstanding. You didn't love me, and you had to let me go to be fair to me.

I lost myself for a long time after losing you. I became someone I didn't recognize, someone I'm not proud of. But slowly, as the years rolled by, I found love again. And you got married. And in wishing you the best, I rediscovered the best in me. I realized you never meant to be cruel— but that you were lost when we met. I was never meant to be the one to put you back together. You were marble, and my hands were simply used to clay. I realized that it was ok to be myself, with anyone, at any time. I didn't have to hide because I am worthwhile just as I am. You knew that, and you selflessly let me go when you wanted to hold on. You couldn't give me what I needed, and I thank you for that.

I've seen you a couple of times over the years, but there has never been an opportunity to tell you goodbye, until now. To tell you about him. He challenges me every day and pushes me toward my dreams and goals. He makes me laugh. I'm grateful for him. But I'll always be grateful to you, as well. I'm not in love with you anymore, but I'll always love you. Thank you for teaching me that I can be happy without you. Goodbye.

It's such a relief to let you go.

A.
United States

MAVDEN,

I knew what it was, even when I didn't know your touch, your scent, your eyes on mine...

I knew what it was, when we felt our souls from far apart,

when you knew I was hiding it.
I knew what it was, when you showed up in my dreams, but never here.
I knew what it was, when it taught me more than I ever knew.
When your presence was louder than anyone present in front of me.
I knew what it was, when we were part of each other's prayers.
I knew what it was, when I let go but never waned.
I knew what it was.
I know what it is.
Love.

Forever grateful for having you.

FAKE DUCK <3
Sudan

P.S. A letter to an amazing online friend I've had for a long time. We shared all the happy and sad moments, but I never admitted how much he means to me. I wish to meet him one day.

DEAR BODY,
    that holds me together and all my love in,
    that I have looked at my whole life as a shell, a carrier,
    separate from me.
    I now see that you are my best friend,
    that there hasn't been a second you haven't been looking out for me,
    fighting on my behalf,
    sending me signals in the form of intuition.
    I used to hate you
    and because I am you and you are me
    I thought you were making me hate myself,
    but you have always loved me.
    And now I see that in those moments I was feeling hate,
    that was the outside world
    and outside people telling me I wasn't enough.
    It was never you.
    You've carried me to all my dreams,
    steered me from danger,
    warned me from going back to pain,
    because you always remember.
    You bring me the capacity for pleasure more divine than the sun,

for smiling and laughter and dancing.
You are not the enemy.
You are a friend.
The dearest and most loyal friend of my life
and I am finally learning
to hold you and feed you and rejuvenate you
in a way that makes you feel as loved as you've made me feel.

J.E.K.H.
United States

P.S. A letter of self love.

Dear Nanna Neen,

No godchild, Buddha child, or Cinderella should ever have to wonder if their fairy/buddha/godmother is alive or not.

No child should have to fear the day that the "just in case" adult chooses not to care anymore. Not to be there anymore. Not to answer the phone or reply to emails or even the letters. I know the world has been crazy, and I'm sure you're just as worried as the rest of us - but I'd love to hear from you. To know you're doing alright. That you know where I am these days and what brother and I have been up to in the last five years. Just because we're "grown up" didn't give you any right to disappear - to give up - to forget that we exist and so does your title.

Crunching leaves and tiny cups of piping hot tea betray me. Convince me you've come to visit unannounced - and I'd be okay with that. I'd be okay with the questions and the awkwardness and the confusion-laced anger as well.

Halloween reminded me that we can indeed be anything - anyone - we want. Something you loved to tell me when I was young so I wouldn't grow up to be like my father. Something you used to say any time I'd put pen to paper. Something I should know by now.

And Thanksgiving brings with it the lecture that we do NOT have anything to celebrate on that day because America's triumph is not ours. Because we have not yet done right by any tribe of our ancestors. That even our family and friends should not be gathered so ceremoniously, because you may have been a storyteller, but you value history far too much for these twisted lies that spread like wildfire. I understand you - I do.

But any excuse to spend time with the far few who motivate and inspire me is an excuse I'll embrace. Not to mention - we all need a break from the rest of the world from time-to-time. Surely, based on your radio silence - your mysterious absence - surely you of all people can understand.

Soon, the seasons will change, the stage will be all set and ready for Winter. I cannot bear it - winter seems to hate me in ways no other time of year can manage. Christmas will roll around and I'll watch my mother's heart break all over again because there is no extended family here and we were not invited elsewhere. And you still will not have remembered how to to call, to respond to an email, or send a greeting card (even though, you're the reason I love sending them.) The reason I reach out as far back as my address book will take me. The reason a new family in the house on Madison Ave gets love-letter-laced cards for EVERY winter holiday - because I hope he will return. Or they'll still forward his mail. The one you said was no good for me cause I'd never hold his hand or been out for coffee - but his precious heart is what made him so damn lovely in the first place.

I digress - there's just so much I have been dying to say to you for so long.

This next season - Winter - Christmas - the New Year and mom's birthday - even Valentine's too - they will all come for my heart with a vengeance because none of them will be celebrated or discussed or shared with you. Or Papa Bob. Even his February birthday will go on unobserved. I miss his hugs and the way he refused to stop reading to me no matter how old I got.

You have been so silent for so long that I've started googling obituaries in your name every Friday. That I send you postcards three times a week just to see what might coax you out of whatever phase you're in - whatever is going on. I write you letters like this every month - only I've finally stopped sending them because I'm so angry. So furious. So completely and totally livid - I remember when you taught me that word. I couldn't bear to have you see me like that. Though there are hints in this one, I'd definitely say this is tempered down and maybe, just maybe, that's acceptable considering the circumstances.

I miss you. I love you. I hope you're just busy.

Write back soon, okay - the worry has a way of getting away from us.

M. RENE'
United States

P.S. To a godmother who disowned her friend, thus disowning the godchildren during the most challenging year of their lives.

TO THE CAREER,

I always wanted you, since I was young. As long as I can remember it was you, you were the dream. I remember being asked, "What do you want to be when you grow up?" It never not being you. The television shows, the movies, the fictional heros, I wanted to be them. I wanted to be you. I wanted you.

I set my life up for you, school, college, degrees, I made sure I followed the rules. Kept my background clean. In 2016 we met, in 2019 - it shattered - my dream, my heart, me. You.

You shattered me.

By 2020 we were over.

So what's next? Once more, the journey begins.

D. JUANITA
United States

P.S. When everything you ever wanted just wasn't the right fit.

R.M.,

Saudade.

Please, can I have you? Can I have you already? I don't know how much longer I can stand it. This silence between us. This pain. The pain of missing you. The pain of the desire to have you here with me. You don't know it. But I counted down the minutes and seconds just to wish you a Happy New Year! But I wished it silently from across the world in another country as I was laying in my bed dreaming about your words, words that never reached me, words that never came. Like mine, that never got sent.

MAYARA K.
Brazil & Japan

January 7th, 2022

DEAR GRAMMY,

Hello! How are you? I wish I could hear the answer to this. I wish I could still send this letter to you. But I can't. You've been gone now for almost six years. It's hard to believe it's been 6 years. The last day I ever saw you was the hardest and saddest day I ever visited you. It was hard seeing you just lie there on that bed, in the nursing home. I had to hold it together, keep those tears inside. I don't think I really talked to you much that day. I knew if I tried, the tears would come. And I knew, even if I didn't want to believe it, that would be the last time I saw you. I am sorry I didn't say much then and I am sorry I didn't visit much as I got older. And I wished I could remember what all we had talked about, but I do remember a lot. A lot of great memories. From hopping on a bus and shopping at the malls, going out to eat with you, my sister, and friends of ours, watching TV together, playing bingo for pennies.

I remember you always had potato chips for me because I love them. Also, you would always cut up tomatoes and cucumbers because I love them too.

I remember spending holidays there, mostly Christmas, but occasionally Thanksgiving or Easter. Christmas was especially fun. Your tree was so pretty and I loved playing with your train with Chris. Even if we got it stuck in the tunnel a lot. Sorry about that.

I know you always said I was beautiful even though I never believed it. I still have trouble with thinking I'm pretty when people say it. I'm trying, but it is hard.

I love you so much and miss you a lot too and wish I could see you again and tell you all about me and Hurricane. He is my new cat. I know you remember Jasper. And maybe even Eli, since he was around when you passed. I wish I could share my poems with you and so much more. Again, I love you so much, and please know I will see you again when I come up to heaven.

Until we meet again, Grammy, remember I love you so much and miss you lots too.

Love, your granddaughter,
Missy
United States

S.R.,

Was it the way you looked at me. Or the hidden stories in those deep dark eyes. Or the gentle touch we shared in a bowl of chocolate covered almonds. You shook my hand and you smiled. You made a joke and we shared a laugh. You had me. 01.11.19

You were always enough.

From the moment we met, you put me on a pedestal. You taught me to be selfish and selfless. That I was worthy of a kind of love that only you could give me. You told me I deserved better than him. I deserved the world.

And you loved me, oh did you love me. For me. For all my faults. Imperfections. You said I was perfect. "My perfect."

You had a soft heart. You wore it on your sleeve. You were gentle with your words. You put everyone above yourself. You cared. You were funny. Oh boy, your wit. You made me smile. Really smile. And though I never doubted you, you always reassured me of your love for me. You unfolded me. Saw between the layers. And you kissed everyone one of them. You gave me your heart.

The kisses on the forehead. The gentle pecks on my lips. Your arms around me as my safety net. I could always count on you to make me feel heard and seen. You reminded me that the world could be gentle and kind as long as you were in it.

I longed for those late nights. I longed to have you in our four walls. Where the world went quiet and I could only hear the sounds of our breaths as you took me. Passionate and breathtaking. You knew how to make me feel alive. I could be so vulnerable with you. You made loving you so easy. We easily forgot all the noise around us.

Those walls knew our secret. They knew what we shared. I could lay for hours on your chest. Listen to your heartbeat. Telling me we belonged together. There was no fighting. No fussing or nagging. We only knew each other in those moments. I loved our moments. I loved you.

And I wanted it to be you. It was always you. Don't you see? We were meant to find each other. Although, our love story was tangled in a mess of our relationships, we needed to find one another. To remind each other what it was like to feel a pure, honest, intimate kind of love. There were no boundaries. No conditions. Selfless love. The kind of love felt deep within your bones. We were consumed by one another. If only time stood still for us to be in those moments forever.

Everything about us made sense. We were the perfect kind of love. You completed me. We are soulmates.

And yet, I hurt you over and over again. I only hoped you'd walk away so I wouldn't cause you more pain. But you stayed. You told me you wanted me in your life one way or another. We were constantly reminded of the pain. Of the thought of "us". You and I. For so long, I watched you ache at the thought of us. Of what could have been. Our dreams. Our future. And yet, you remained my constant. You held me up. You continued to love me. Don't you see, you were always enough.

I was scared. I was bound by my own insecurities. Everything that held me back to take that leap of faith stemmed from what I didn't want to believe. But you believed. You knew if I stayed I'd be miserable. I'd fall back into a vicious cycle of forgive and forget. You were always right. Your words echo through these walls. I only wish we could go back in time. I'd do it again. Only this time I'd choose you. A thousand apologies could never turn back time. But I'm here. I'll wait till we find each other again.

People can say that they love you, but it's what they do to show you and how they make you feel on the inside that truly matters. I love you, Bub.

And though we say we'll find one another in the next lifetime... my love, our love story hasn't ended.

JAANU
Canada

P.S. The best thing that's ever happened to me...

X.D.V.,
Hope.
I keep asking myself.
Going back and forth.
Do I even dare?
After you broke away from me?
I feel you'll have to prove yourself.
Maneuver differently–
make up for the mistake–
If you ever plan to communicate.
A space will be held,
for how long– I do not know.
But not too long, please know
another entity might fill this .
I know what I felt and all the signs are chanting
that you did too.
Nothing was done for it.
Left in limbo.
Left to disappear.
If you truly love something, you have to release it–
a process I know.
But I must embark on it.
With hopes you'll swing back to me.
If not, a new connection will elate me–
for I know now what I deserve–
and at the time neither parties had the nerve.
Not taking it negatively but,
indifferently.

I don't resent you for needing to go your own way.
I am now doing the same.
I'm releasing this for good and focusing on other aspects.
You are free.

A.J.X.
United States

Spencer,

Each night, as I lay down to rest, I go over my day in my head and I try my best to keep my thoughts from wandering back to you. In my dreams, there's no reality, no hurting, only the brightest versions of ourselves shining through. Even in a crowd full of people with brown hair and green eyes, I'll always be able to recognize you— as your aura is so bright and singular, so chilling and compelling. I constantly get deja vu. It must have something to do with you. They say, *What you don't know can't hurt you,* but what good is that to me when I constantly question what this could've been? Who we could've been. I beat myself up over how the universe could be so mean.

The only things I have left to remember you by are a single infinity sign and a horseshoe. Out of all the words I can utter at this moment— I just want to say, I love you.

Aura
United Kingdom

Shishir musu,

I wish to hug you tight in the nights I want some warmth. I wish to hold those hands in the nights I can't hold myself. I wish to see your smile in the nights I can't fake one.

I wish to love you in all the nights that could be my last.

Jen musu
Nepal, where the Mount Everest lies.

P.S. I would have held you tight if I knew that day was going to be the last day with you.

To the me I used to be,
   All of the things we're doing I can't wait for you to see
   what we can be.
   I found our voice and I let it be heard.
   I write poetry without fear
   so I can help the ones I hold dear.
   We're published and we're helping others like we always wanted to
   with our words and our stories.
   Never knew if we'd make it to our forties,
   now the way we be inspiring, oh Lordy!
   When we decided to leave that town
   we finally got to look around,
   the world is big and full of love
   and more than we ever dreamed of.
   The abuse we went through helps us to relate
   to help others change that 'fate'.
   We're not building shelters or doing social work,
   but we're creating and living a life that inspires others to do the same.
   Remember looking in the mirror,
   all the flaws you'd see?
   Now we make a point of loving every inch of *we*.
   A model, on the runway.
   Don't you see?
   We're doing exactly what we're meant to be.
   The art that pours out of me
   finds others who needed to see
   and the knowledge I have
   has grown times three.
   He said he controlled your life,
   but you knew all along you and your choices shape it.
   I've fought for those choices
   and we make them everyday.
   No one will ever control us in that way.
   The punishment and the poverty
   makes us appreciative
   and resilient.
   You will find you're stronger than you ever expected.
   And you won't let you or your family be disrespected,
   no, you don't let them disrespect you.
   You show them all you do
   while reminding them they can change too.
   We are love and we are light.

Every piece of us is worth showing and saving.
The scars heal and the addictions fade.
You won't keep questioning why you were made.
You find friends and community,
things you have always attracted.
You teach and learn and have energy to burn.
Missed a childhood.
Don't have a child, good.
For us.
But as a nanny we gained some trust,
truly believing in ourself is a must.
And keep reading them books,
you'll find a few that will truly change you
and then a couple that will contain you.
And your works,
it gets better, yes.
You even find a way to channel that energy.
you act in plays, immersive theatre, music videos, and films.
All of those dreams of 'being someone'
becoming so real.
When you lose them it'll be hard to feel,
like saying anything besides *why*,
why them, why not me?
Why does it feel so lonely?
But you carry them with you
and their strength too.
They're a reminder of the beauty we bring,
the light and love we can be.
Making my own stories to share someday
in a way we're happy today.
That we went through the stuff we did
and learned to love life in a real way.
Just don't give up, kid.

> KAYLYN MARIE
> *Colorado, United States*

P.S. To a younger version of myself.

My Daughter's Dad,

To the one I thought would be my forever… now that I look back at everything our history holds, I realize that perhaps I wasn't ready for the love you had to offer in the beginning. I don't mean to justify the hurt we caused one another, but I do believe that if we had met later in life perhaps you would've been my forever love. It saddens me to witness how something that once meant the world to two people can turn into something so dark and resentful. I wish we could see past the pain and that hurt that haunts the memory of what once was so magical.

Sharing that love that lead to a new life within me was an experience unlike any other, it is the bond that forever unites the ashes of our once true love. I don't regret our baby girl, she is the color of my life. I do wish that one day you can learn to forgive me as I have forgiven you for any pain I may have caused.

It no longer hurts me to know that your life no longer involves me. We grew apart and that happens, but what I don't want is for our daughter to grow up witnessing resentment in the people she loves the most; mommy and daddy. I wish you all the best in life. If I had one wish it would be to know that you can wish me the same and learn to let go of the pain that continues to haunt the only relationship we now have… for the sake of our daughter.

I wish to let go of any resentment and move forward for that precious little girl we now share forever. I send this letter off, hoping that perhaps you will come across it someday in some mysterious way and that it will sink into your heart as you realize it was written for you without having to say so.

Steph
United States

P.S. We were young and in love. We hurt one another to the point of no return, but not before we had a child. I wish to let go of the pain and move forward for that precious little girl we share forever.

Dear my guardian angel,

Are you out there? Out in the dark? Or right by my side?

If it is so, can you hear me? My silent whispers? I am hoping so much, that you can hear me and maybe even listen. There is nothing I wish more, than for someone to just listen. All the time I am wondering, if you are there. By my side. Sometimes I feel a strange brush at my arms. Like somebody would try to take my hand, but doesn't really reach. Or at least it feels like that. But maybe it is just the cold wind, which whispers that a sweatshirt is not enough to keep me cozy this night. But sometimes I feel something warm in my chest. I think, right there, where the heart is meant to beat. I feel it most, on the nights when there are only hot tears, streaming down my face— keeping me company while falling asleep.

So please let me know, my guardian angel. Is that you? Right by my side or out in the dark?

>   Love,
>   Ness
>   *Germany*

To Sixteen,

Honey, what are you trying to prove? Why are you so scared to show them who you are? I know, you've been told you're the silent, shy girl. If only they knew that was just your armor. I know, right now, you feel stuck. You feel like it'll never be your turn to bloom. You're scared no one will ever choose you. No one will ever want you.

But have you asked yourself– do you want them? Do you want him? Really. Or do you just enjoy the attention? There's nothing wrong with that but honey, take a good long look– he isn't worth your worries or affection. I hope you know that in ten years time you'll look back at these years and be proud of yourself. You did the best you could with what you knew at the time, and every child in some way, is conditioned by circumstance. You can't help so many of your insecurities because you can't escape them. You haven't had a chance to figure out who you are without being under a microscope of your peers– but you will. My darling, you will.

So keep your head held high, your braces look fine, please stop using the straightener everyday and for the love of god– wash the makeup off your face before you go to sleep. Some of the biggest changes in your life are headed your way and you won't be ready for them, but you'll make it through. Trust yourself a bit more. Listen to your intuition. Please, stop lying to yourself. Release those fantasies– they aren't real.

Being sixteen is hard, I would never go back and choose to do that again– but the one thing I can tell you, hold your friends close and hug Granddad and Granny for me. They won't be around forever. I'll be here, waiting for you to arrive.

Take your time. Enjoy the ride. xx

Twenty-Six
United States

To Thirty-Six,

I wonder if you'll even remember I wrote this. I wonder if you'll remember where I'm sitting, or what pen I'm using, how I'm feeling? Do you remember my dreams and regrets? Do you remember my fears and anxieties? Do we still have the same ones?

Are you still scared of driving? Still afraid of intimacy, of being touched? How long does that trauma stay with a person? Surely you've been able to sort through it by then, right? There's a few things I'm scared will keep me from being able to ever love or be loved in return– I wonder if those things are still true for you. I hope you're still writing. I hope you never had to give up and cave in to the system and get a job that you hate. Have you moved? Do you live by yourself? I never thought we'd be too good at living by ourselves– we love talking too much. Always wanting to chit chat and tell stories. Please tell me Mom and Dad are well. Give them a hug from me.

I'm always so worried about some freak accident or worse– a slow illness. May neither ever come to pass. I don't think I could handle it again. Not after watching dementia take Granny.

This is the year when three of our closest friends are getting engaged (they don't know it yet). Do you remember each proposal? Did they all go well? It's funny how all these boyfriends came to me to help plan the proposals. It's nice to be included. I'm happy for them, but also worried we will grow apart. I don't know how to tell them that.

Please tell me you're all still in touch. How are they? Do they have kids? Did Liv use the names Ezra or Valerie? Did she build her house behind on that plot of land she told us about? Did Lou move to Atlanta? Did she get married first? (We've got five dollars riding on who gets married first!) Did Red say yes? Did she finally get that job and the dobermans she's always wanted? More than anything– are they happy? Are you happy?

I hope you're over all the boys that broke your heart, I know I still write about them from time to time and I wonder if you do too. I wonder what you think of me. Idealistic, delusional, determined, ambitious, anxious, impatient, feeling like I have to keep all this momentum. I don't want to be forgotten. Left behind. Can you still hear me, this version of you, inside your head? Do you remember what it was like? Is it all so different?

I wish you could speak to me, offer a few words of encouragement, validation, or advice– but that's not how this works. Wherever you are, you get to look back on me whenever you want. But for me to make it to you? I have to go the long way. That's all right though, I've always loved the scenic route.

TWENTY-SIX
United States

DEAR M.,

It's been two years since we said goodbye in London and not a word spoken since. In the taxi to the station, I cried, and you held my hand, knowing we may never see each other again. We went our separate ways, standing on opposite train platforms. When I blinked you were gone, but you'd left your suitcase on the platform and came running back down the stairs to hold my face in your hands and kiss me. I guess that's the last time I felt loved. Clear as the waters, I sink into hoping your reflection might stare back at me.

In the stillness and solitude of this pandemic, the memories of you light up all the endless nights, but with a fire that scorches my insides. That blaze stretches from my side of the world to yours, over miles of clouds and ocean, so the distance between us feels insignificantly small. Even if, in reality it's not.

I know the right thing for both of us is to experience everything life brings in the short time we have it. To not wish it away somewhere else. We both are where we are, in this moment, where we should be. Ekhart Tolle says, "Whatever the present moment contains, accept it as if you had chosen it." Because we did. So I accept the sadness that comes from loving you... it's not something to push away. There will always be a dull ache and a heaviness in my bones. It just... is. Like how the grass is green or the earth spins around the sun. Gravity exists. So does the pleasure of having known you and the pain of your absence.

The best word to describe this feeling I've stumbled across is the Portuguese word, *Saudade*, which has no direct translation to English...

"Saudade is a deep emotional state of nostalgic or profound melancholic longing for something or someone that one cares for and/or loves. Moreover, it often carries a repressed knowledge that the object of longing might never be had again. It is the recollection of feelings, experiences, places, or events that once brought excitement, pleasure, and well-being, which now trigger the senses and make one experience the pain of separation from those joyous sensations."

I had a procedure recently and when they wheeled me into theatre it felt like I was having a complete out of body experience. I was holding my breath in silent tears (you know I love a cry) and the doctor that was trying to put me at ease said, "Think of anywhere you would want to go in the world and you can be there in an hour. I want you to think of that place as you go to sleep." I thought of London and I thought of you. In the presence of those big life markers, I guess a heart can reveal itself as mine did that day, and it made me want to tell you that, with no shame or expectation, other than I just needed you to know the significance of that moment. Even if I don't feel like that in a year or ten, or ever again, I felt it that day on the operating table, and that's important.

As the years have passed and will continue to, you should know, there is someone that thinks of you fondly in their darkest and happiest times... I figure that's too visceral to be shameful, even if it is equal parts crazy, magical, absurd and inexplicable. I like to think of it as our own tortured, twisted, modern-day version of a 1950's long lost love story, however fragile and fleeting it was. There are other flashes of love in this world that blazed like ours. I don't believe them to be any less important or real than ones that go the distance. What is "the distance" anyway? The distance is however far you go. And we ran ours with a boundless freedom that many aren't ever lucky enough to know.

Each memory of you is clouded in a love untested, it's a rare situation where we can live in a place in our minds having never truly disappointed each other. And there's something comforting about that. I'm not sure I would want you to see the not-so-great parts of me. So life hasn't tested us, broken us, revealed our darkness, forced us to give things we weren't capable of. To scream and never be heard, to fight about dirty laundry and who's done the dishes, or sit in silence like strangers across a dinner table.

Instead you'll always be a living memory of irresistible sunshine, song, recollections wrapped in music, long hazy nights, quiet comfortable moments, lazy days at the Heath, morning coffee, lost cobblestone streets, rash decisions, dark bars and reckless abandon. The feigned absence of expectation, total and complete presence, pleasure, pain, a comforting lie, an unending whim, the most beautiful untruth, forever a half-read book and unwritten chapter, the saddest maybe, a blinding illusion. Pure concentrated form. Saudade.

I feel someday we will meet again, perhaps in a different form, another lifetime. I'll know it's you when the time comes. If ever I'm stuck in the monotony of the every-day, these memories remind me we once took our chances and lived a whirlwind, ran our own race, the perfect distance.

ALWAYS,
C.
Austraila

P.S. This letter is to a love who was never an official "relationship"... there was a significant age difference and I feel we were both too scared to really try. The stars never aligned for us to progress, but they did in so many other ways.

Mak,

There is an ache in the cold. My bones feel softer today. More malleable.

Is there a method to understanding how our hearts billow and wilt in the same breath?

Yesterday I was all clouds, all endless and alive, all gentle, all sunshine. Today I am soil. I am lost in the earth. I am tasting the rain but I cannot get used to the absence of your name.

I am in a crowd and I hear your voice over and over again and I am trying not to pour across the pavement. Trying not to ease into growing old without you.

There is an ache in the cold. Summer is keeping its distance and I was never good at letting go.

Matthew
United States

P.S. Words she will never read. A realization that the changing of the seasons leaves an emptiness we can never return to. Summer is too far away to hold and so are you.

Hey brownie sundae,

There is so much I want to tell you, but I don't— because whenever I see you, it feels like everything for me has stopped. All I want to do is be there with you in your madness, listen to you talk, and hear about all your problems. You will never know how many lame excuses I have told myself, just so I could see you.

The thoughts of you and I holding each other's hand and having our favourite ice cream still makes my heart skip a beat. I know, in the real world, these thoughts do not have any place. I have tried, tried to stop myself from dreaming about you— about you being close to me. You filling up my senses. You lighting up my world, but I have failed every time.

I know you must be feeling sad because I am not spending time with you anymore . I also know, now, someone else is there who makes your heart skip a beat. The clock is ticking and I have to let you go because I know how you feel about her. You stupid boy, it is all there in your eyes— how much you love her. Truth be told, it does not make me feel insecure or sad— because I know your heart is in a safe place.

So, I have to end these dreams and close the door forever.

I am not a coward and neither are my feelings for you. It's just who I am. Long ago, I knew my feelings for you and I have accepted them. I know how you feel about me. I also know where I stand in your life. During the hardest days, you have always made me laugh. I will always remain grateful for that.

So give me some time, for now I am ending this chapter and letting you go from my heart— because I can't fight against my faith.

Your smile will always remain my weakness. Thank you for teaching me how to love you secretly.

Your secret lover,
K.
India

Hotstuff,

I love you. I'm in love with you. I know my confession is making you want to turn away... not that you were ever truly facing me, or even my other half. But what can I do? I'm in love with you— even though I wish I weren't. I have to confess, to try and get closure. For myself. I already know you're unconcerned by this. But for once, I'm thinking about myself. About my mental health & about my heart.

I'm shocked that you blocked me so suddenly... we didn't fall out. We were speaking more than we had in months. Actual words, conversations. Short, but there... and then you disappeared without a word. There was no inclination of this. I have to admit it felt like a slap in the face. I can't deny I wasn't planning to ask you to block me eventually, but I would have at least had a heads-up if I did. Instead... you just blocked me. Like not even a goodbye or a warning. I'm lost without you.

I've been turning to things I'm not meant to believe in. Like psychics and tarot. I know they just tell me what I want to hear. But you've driven me to it. My feelings for you have both healed and devastated me. I don't know what's worse... the pain I lived with before you or the pain I live with now.

S.F.
England

P.S. A man who literally changed my life. It was meant to be fun, a rebound. It turned into my greatest love. Unrequited love.

Hey you,

I hope you're doing well. I know it's been years since we met and years since you blew that second chance but I swear some days it hits me, and I can hardly breathe. How do you manage to do that after all this time? Why do you haunt me so? Do I drift through your mind like a ghost, some days gossamer and some days almost solid to the touch? That would only be fair, I suppose. A tiny part of me hopes I do. That I'm your "one that got away" story.

You've always been a writer; perhaps I'm tucked away in a journal somewhere, with you finally voicing the things you didn't say. Do you wonder what one more thing said might've done for us? If you had realized things sooner or I had the gumption to say, "Yes, of course, I still think about us." But it's hard to be vulnerable again after you've been hurt. We both had our walls. We were both a little more cactus-like. It doesn't do any good to dwell on the past so I hope you're happy. I hope you found someone that can make you roll your eyes and smile. Even if we never cross paths again, I hope you're out there, reading books in your favorite chair and falling asleep on the couch early with someone you love and I hope once in a blue moon, you think of me and smile a little wistfully.

We were good, you and I, I just wish we could've held onto it. I first met you in the winter, a cold February night that stretched on for hours and coincidentally— I left you there too, almost a year later. And a year after that our paths crossed again, all cold winds blowing and rosy cheeks, hesitant but delighted to stumble on the other.

You were bolder than you'd been the last time, so much bolder. Our lips met and suddenly it was as if no time had passed. We were the same two people that had met before, our souls reuniting like they might've for millennia— for no one can feel so familiar right from the start. Not unless, perhaps, we'd been stardust together once before.

Maybe in a distant past we had made it work or maybe we're doomed for eternity to meet, the stars always turning a little out of alignment, doomed to pass each other by, close enough to touch— but never close enough to keep. Maybe in our next life you'll be happy and brave enough to say everything running through that mind of yours. Maybe I'll be brave enough to say that yes. I miss you. Yes. I want to see you. Yes... Maybe in that next life.

But in this one we're mere whispers heard in old songs I'd rather forget. *Wicked Game* will never sound quite the same to my ears again. I wonder, is there something that triggers memories of me? I see you in the book shelves we'd browse on a lazy Saturday and in every guitar, I still remember you playing softly while I moved about the house. I hear you when the Raven is at my chamber door and how I felt when I truly made you laugh. I remember that smirk, and that smile for when I said something particularly eye roll inducing.

I can only hope that maybe that next life will be the one where we stay.

I MISS YOU PUNK,
C.
United States

P.S. A letter to the old flame who will always have a little piece of my heart.

R.M.,

Why should I talk about the stars and the moon if since the first day, you've been my sun and as I walk to work in the light of day it's you who's on my mind. More specifically, that day when I woke up and told you I missed you. Not because it was the first day I was missing you in the morning, but because I wanted to see if you would reply to me. I knew you were busy. I knew you were at school. I didn't want to bother you. But God, I needed you. And you replied, "I miss you too."

If you only knew the power that those four words had over me. More than your words, the breaking of a time pattern between us— and I'll tell you now why I never asked you about your time schedule, why I never asked you about the things you did during your day. About how you'd go to school— walking, driving or riding a bicycle. How much free time you had between classes. How many minutes for lunch.

I knew the time you'd wake up and I knew the time you'd usually go to bed. I knew we were together at those two moments of your day. I knew you were free to have me as a company, and you were choosing me every day… but what if I found out that you were less busy than I thought? What if I found out you were choosing me just when you had nobody else around?

I couldn't handle getting the answer, because I was already counting the time between seconds to talk to you just two times a day. And if I knew exactly when you were free during your day, it would hurt me too much. To acknowledge that I was getting no messages from you. I needed you then. I need you now. I need my sun back.

MAYARA K.
Brazil & Japan

P.S. The pain of being forgotten.

Dearest Snow,

Unlike my letter from before, this one might not reach you. And it might be for the best. Not that I have anything bad to say, but because this letter might scare you.

You have always been a good friend. Well, most of the time. Our time together has strengthened our friendship, maybe like how a glacier is formed. And like glaciers, there is so much more underneath. Things unsaid. I don't think you know how much you mean to me. I might even call you my best friend. But do you know why I dare not say it aloud? Because I'm afraid I'm not yours. And I do not want to assume. Not again, perhaps.

But, there is so much I want to do with you. Travel to so many places, work together, live together. And not in a romantic way, but in a way where we remain friends. Oh, imagination.

There is also much that we know about each other, much shared in classrooms, during walks, in McDonald's, and in your home in the province. It is always a special moment when you open up. And I can't wait for more moments like those. Remember when you treated me to McDo when I felt so bad after losing for the second time in a spoken word competition?

As much as there is good, there is also the not-so-good. You're stubborn in your own way that I have to defer to you. This compromise dance that we sometimes do I deem essential to preserving our friendship. Also, you hide your emotions way too well. You can be cold as ice, or at least that's how I perceive it to be. Nowadays, at least, I understand you more or less. We get along more, even though we are apart.

I guess this letter is not as frightening as I once thought. Somehow, though, I was able to settle these thoughts, and you were able to know them (indirectly).

At the very end, you are still one of the closest friends that I have. I am ever grateful for you. Cheers and warm hugs this winter, Snow.

Your Confidante
Philippines

P.S. Just some random thoughts I have about a dear friend that I don't think I'll be able to tell her.

Dida,

I stare blankly before me. Trying to string together some words.

But, everytime I think about you, tears tend to run down my cheeks instead. From the same eyes that I've been told countless times resemble yours. But I don't think I will ever be you.

There is no other you.

I've walked every step since you left searching for the same comfort I felt when you would sit me down and wrap yourself around me like a blanket in the cold winter. When you would hold your hands together and teach me how to pray.

And you took all of that away with you when you left this world. Leaving me alone, when I could barely understand how someone could just stop breathing.

I've always thought of you as my umbrella on a stormy day, to keep the harshness of this world from pouring down on me.

But now I cry endless tears just at the mention of your name. And I know. I know that's not what you want. You hated seeing me cry, hated seeing me sad. Would fight everyone and everything to have me smile again. But a deep hollowness is left in me and I know that it won't ever be filled unless I get to hold your hand again.

You're the closest representation of an angel in human form that I've ever seen. You loved me and all your grandchildren with everything you had in you. So unconditionally, so completely. I don't know how someone who has lived through so much pain could still care so deeply. I must have inherited it from you, this loving too much. It's my greatest weakness, and my proudest strength.

I feel like the older I get, the more I miss you. The more your memories come back to me. And all I want is to go back in time, when I still had the chance to breathe next to you.

I remember everything. How I used to climb on your back while you were praying. You never complained. Even though dad would always scold me, you would take my side instead. I can't help but smile thinking back. These small acts of love and kindness were just a glimpse at how pure and beautiful your heart was.

I remember drawing all across the white walls of our house, and the moment I was caught by either of my parents you'd say "she's just a child, let her be." You never tolerated anyone saying a bad word to me. If they did, you'd take it to heart. So much so that you refused to eat one day.

I remember holding the phone to my ear and trying to speak to you. Only to hear back something incoherent. Those were not words. Yet, in that state, from the other side of the planet, you still wanted to reach out. The desperation in your voice was clear enough.

I remember seeing you in a wheelchair for the first time. The strong, wise woman that once held my hands and taught me to pray, that gave me my name, cooked for me, and walked me to school, now could barely even take a step by herself. Perhaps the most painful part was not being able to see you smile, when yours was and always will be one of the most beautiful ones I'd ever seen. Now your mouth was lopsided, your head hung slightly to one side and most of your movements out of your control.

I remember that day clearly. The day I was standing by your wheelchair, my small young hand holding your aged one. The smooth texture of my palm against yours which was etched with lines of wisdom and pain gathered over the years. I remember holding onto it for a while and once I thought a long time had passed, I stood up to walk away. I slowly retracted my hand and your grip instantly tightened, silently asking me not to leave you.

The realisation hit me, that even though there were countless things you were no longer able to do, you never stopped loving me.

I remember staring down at our joined hands, and thinking "I can't leave yet. Dida wants me to stay." So I did. I stayed there a little longer, holding onto you. Not knowing that it would become one of my last memories with you. Because if I had known, I swear on my life I would have never let go. I swear that I would have stayed there kneeling next to you with both hands on yours and I would have never left. I would have kissed the back of your hand and laid my head on your lap and just stayed there. I would have just stayed and forgotten about everything else. That the Earth was still orbiting around the Sun, that the clock was still ticking. I would have stopped there even if time wouldn't. Even if it meant that you would still leave me. Maybe that way I could have been there when you took your last breath. I wouldn't have been miles away from you.

I just want you to know that I will always remember. And I will always try to match the size of my heart to yours. And if I could give you my heart just so yours could beat again, I would. Believe me I would. Without a second thought. Without a single doubt in my mind.

My Dida. My hero. I hope you are still smiling just the way I remember, wherever you are in God's kingdom. I hope you're in that place in Heaven you've prayed for all your life.

I love you.

Always and forever.

A.A.
London, U.K.

P.S. Unspoken words to an ever loving grandmother.

To Ely,

Hey, Ely. I hope you're doing okay. I just listened to your podcast episode where you talked about mental health. Very good stuff– very accurate– but, what I wanted to tell you was– you looked beautiful. ~Even though you also look like such an idiot XD~

Well… I have finally accepted that you're gone, and that you're never going to come back. But IF the situation ever would come— I asked myself what would I do? I loved you in a very selfish way, Ely. You're the first person I loved– so selfishly. I think that's what makes it ironic, you know? Like I told you– I lowkey sympathize with everybody. This causes me to be confused– is it love or empathy? I think, with you, I know it was love.

Maybe five years from now or even just three years from now, if I still have these letters and I read them, I'll laugh at myself. Adult me will address it as hormones or a dopamine rush. Maybe it is. Maybe there's no higher calling. Maybe, like you said, it's all only delusions– just an infatuation. However, I would still like to think that you were a piece of my heart that I was meant to find. A little scarred. A little broken. A little cold. A little too itself– a little brutally confident.

A part of myself walking around in this world and that was you. So, I guess I would not necessarily say that I'm over you. How can I ever be, entirely? Although, I think I'm starting to get over the idea that there's ever gonna be any *us*. Maybe it was never meant to be in the first place– but we can't deny that we hoped, right? I know you well enough to see you were in more denial than I was. It's okay to hope, though! You could've just let yourself believe in the idea of us. But you believed that things like forever and soulmates were never possible. You were the guy who wanted an explanation for everything. A scientific explanation. Maybe, after all, you've found one– for you and me both. But– let this sink in, that for a brief moment, you wanted to have no reasons, no scientific explanation, to love me. To believe that love– not just dopamine– exists. That the love we read about in books– exists. Please, just accept this for a brief moment and forgive yourself. My Elyaan with an E. The guy who tries to find a scientific excuse for everything that happens on this inside and out. (I'm not saying that there's *no* explanation. For it. There is. But just for a brief moment, listen.)

Let yourself believe that you're less of a robot and more of a human. That you have feelings. That you're *bound* to feel. And it's okay.

Maybe that was something that wasn't healthy for you, because as a person– you're constantly trying to find a meaning, a reason. A logical reason. Evidence. A scientific answer to every idea. To everything that goes on— all because you don't want to feel... lost.

But oh, we are lost, Ely. Maybe that's why love made you feel so *lost*— because you couldn't explain it.

I must believe that what we felt was love. I am quite certain it is. Please hear me when I say, I am so proud to know you, Elyaan. God, in this moment I just want to look at you. To admire you. To run to you. To feel that you're never going away. To feel that you're mine forever. But our reality is different. I'll always be proud that I met you, Mr. Ely. Half of my heart.

Maybe someday I will find somebody that I can love again. (Though I don't really want to.) Maybe when that day comes, I'll love him more than I love you. Maybe. Though I *really* don't want to— beause in this moment, my heart is yours. I only love you. I only *want* to love you. In this moment, I want it to be just you and me. Nobody else. Nobody better. Just you and me. Ordinarily broken people, imperfect— but human nonetheless. Lost— but constantly finding new ways to feel it a little less. Ah, I wish I was there with you. That I could hold you. As long as this world exists I will pray to god— as a sinner, as somebody who's flawed— to make you forever mine.

Even though I'm not a good person, my prayers always somehow get fulfilled. Maybe not in the way that I want them... but they still come to pass.

I love you, my Ely. The Zahru of this moment loves only you and wants only you and doesn't want anybody to ever come close to the kind of love that she has for you. But boy, oh boy. How lost she is. How lost are you.

YOUR ZAHRU
Pakistan

P.S. A letter to a guy that made me believe I could be loved. Then he dissapeared, because I made him think I wasn't ready for that kind of love, when in reality— I ached for him. It took me too much time to realise I how much loved him. By the time I realized this, my fairytale was long gone.

M.E.H.,
Valentine's Day. Chocolate. Flowers.
Love poems and proposals.
Relationship posts on Facebook.
I stayed home (alone) and watched Bogart films.
February 15th. I went to work, thankful the reds and pinks
and couples locking arms would be (mostly) gone.
I was reading Kerouac's "On the Road"
when you walked in the bookshop.

You ordered coffee (with more cream and sugar than coffee)
and as we made small talk; my soul sighed.
I knew. We would write a love story.
Thank you for these chapters of love and adventure.
Thank you for feeling like home.
That cup of coffee changed my life
and I'm so grateful you became part of my world.

> STEPHY NICOLE
> *United States*

P.S. To the love of my life.

HER,

When I first understood love in a romantic way, I moved so slow and so cautiously. After finding it and then losing it, I started to move too quick. Maybe I was excited by having that feeling again, or maybe I was scared that it would slip through my hands. Either way, I know now that I don't feel homesick for places, but for people. People that I can laugh with, people that make me feel seen, people that I love too hard and too fast, people that I can never have, people that I've lost. People like you.

> M. MILLER
> *United States*

P.S. To the one I can never be with.

DEAR G.,

I thought letting you go was the easiest thing to do, but I am having a hard time with it. Watching you live your life. Envious of who would love you better – better than I could have offered you. I wanted to give you the world, yet, I couldn't even offer you mine. Letting you go was necessary, but it still pains me to see you go. I still long to be with you, to give you the world– the world of love and hope.

> LOVE,
> F. WOLF
> *United States*

P.S. A letter to an ex-boyfriend that I am still friends with.

To the boy I tried to love,

Why did you make it impossible to reach you? What happened to make you push away so many people who just want to care for you? Why do you treat me like a stranger?

I held on for so long because you were the last man that I was close to before I got hurt– really, badly hurt– and so my little heart latched onto the idea of you. I desperately didn't want to lose my trust in all people just because one person hurt me. It took me years to figure that one out, that it was just the idea of you I was holding onto.

That's the thing though– I've known you for almost five years now and yet I barely know anything about you. Your favourite colour, your favourite film, the kind of music you listen to? No idea. When we first met, I wouldn't let you in– then years laters, you wouldn't let me in. Our timing was never right. Maybe all this trouble was the universe keeping us apart, because the truth it– we were never meant to be.

I let the idea of you take on a life of its own– in the end, even you never stood a chance against it. It's foolish, I know, but that idea of some version of you that I could trust was my eye of the storm. As I sorted through trauma and rode out the waves of panic attacks and nightmares– the idea that you were a man I could trust helped me from filling my heart with cement. But then the world started spinning again and I found myself basically at your front door and yet– you couldn't even spare an afternoon. You blew me off– you stood me up– it had been *years* and you didn't even make an effort. You *broke my heart*.

Standing in the cold– watching the minutes tick by on that stupid giant clock in the middle of London– and you, never showing up. Then hours later– seeing you, by chance from across a crowded room– you coming up to me as if nothing had happened at all– and in your world it hadn't. You're so blissfully unaware– you hurt those around you and don't even feel it. I felt your walls go up when you got near me though– that broke me in two all over again. You actively ignored me and talked to anyone other than me when you knew you were the only person I knew in that bar (and in that whole damn city). All I wanted to do was curl up and hide.

My feelings for you, that I thought were long gone, completely relapsed the moment I was near you again. All these chemicals flooded my brain and I literally felt rational thought leave my mind. Do you know how inconvenient it is to love you? I felt like a crazy person. You made me think you had never cared for me at all when years ago– you were the one who started all this in the first place. You even told the story of how we met in a different way to your new friends to downplay how much you pursued me— that shattered me. Humiliated me. You let me stand there in a sea of strangers and feel so out of place, judged, belittled— I felt so unwelcome— and you said nothing.

Do you even realize how much that hurt me, how much that night rattled me for days after? Weeks?

Only now— months later— am I finally separating the real you with the idea of you and convincing my poor little heart that they are not one and the same. The real you ignores me. The real you refused to kiss me when not too long ago you could barely stop. The real you humiliated me. The real you stood me up. The real you breaks his promises. The real you let me down again and again. The real you made me feel like nothing but an afterthought. The real you doesn't deserve me and one day you're going to realize you messed up. On that day, when you come back and say, "I'm sorry, please trust me." I will say *no*. I will never trust you again. That is why I must drain the real you from my heart— to be left with nothing but a trace amount of sweet memories and double the bitter ones to remind me not to be fooled again. I tried to love you, you know— I really did.

I would have been damn good at it too— but now— I'm glad you never gave me a chance to prove it— because you never would have loved me right, and I never would have said anything.

So, this is it. All I have left to say is— I'm sorry. I hope whatever holds you back from being able let people love you gets resolved before you lose everyone around you. You'll never know it (not for a long time at least) but you've lost me. For good this time. My heart no longer longs for you, for when you cross my mind— all I feel is disappointed. If only you knew. I'd like to think you'd change, but I know you won't. I've known you for half a decade and I may not know much— but I do know you've barely changed or grown at all. I wish I saw that sooner. I wish I gave up on you sooner. So much time longing for you and I probably didn't cross your mind for weeks, months, years. How silly. How tremendously sad.

I can feel myself detangling you from me— one heartstring at a time. Soon I will no longer be attached to the idea of you, or the real you. You will simply be someone that has happened. Like all the rest.

It's about time— it got to the point where even your own friends told me I deserve better. As someone who believed in fairytales, I never thought I'd tell anyone this— but darling, you really need to grow up. If you don't, you're only going to keep losing people. They'll be long gone before you even notice.

Just like me— right now— I'm walking out the door. Fading from view. Never even turning back— and you're off somewhere, miles and miles away, drunkenly unaware that you're losing me as I write these words. I wonder—

will you even notice I'm gone?

>   Kore
>   *England*

S.,
   And each year–
   in darkness we heal
   as leaves cement themselves firmly into the earth's depths,
   shadows allow rest.

Another season without your body against mine.
The years continue to pass,
the pain doesn't fade.
Our fire burns.
324 days.
The longest time we've failed to speak.
A moment, a feeling deeper than the ocean tides
and we whisper once again.
The flame.
My flame.
I often wonder how your hands feel wrapped around hers–
does she hold you as tightly?

I should have never let you go.

>   J.
>   *Australia*

P.S. A letter to the one I let slip away.

Dear Stranger,

I know, I know— you're anything but a stranger to me. But what else am I supposed to call you when we don't even have a word to define the relationship we had? I swear to god, I never planned to go on that trip until I found something to run away from. Only then did I pester my friends to death until they agreed.

So there we were– me and my friends– all on a trip (a trek to be precise) with 40 other people I'd never seen before (even though we studied at the same university). The trip was meant to be a week full of listening to my music and writing poetry, plugging in my earphones and wandering off aimlessly. Or a trip to just spend some more time getting to know my few friends who'd tagged along. Little did I know that it was going to end up being so much more than just that.

For the first day or two, I was determined to follow through with my original plan– putting on a brooding stoic face and keeping the earphones in. Almost no one wanted to– or would even dare to try and pull me out of the bubble I'd created.

Then, one day, I saw you playing with a dog outside of where we stayed during the trek and for a second– just one split second– I saw *you*. No, I didn't feel attracted to you or fall in love at first sight, but *I saw you*. In that moment I didn't, no, couldn't think or see anybody or anything else. The confidence you carried, it fascinated me. How you portrayed yourself intrigued me and seeing you play with that adorable but scary dog (because I find new company scary, let alone new stray pets) made me go all warm– internally the *awww…* alarm going off in my head– and fuzzy inside.

But being the person I am, I did not approach you. Probably because you were out of my league, even for a friendship? I don't know…

What I do know is that after that point I looked for you wherever I went, when I found you– I gazed. After a while I caught you looking back. Probably because you'd caught me looking a few times. Maybe you were contemplating whether or not to approach me?

Then the trip ended. I hadn't spoken a single word to you, but I was filled with strange emotions of happiness that we went on the trek together and sad regret that the trek had ended. Not to mention, a little bit of jealousy for the people who ended up making acquaintainces with you during that week. Mainly, though, I felt a whole bunch of emotions bundled up together– indecipherable, besides the one that was caused by the truth that we won't be able to cross paths again– which made my stomach twist just the tiniest bit in regret.

I would never be able to see you so upclose ever again. The trek ending meant that all reasons for us to ever come across each other again, except for that fact that we studied in the same university, had disappeared. And so I write this to you, or not– since I don't know if I'll ever send it you.

You were one of the few people who ended up making the trip memorable. It'll stay etched for a long time, and for that, I'm grateful. Your attitude, confidence, and personality in general is so admirable and you just made me want to try to get to know myself enough to be able to carry myself like you. But even after all this is said, I wouldn't turn back time and talk to you, not because I might be disappointed to find the portrait I'd painted of you so wrong— but because on the trip I was finally able to heal a bit. I was finally able to face the things I was running away from back home, and the truth is, I didn't have it in me emotionally to be ready for another person to enter my life— at least in that moment.

So, I will let that time in my life become a memory, a magical one, so that when I do revisit it through the years, I'll remember the beautiful parts alone: the peace, the warm fuzzy happiness, the snow all around— and you.

> Your Nobody,
> K.
> *India*

P.S. This letter was to a person I will forever be a stranger to. Where else would I let out all of the words I had for her? It must be here.

To a crush,

The urge to love you was as strong as the pull to go outside on a winter's eve and stare at the moon for hours.

The urge to hug you was as inviting as a copse of trees bathed in afternoon sun, burning like oil on the leaves, turning the grass emerald, tempting me into its arms from the hidden forest path. The urge to hold your hand was like the lake inviting me to put my fingers under its surface, to caress its heart. The urge to tell you that I love you was like the wind pounding against my shoulders, shouting reminders of you in my ears like thunder.

The urge to drown in your gaze, with that lake-like glow, was as enchanting to me as finding the very depths had the same color as your eyes. Completely by surprise, just like I found you.

The urge to kiss you, to pull you in, was never compared to anything, except to wanting to watch the sunset every night, hoping it caught fire against the clouds that reflected my soul whenever your gaze met mine— rays hitting clouds of orange peels and castles of ice and fire.

That's how your presence brushes mine, when the last light of day pours itself over skies, yet to show stars. It burns me aflame, washes me in golden glows, drowns me in lake-shine water. I feel that quiet urge to say something, and, tragically, I do not have a voice in this silent desire.

> To never be yours,
> M. C. Flora (someone who loved you once)
> *United States*

P.S. I've had a crush on a boy who turned lakes into reasons to need his eyes in my line of gaze more. This is for him, I loved him like I never loved anyone before, at least I thought I did. This is the Lake Shine I've written about, but I've given the title as crush instead. He's a friend of mine, needed when he was needed.

X.D.V.,
   It's not about you anymore. You're not coming back.
   I think I realize that now. I'll be okay.
   This is about me and I have to put myself first.
   It'll get easier in time.
   One day, I'll send out the painting.
   Maybe in March.
   Maybe before then.
   I'm just tired of my mind wandering to you and this situation.
   It frustrates me.
   I can't put a time limit on your healing or you needing space,
   but I have to honor how I feel.
   I don't like this feeling.
   So, you've got your space and your time for now.
   I just won't be here by the time you come around.
   If ever.

   A.J.X.
   United States

K.,
   I dreamt of you last night. Again. The third night in a row. This time, I felt the shape of you in my arms. That doesn't happen much.
   I woke up guilty, slinking out of bed like I'd done something wrong, but gripping that feeling around me as it slid, like a blanket off my shoulders, as dreams do. The more I woke, the more it slipped away. So I hunched.
   I sat at the kitchen table, stared out the window, and imagined a world with you and me in it. Felt the ghost of you still on me like a scent.
   And I breathed it in.

   Me
   United States

Dear Grandfather,

Sometimes, in my heart, a thought emerges— if you were not in existence, love would not exist for me either.

Would the heart flutter from its cocoon to create selflessness, if it hadn't been taught by you? Would words be an inexhaustible source of magic, if you hadn't shown me how to create that? Would the mind draw imaginations and rich imagery and travel the world, if you hadn't shown it possible?

Yes, sometimes, in my heart, a feeling emerges— if you weren't alive, love wouldn't be alive for me either.

Sometimes, in my heart, a feeling emerges— would beauty be so beautiful if you hadn't taught me how to appreciate and cherish life the way it is? Could this angry narcissist have become an empath and connect with the life of everyone, if you hadn't motivated me? Could this ordinary boy have worked his magic on the hearts of hundreds, if you hadn't recognized him and brought out the best of him?

Would he have been loved if the onlookers had not seen him in the same perspective as you did?

Yes, sometimes, in my heart, a feeling emerges— that if you hadn't been a part of my life— then beauty wouldn't be so beautiful.

Sometimes, in my heart, a feeling emerges— would time hold so many memories, would connecting with and meeting people be just a coincidence if you hadn't taught me it was destiny? If it wasn't for you, could I have learned that a mere coincidence could turn into a life long bond?

Yes, perhaps, if it wasn't for you, then coming across people in my life would not have been destiny but just a mere coincidence. The dreams that you pointed out to me on that starry curtain of the night sky— in those dreams, that sky, you showed me what is worthy, what is possible in this universe. I could see it all, in your lap.

Thank you for teaching me to see God in everything. Perhaps, if it weren't for you, life— and anything existing in time and space— would not hold my indebted love if I didn't see God's blessings, infinite wisdom, and love in them. Yes, sometimes, in my heart, a feeling emerges— if you hadn't taught me— then the connection of man with God wouldn't involve loving and cherishing God's creations as well.

Love,
Wolf in the East
Pakistan

P.S. A letter to my grandfather, who is greatly responsible for my character building and inherent courtesy and morality.

Dear younger self,

Slow down and know that in everything there is a lesson. Especially in things as simple as gardening. It is hard work to say the least. You'll sweat from all the weeding, digging, and cutting roots, you may get blisters from all the raking and watering every day, and some plants still may not last more than one year. You see, there are plants specifically designed to bear their beauty for only a season. It's crazy how all that hard work is in vain for 'annual' flowers. It is easy to believe if you work hard enough, and treat them just right, that you can save them and make them last. But even something so trivial as that is out of your control. People are similar, except people aren't so easily read. They don't have a tag letting you know whether they will last for a season rather than a lifetime. If anything, learn the consistency, hard work, and time needed to make relationships grow, even if you cannot truly discern the perennials from the annuals.

Or what about the blind? They have to learn to trust and know people based on tones in their voice along with short breaths and sighs. But even more challenging, they have to read braille— which is just moving their fingers over small dots. Each pattern of dots is intricate and has meaning, in its own way. Maybe that's how you love. If you can fall for the simple things, then even when the big things go wrong, you will still have love and be okay. That's the problem though, most are too quick to fall in love with big things like a certain body figure or a voice or a talent, but when those end or become harder to achieve they lose hope and just end something greater. Think of twirling your fingers around your palm. When you are deep in thought, simply brushing your fingers against each other is something amusing, and even if someone leaves or something happens you can always return to that simple enjoyment.

Finally, I hope you know that each person is intricately their own, singing their own song. Their tendencies are rhythms and their actions are keys. Each idiosyncrasy that someone possesses; the way they say common greetings, or the way their nose scrunches up when they get really excited, or the way they swallow to keep the flow of their conversation reflecting their innate passion, can all be compared to notes. The simplistic bliss of excitement over the mundane things that are easily overlooked. Those are keys, maybe a chord or maybe a couple second flow of music that hits emotions so deep. Why does it do this? The comfort, the trickle, the harsh dance of notes as the tones amplify emotion. The way each press, builds and falls, digs and relaxes to befriend emotion known by few. Other times, many people enjoy those things too. There are beats and keys and notes and chords that many people find delightful, lovely even; but it's not about adjusting to how they perceive it. Or playing the same song as someone else, but letting tones or notes inspire you as you merely play and learn new songs.

At the end of the day it's not the CD player's responsibility to choose what song to play. The tracks are preloaded. It just keeps playing. Like when those players get stuck, and you can't change the CDs out. Or even switch between the ones in them. It just keeps playing. Some people walk by, hear the song, it's not for them and they walk away. Some stop and listen for a minute because they appreciate it. They really do. But after 3 times through the same song, they're looking for a different one. Eventually, someone will walk by and hear that their favorite song is playing. The one that gives them goosebumps every time they think about it. That never fails to cheer them up or remind them to breathe. The one they blare at full volume and dance around the world to. The one they never tire of. The CD player didn't change what it was playing. It just had to find the right person to listen to. But it's not even that extravagant.

The goal shouldn't and can't be to find a person that is moved that way by every song. Realistically, it's going to be someone who recognizes their favorite song is up in the rotation. And even though they may not enjoy all the other tracks to the same extent, they're willing to sit and listen and wait for that one to come back on. You must find someone willing to choose to listen to every song. The good or bad. The danceable or cry worthy. Either way. Don't toss out any CDs. Then you're left with silence between the music and no one, not even the CD player, enjoys that. Finding that friend, that person to listen to all the CDs. That's so freaking hard. But in the meantime, I still think that each person can have their own CD, right? Like every one of your "songs" doesn't have to go to one person. But every song on one album can be fit for a specific person. You build a community that way.

SINCERELY,
B.E.
United States

P.S. Just a couple analogies that I have been thinking about a lot lately that have shaped the way I love those that are in my life for a moment or a long time, the romantic thoughts of love, and then how we can build community based on our innate idiosyncrasies. Lesson's I wish I knew earlier.

V.,

I have the honor to message you every day. However, we don't kid ourselves. It is not the same as it once was. We avoid saying it. We do our best to be there for one another and sometimes I sense that you want to give up. I don't know if I am writing this to you, for you, for me, or to what we used to be. I will say this. I am sorry that my love was the spark of a war. If I am to be collateral damage in the path to your happiness— promise me you'll find your happily every after.

ALWAYS,
LUCILLE
United States

P.S. The words we wish to say but don't.

March 11th, 2022
9:56PM

DEAR DONALD,

I'm writing this to you in the midst of our break-up. I'm driving to Ouray for the weekend while you spend a few more days contemplating how to articulate once more how tired you are of working on our relationship and maybe on Monday when you explain it to me yet again, I'll finally stop wanting to believe we can work.

It's been a week since your decision to take some space turned into two phone calls on why we are wonderful partners, but are not good for each other. I spent those two conversations fighting for our relationship and wanting to work through things. Yet, your response leaves me with driving to Ouray on the very weekend we should be together, turning your house into a home. It's difficult to fathom a future without you in it.

It's been a tough few months with work and looking for a new job. I felt so emotionally and physically drained. It's weird to think that while I was grateful to finally have a partner that I could rely on, someone who would support me during those not-so-great moments, and for you, those same moments were also contributing factors that built up to us being over.

I wish I would have known a few weeks ago when we said we wanted to keep working on our relationship, our life together was already at critical point. I wish I didn't walk out of the house ten days ago because I didn't know that was the last time I would get the chance to hold you.

It's now 4:09AM on Tuesday. Yesterday evening, I watched as you said goodbye to us and walked out the door. I peeled myself off the hallway floor two hours later just to end up calling you to ask for you to come hold me. You didn't think it was a good idea and didn't waiver in your response, but after so many lonely nights and now countless more ahead, one night of feeling loved, even if you are no longer my partner, was worth that to me.

I know I'm going to have to eventually figure out what to do with all this love I have for you and for us. I'm just not sure yet where to put all of it and there are moments when I feel like I'm drowning in it from the inside out. Loving you changed me and it should come as no surprise that losing you has done the same. You became a rock in my life. The one who could make me laugh till I cried. The one I tried new things with and looked forward to seeing the most. It's cliché but you weren't just a partner, you became my best friend. The one I could tell anything to. The one I could rely on for advice and hard-truths, even if they hurt.

The hardest part was not being able to celebrate our successes after what felt like our worst hump. This next chapter already feels so much lonelier without you. I'm going to miss the way you would talk first thing in the morning, how you always said you "needed" cuddles. The way you put yourself together for a hike. How you call Eleanor all these weird names and treat her like a toddler, oh— is that dog going to miss you too. Your pancakes and how you never seemed to mind that I couldn't ever make up my mind about dinner, even when I already prepped for a meal. The way you knew how much it turns me on when you nibble my right collarbone. The way when we reconnected, I completely forgot anything else happening in the world except for you inside me and us being together. The way we talked through almost everything. Even when the conversations weren't easy, I always felt like we were a partnership against the issue.

All the weekend trips with you listening to the risk podcasts. The way you would tickle me or have me laughing in bed. The night in Sedalia, when we were laughing hysterically together in bed for no true reason. Learning to climb and learning to trust you because of it.

Good morning texts and learning about facts with your job and degree. The way your family made me feel like a part of them. It's been such a long time for me since I experienced that. I know it was best for you to not have me around this past weekend, but not seeing your mom while she was in town and helping you paint or pull up carpet brought on such a different type of ache.

The stories you tell and how I always felt closer to you, even if our worlds couldn't have been more different with our childhoods. The way you included me in everything and how I felt so honored to be your partner.

That bottom lip of yours. I never did tell you how sexy I found that combination of baby blues and bottom lip to be. Most of all, your consistent and unwavering love. The way you show up for everyone in your life and how you showed up for me. The evening phone calls and all the moments you shared cute cat videos or how you even started saving reddit finds to show me when we were snuggled up with each other.

I might not have been able to articulate what I meant about how at times it could feel like I was on the back burner, but I always knew for certain I did and still do want to be apart of your life. I never wanted to stop working through those conversations and quit us because it was just about figuring out our own rhythm and what works for us as a couple. I'm sure it felt like I was dissecting everything, but at the heart of a muddled relationship challenge, I was trying to protect what was and is still great about our love.

Thank you for the love letters, I know to some people it looks like a tomb of depression to keep them after a breakup, but all I think about is the love we built. I think about a life with you that opened up so many new interests, explorations, experiences. A life still unfolding with one another. When I read them, this life feels a little less lonely. I look at the letters and I feel surrounded by love.

I love you.

KAYLA
United States

P.S. Mid-breakup love letter.

DEAR SOULMATE,

I am grateful that God gave me *you* or *us*. This letter is dedicated only to you. I wish we lived together to the last breath. I remember you said, *I love you, not your position.*

The majority of time in our relationship was spent missing each other. We miss *us* a lot. I know our relationship is different, complex, and complicated be able to meet each other. But our feelings are crystal pure.

Your every touch makes me feel peaceful. I am grateful to you. You make me laugh, cry, get angry, feel positive, energetic, and strong. I genuinely give all my love to you. I adore you so much. I know our circumstances do not accept us. I don't know about the future, but one thing I do know is that my love is always for you.

I want to share our untold Best Memorable moments:

- Our first kiss
- When we were in the theater watching the movie, "Spider-Man: No Way Home"
- Our excellent sense to understand each other.

I also want to share an untold Worst Memorable moments:
- When you talked with others and made me jealous
- We got caught in front of our bestie
- I was missing you and didn't have you with me.

Honestly, I don't believe in soulmates, but you changed my mind completely. I am so grateful to you. Sometimes you irritated me while you were under stress, but I can handle it. You know, you are the best person I have ever met in my life.

HALF OF YOUR SOUL,
RAHMAN S.
Bangladesh

P.S. A letter from a girlfriend to an adorable girlfriend with some untold words.

DEAR YOU,

Hey. It's been a while since we've spoken to each other. I miss you. There are days when I feel like just texting you and letting you know how much I miss you, and there are other days when I feel like hating you for leaving me behind. This is the first time that someone's absence in my life has made me cry so much that my eyes are all dried up. Please, for once, come back and tell me— why did you cut me off? Why did you leave me behind? Why do you look so carefree without me in your life? Why did you make me see a future with you when you didn't want to be there? Did you ever even care about me? Or was that all a lie?

And this time, please, if you come back, make me hate you before leaving. I don't want to stay like this. Please. I will be waiting.

YOURS,
ANA
Nepal

P.S. A letter to someone who forgot me.

My Pretty Talker,

It's funny to think that, in the moment, you meant the world to me. I woke up thinking about you and couldn't fall asleep until I replayed the conversations we had. The conversations... nothing salacious, but just being near you enough to talk about literally anything, made my heart race.

For years, you were my favorite person. I'm sure I told you that. It wasn't hard to see that I was obsessed with being near you. We would play word games. It made me love language. It actually pushed me to go to college. I didn't know I had it in me; the desire to further my education wasn't within me until you came along. You used to read "Me Talk Pretty Someday" out loud to see how long you could go without laughing. You couldn't go long without cracking a smile... and I held my breath waiting for those moments. I let you trace words on my back with your fingers. You would spell out a word and I'd pretend I didn't know what it was so you would write it again. Over and over: "love, love, LOVE."

We moved in together for a couple weeks before you moved away.

It was quiet when you left.

We didn't speak much after that, until you heard I was graduating. I saw you, of course I noticed you, in the sea of friends and families there in the stands for my classmates. You stood out, brighter than anyone.

And just like that, you were gone, all over again.

You talk pretty, and that will always stay with me.

love, love, LOVE,
A.K. Bay
United States

P.S. Reminiscing of a simpler time with an old flame.

To the bullet I dodged,

I never thought I'd write to you. Ever.

You crossed my mind so I suppose, there's something left unsaid. Maybe I'll find it in this letter. Then I can forget you altogether, all over again. It's been almost ten years, ten years since we met. A decade. 1/10 of a century. Sometimes that feels like a lifetime has passed, and sometimes just a few weeks. When I think of you now, I don't feel much of anything. A bit of anger for the hurt you caused— a bit of shame— knowing my naive heart could have only ever ended up being broken— but why you? I wish I had made it through that last year of high school never knowing you. Never spending hours on the floor of the band room talking about who we wanted to be when we grew up. Never looking for you in the hallway. Never spending extra time in the morning fixing my hair, hoping you'd notice. Never realizing that all along you were after someone else and just leading me on. Was I an ego boost? A joke?

I know I was shy, quiet, timid, sheltered, small-town. I wasn't the prettiest and I second-guessed everything and over-shared whenever I did have a moment of courage to talk— so why couldn't you have just ignored me like everyone else? If you were so into her, why did you ever even look my way? I was seventeen and you broke my heart and it had never been broken before. I cried and cried. I shattered. I was never quite the same. My family and friends noticed, I wasn't myself after that. Not for a long time. It'd be months before I got over the mind games you played with me— years even. You betrayed me, you destroyed me— all our friends stood witness to it.

You know, I really thought it would be you. I wanted it to be you. I actually believed I loved you. I even put a pathetic love lock on that damned bridge in Paris— with your stupid name on it. I never told anyone about that— but that's how bad I had it. To me, you were everything. To you, I was a pastime that got boring. We were kids, and you broke me like a favorite toy you had outgrown. I never knew I could feel that empty and unwanted, that unlovable, until you cast me aside. Ignoring me daily, twisting the knife deeper. I wonder— do you regret it? I hope you do. I bet you do— especially after a couple years ago when you messaged me on social media— wanting to meet up at a concert we were both going to. Asking to see me. I didn't see your message until after the concert was long over and you should count your blessings.

Maybe that's it— that's what I'm trying to say to the silly boy I thought I loved so long ago. That girl you knew? The one you told wasn't the kind of girl you could fall for— the one that hadn't done much yet, didn't say much in school, the one that wasn't enough for you? She's gone. Long gone.

If you met me now, you wouldn't know what to do. The thing is— I became everything I told you I would, that afternoon in the band room. She was well-behaved and sweet. I'm unkept, unruly, unpredictable, insatiable. I'm passionate and loud and cunning and everything you wish you never let go. It was foolish of you to ask to meet me— don't you know what would happen? A shy, timid girl would exchange pleasantries and say she hopes you're doing well. I'd eat you alive. I'll tell you *exactly* what would happen if you're so unlucky as to meet me at a concert:

You see me through a crowd of people and make your way to say hello, it's been too long. I talk a little too quietly so you have to lean in closer. I look at you like you're the only man on earth, I wait until it gets loud and dark and the world gets hazy before I get a little too close and press my body against yours. You can feel the bass pounding in your body and I run my fingertips lightly up the palm of your hand. The dense crowd holds us steady. You'll hear my breath, feel my warmth, you may even taste my lips– depending on how much I want you to remember– and you'll ask for more. Beg for more. You will ache for me and I will leave before your favorite song is over. Every time you hear that song on the radio, you'll think of me. The scent of my perfume will hang all over you to haunt you like a ghost. I will be the last thing in your mind as you lay awake at night.

You'll curse yourself for ever hurting me, for losing me again, for ever pushing me away in the first place. Your mother will remind you each Christmas that you should have never let me slip through your fingers and you will smile at your brother's wedding and get a little too drunk looking for the color of my eyes in the bottom of that bottle of bourbon and you will go home alone. You will always go home alone because she's pretty but she can't kiss you like I can so what's the point? Your hands will be cold and you'll look for me in every crowd of people– but you will never see me again. I will be your lifelong regret– so you should pray to any god that can hear you that you never see me again.

THE ONE THAT GOT AWAY
United States

March 13th, 2022

MY DEAR SHAH,

The reason I'm writing this letter is because I'll never be brave enough to face you again. First, I want to sincerely apologise that it took me some time to realise in what way I see you. I seemed so disinterested in you from the first time we met. I only realised what I felt or wanted to feel for you after I often couldn't see you around anymore. I realised I lost my gem.

I remember the exact day I started to look at you in a different light. Right after my aunty died– I was drowning in grief and was out for the first time after her death– seeing your familiar face and you just standing there looking at me with the calmness you always carry within you. You looked at me with such peace, as if you knew what had happened without me saying anything. Even though it didn't show on my face– that moment felt like it was only you and me there. Everything else went blurry. If it wasn't a public place and your friends weren't around, I would've just hugged you tightly for the longest time and cried. Your existence is comforting to me.

From the way you carry yourself, your ideals and your amusing (but bad) humour and just the way you look at the world with such peace and calmness and humbleness. It made me want to be by your side always. I've still not been able to process what happened. Only two days ago– I found out you are happily committed in a relationship with an amazing woman. I hope you're genuinely happy and at peace, finally. I wish I could have told you how much love I wanted to give you. You're just so lovable, even though you don't see it sometimes.

I haven't seen you in almost two years, but everytime I leave the house I hope to run into you– especially when I'm around the area where we used to hangout before the pandemic hit. I thought I was the only woman to say, "Only I can understand and love him the right way." I still wish that was true. I'm wondering, if I had told you that I really cared about you, and wanted to fall in love with you so badly, and already *had* fallen for you– would it have changed anything? I had the notion you were waiting for me as well, but maybe it only was my own projection onto you. I have regrets and so much anger built up in me right now. Regret of not telling you when I had the time. Anger that I missed my chance. I'm angry at myself. Maybe if I didn't overthink so much and just swallowed my pride it would've been easier to tell you what I feel, but I was scared you had moved on already or that you didn't want to settle down. But also, some anger towards you– that you didn't give me the right opportunity to express myself and just slowly, then suddenly, drifted away. I wonder if and for how long you were waiting for me as well.

I cried on the bus today because it just hurts to know I missed my chance. I couldn't even listen to the song that I loved so much as it reminded me of you. Life right now feels like a nightmare. But I should be happy, at last we both finally have parted ways after five years of uncertainty. If I ever run into you, please don't look at me the same way you used to, as it'll make things harder for me. I know for sure I'll never be able to let go of you, but I'll try to move on. Still...I wish my story had ended with you, Shah.

P. S. I wish I had a time machine.

Sincerely yours,
Shajia
London, U.K.

P.S. To the only person who made me feel understood and at peace.

Letter to you,
Have you ever imagined the snow melting? Did it look like the ending or the beginning? Although I've never witnessed an actual snow, I can feel it.

The darkness of night wraps me in a kind of freedom, and I am undecided on whether the day is at all different. You know, the trending reels on Instagram have jumpstarted– seen by so many– but the reels of my past are guarded safely under piles of dusty films and all the fear in my head. What is amazing is, they keep replaying– uninvited. A tornado of destruction follows them– always. Your love for me was like a fruit jam, so sour and sweet, and the fresh brown bread so tasty. A love only available for breakfast (and dinners were a buffet). But as breakfast should be the most appetizing one, your presence made it all the more dear. Now the candles are afeared to be lit, darkness craves to visit, and the only emergence is grief– to which I hold so dearly, in hopes it doesn't slip. A masquerade is told in stories as a grand ball, yet I am always masked from all. Masked to hide my tear-soaked face in a gilded mask of grace. Sunny days are gone, there are now only storm filled days. Tears may have dried, but the thoughts that were once blurred are now clear– the fact that you are gone.

I didn't know that those two months would be a beginning and an ending in its own way. I didn't know that the curry you cooked would be the last one I would ever taste. I didn't know you would be gone so soon. Now, the fading memories and precious clear ones are all I have left of you. Remember? The day I refused to give you honey when you had that terrible cough, or the times I said no to helping you with your phone, or the times I gave you work without realizing how sick you were? These are some deadliest thorns in my life, ready to prick with slightest remembrance. I don't understand why you never said anything and how I never knew?

Do you remember that time we planned our trip to go to India in coldest weather? That time when you were freezing and you jokingly said we'd never return to India in the winters. I think, maybe, that was the last time we gathered as a family in a wedding season. Do you remember the times we played business and all the times I would fight to occupy the front seat in the car or the times when I would argue with you for the electronics or the time when everything was perfect and you were here. In the grand scheme of things, time now vs time before is the same, logically, but the bruise of your absence in my heart can never heal overnight. I remember the times when I saw mom, after you were gone, for the first time in three months. She was in the palest of colors and had the whitest of hair.

I realized the emotions to be felt in this grief are not few and far inbetween, but oh so engulfing. It's true, the windows in the house allow fresh air to circulate, the door allows the guests to visit but there is no window, no door, no pathway to swallow the distance between us and I know it all too well. Because you are gone! I feel as if my brain has gone on mute and the situations in life on auto, because everything falls– the friction in my hands– erased. My grip has lost its strength, its power. In this journey of life, the only valuable treasure I have is your memories. I couldn't meet you for the last time and you couldn't see me drive. But I want you to know your strong *raja beti* still captures her life in a series of photographs, like an autobiography– where you can see some days are empty, some filled with laughter or pain or, some filled with the distant, floating memories of the past or dreams of the future and I'll never stop– because you wouldn't want that.

This is the kind of pain that will never fade, for losing you is nothing compared to a mere injury. You're memory is faded, but I can still feel it. Our time was the greatest of all– and the time I spent with you will always be there, maybe a bit distant, but still present– because love never fades and it never gives up. I need you to know, though, that now I am okay. I don't want you to be burdened by the thoughts of your old life or by us and I hope the peace you deserved on earth will be everlasting, wherever you are now.

I don't know whether you are reborn or in heaven or a wandering soul, but no matter what, you will always be my dad.

I will see you again one day, I promise.

> Your daughter,
> S.S.K.
> *Dubai, United Arab Emirates*

P.S. A letter to my dad.

L.L.,
    as the railroad sticks out
against the fallen snow
eyes watering in the bitter wind
my boots sunk inches below
I continue to wonder
how long I will have to wait
until I don't have to miss you

I say that I'll erase you
with less conviction than I meant to
the winters felt less lonely by your side
but no season can last forever

as each snowflake melts away
and spring sings her greeting

I'll be there waiting
for the morning sun to rise
and a new day to arrive

> Bonnie Fay
> *United States*

We were caught somewhere between luck & destiny.

Who knew if we were destined to be together or not? Still, all I wanted was to dive right in, completely fearless, no matter where we were headed. I would've chased clouds with you until we reached another set of skies, and boy did we ever. You painted my life with an abusrd amount of wonder. Everything became brilliant with you. Everything about you is beautiful.

Your eyes. "Brown" would never suffice to describe them. They were the colour of sunlight shining through a bottle of whisky. Forget eyes that reflect the ocean. I could drown forever in your dark gold spirits.

Your silhouette. The back of your head is ridiculous against a sunset. Your lips. They never fail to break the sound barrier, and all of a sudden my head is reeling and we're in outer space. Your hands. They encompass the world, and in the crevices of mine, I still find pieces of our sky. Remnants of a life full of adventure & unknowns, yet the safest place I've ever been.

Incredible, isn't it? That you exist, that you make me believe in magic, & that you are the closest thing to it in the world. Tonight, I sat up on the roof & poured my heart out to the moon. I told her all about you. How I look for your eyes in every shot I take, your sillhouette against the heat of a thousand fires descending, and the feeling of my soul igniting from your touch when I remember to look up at the endless blue. Now I'm certain the moon is shining a little brighter now.

Still, I despise the little piece of hope that I have after all this time, after all these years. All I know is we were caught somewhere between luck & destiny. So maybe, we were just lucky. Oh so lucky, because I wouldn't trade anything for loving & having been loved with such intensity & passion; even if I fully believed we would always have it. We were destined to meet, lucky to be in love, and if our paths don't ever cross again, I am eternally grateful for having been caught with you somewhere in between.

C. Le

P.S. I thought of yet another unsent love letter & I felt completely compelled to send it to you. Forever yours in the fight to feel anything at all.

Spring

Dear Donald,

Winter is almost gone and everything outside is trying to show off. The weather is 62 degrees and it's another *Colorado Bluebird* kind of day.

It's been over two weeks since you ended our relationship.

The relationship nor the breakup was dramatic or toxic. Just one of those simple breakups. You told me you felt like our differences weren't going to get better. You wanted a partner who is better suited for your personality.

Oh, it's a tale as old as time— Social Worker falls in love with Rocket Scientist and when it ends, Social Worker is drowning in her emotions. Rocket Scientist is already exploring his next constellation.

It's so hard to find someone with our level of intensity and wit.

March 20, 2022
9:31PM

Dear Donald,

Sometimes love is anything but magic. Sometimes it's just melting.

Today is the first day of spring and I am already happy to hear that snow is coming tomorrow. I have become more gentle with this heart of mine over the past few days. No longer judging myself for thinking of you too often and for too long. No longer trying to pull it together as swiftly as possible when people ask about you. When the tears fall, I no longer become quick to brush them away.

When I reflect back on all my friends and loved ones who have experienced heart angst, I don't know a single male who reacts the way women tend to do during breakups. I've never seen a man tearing up on the treadmill at the gym. Never seen a man work and rework the last scenario before the relationship ended, retelling the same story over and over again to friends. Men don't become so tripped up about future plans that have changed or what they are going to say to friends and family. I want those innate abilities and societal norms that allow for one to push down the emotions, push out the memories and the grief of a possible life unlived. Hell, burying any sign that you were deeply loved by someone who has simply changed their mind.

I still can't fathom typing up a sentence that will bring down your character because I don't want to remember you for anything less than exactly why I fell in love with you. I'm really trying to not doubt the love we created but honestly, it feels so different now. It doesn't even feel like these love letters were ever written by you. More importantly, I don't know if they were ever intended for a life together. Did I imagine us building this life together? Helping you pick out furniture and celebrating major life events. Calling each other at least once a day to hear about the day's adventures. Those sunny, cloudy and unexpected moments that we couldn't wait to hear about. When did I stop being your home? Spring is here, but my heart is still stuck with yours on winter trails and snow-filled nights by the fire.

K.D.S.
United States

P.S. Unsent letter about losing love between seasons.

DEAR N.,

There is something about the way this feels, the way this knot in my chest keeps me captive; I know our time is temporary and I wish I could have held you closer than I did. Your smile under the moon's light brought me solace in a way so unfamiliar, I've hoped to witness it again since the moment we parted.

As I find myself remembering how your heartbeat felt against mine, I swallow the memory in hopes of it residing within me until time itself stills and the chaos settles once more. You are a moonlit drive in the springtime rain, a gentle hand in a world of fire and greed; my spirit is pulled towards you in a way that shouts from the rooftops. When your eyes glance away from mine, I feel a hesitation to dive into the waters of possibility, yet still I write this to you with the intentions of declaration.

Despite the inexorable distance that shall come between us soon, I hope that our time has not ended; you have a beauty to you I wish to behold— and I may do so— if only you share this feeling that our story could blossom into something beautiful, if we let it.

YOURS IN HEART,
A.C. x
Canada

P.S. This letter was written after meeting someone for the first time. An undeniable gut-wrenching feeling that this person could have been someone to fall in love with. But distance is cruel, and timing is crueler.

MUM,

I slouch over my desk again, blodging ink. A sliver of morning sun is coming through the cracks of my closed blinds. It touches my scribbling hand and I disintegrate like a Tim-Tam dipped in coffee.

It's been a long time, Mum. Tears are pushing through my swollen eyes; I forget to blink when I'm thinking, but I don't know what to write.

A lifetime of looking into your eyes, yet, I can't recall the blue mandala of your iris. I can't even remember our last conversation in person. Now, these tears are a waterfall down my rough, cold cheeks— like a rock face. Ask anyone to describe in fine detail the faculties and freckles of their mum. They can't.

If I see you again, I'll flourish them in tattoo ink on my palm, where I jot my to-do list. I'll hug you longer than 3 seconds, and say in front of everyone: I love you, Mum.

Hippie Thinking
Australia

P.S. My Mum lives on the other side of the country, and I haven't seen her in years. We never got along in a close Mother-Daughter bond. I think deep down, I wish we did. I wrote this letter to say, 'I love you,' because we never said those words often, like I should have.

Dear Self,
 If there's something I need you to know, it's this:
The world can be cold,
its leaves dry up and die.
The ground hardens and freezes and the colors dull.
Sometimes your breath catches in your chest, and it hurts to breathe.
Your fingers become numb
and all of the layers don't seem to give you warmth.
And the winters of your mind drift. drift. drift.
Until they settle, deeply, in your soul.
But just as things come and go, the world starts to soften,
the ice starts to drip. drip. drip.
And on the bare, lonely tree, you'll see a blossom
and the golden rays that were immersed in a thick, grey mass
break through, and pour hope into existence.
Watch the sunflowers—
how they turn their face to the sun,
and listen to the birds singing songs of welcome,
as life trickles back in, once more.

If there's something I need you to know, it's this:
the world can be cold,
but it will also be warm
and the frost only lasts for so long.
Keep searching this world for all of the beautiful things,
and when you find them, they will become yours.

>Sincerely,
>You
>*United States*

P.S. I originally wrote this thinking it would be to a future child or younger friend, or someone I cared about, to remind them to hold onto hope. Then I realized it really was written for myself— future, past, and present <3. I have so many words of comfort for my past self, and sometimes think about— what would my future self say to me now? I think it would be something along the lines of looking toward the light and putting my trust in the universe.

B.,

The clouds were gracefully poetic and your embrace was brief, yet warm. I fell in love with the way you handed me a piece of your heart like there was still so much time left for us to keep believing.

Although I have forgotten the sound of your voice, I am still hopeful that one day you'll find your way back to me again.

>P.S. I will always remember your message.
>"Waiting for you." you said.
>"Coming in a heartbeat." I replied.

>Alvin T.
>*Indonesia*

To the loves that had to leave me,
   When your name comes to mind, I smile freely.
   Feel you within me.
   Breathing life into me.
   I thought I lost you,
   but you never left me.

Abandonment issues showing constantly.
To know someone so perfect
and then to be left alone like smurfette.
It was so hard.
It's gotten better, yet
there's a hollowness where the grief ate away.
There's a sadness I feel everyday.
But to have loved you this way,
I couldn't regret that.
I won't forget that.
That love and that support,
nothing better than our rapport .
To be a light like you were to me is all I strive to be.
I'll hold you again someday,
and kiss your cheek.
I'll one day not feel so weak.
It's unexpected to feel a thing
besides pain.
These memories can't refrain
from remembering,
but you're here somehow
lifting me to where I am now.
This confidence, this energy,
I find it inside
where you left it.
Before you, I wasn't shit.
At least I didn't know it.
But seeing the life you lead,
How could I throw it?
I'm in it to win it.
Knowing one day when we kick it,
I can tell you stories,
that maybe you'll think I embellished,
because it sounds too great to have lived it.
But I have and I will,
because living for you has been half the thrill

KAYLYN MARIE
Colorado, United States

P.S. To a combination of great people who changed me before they left this earth.

To Akhil,

Why do you tell me that my tears have a worth? Why do you talk like this? Are you the same person I used to cry for— who I believed would come and take note of each and every tear that I have shed?

Why have you come out of my fantasy world? I know you can never be mine, so why don't you just go back and stay there in my world— the place where I can love you the most?

You don't know how long I have waited for you. What I ached for, but look where that got me. All my dreams shattered in front of my eyes. I have to live in this reality— which is opposite of my dreams. The one I got, I believed was you, so I gave him all my heart. But he wasn't you, and now, what is possibly left of me that could make you want to come and express your love? Just go back to the place where you used to safely reside— inside my mind— where you were so beautiful. I can't give you anything in this materialistic reality. I am helpless to give you anything other than pain.

Sometimes, I wonder if this is all a delusion. That you are not my destination or I have no destination at all or that I've already missed my destination and now I'm just wandering around. Is this my fate? If so, then yes, I've accepted my fate. And since, I've been simply counting my days— so why did you have to come along and disturb me? Or maybe this is all my own illusion, telling myself that I can be loved— when in reality, it's not true. You are only a delusion that I have created to fill the emptiness of my life.

This is all out of my intellectual capacity.

Ask me, is there ever a time when I don't miss you? I really have to think about when I don't miss you. In every moment, I miss you. I want to talk to you about each and every atom of this universe. I want to show you all the pain in my heart. I want to share with you every secret of my life. I want to dress up only for you, I want to look good only for you. I want to cry for a long time on your chest. I want you to give me the worth of my tears.

I want to fight with you for showing up so late in life. Why you made me cry this much, why you made me go through all this pain and now, when this life is closer to ending, you have shown up. Now, I can't love you for long at all. Truly loving you is far away, in another life— because in this one, I can't even express my love for you at all. I'm annoyed with you— just leave all of your belongings behind and come to me. I don't know anything anymore and I don't want to know anything. Just hurry up, this life is already very short to love you.

My love for you cannot be completed in this small lifetime. It's like I've been waiting for you for ages and now that we have met— I can't tell you anything, I can't show you anything. I am so helpless.

That's why I told you to live only in my dreams, you look so perfect in my created world. You come and meet me there, you love me there and listen to me in this beautiful world. There, I will meet you, I will fight with you and I will love you.

Because this reality is not for us. This world is not for us. Please know, our love is not limited to this reality— it exists beyond. In a place that is more real than reality itself. Where you will be only mine and I will be only yours. A place where there will be no confines or bounds. Just you and me. We will live there, together.

It seems as if my identity is for you, I am from you and I am only for you.

This dreamworld is strange— it holds me in place, where I can neither go back, nor can I move forward.

FROM KHUSHI
India

P.S. This letter is about a forbidden love that the writer cannot express as she is in love with a man who is already married. She believes he is the person she has been waiting for since she first understood what love is. She has begun to believe that he is the person who was promised to her by God. But in the present situation, where she is already married and has kids— she cannot express her feelings to this person. She keeps on fighting with her thoughts and then one day she decided to write down letters to him (that can never be sent), so that she can vent out her feelings. In this way, she hopes she can overcome her heart and its emotions.
She's afraid, she doesn't want to ruin two families. She completely understands that this love is impossible. She has no plans to be unfaithful, but still she wants that person to be a friend. Actually, it is a way in which she can survive her own life— how she can survive a partner who has always be unfaithful and disloyal to her. Maybe, this is the reason she has fallen for the kind of love she always wanted.
I hope you understand her, because in this society, nobody has ever been able to understand her and her feelings.

YOUNG ME,

Spring is here and it makes me think. As spring is a time of new beginnings, it makes me want to go back in time to when you were at the beginning of blooming. Your beginning was great, but something went wrong, and while I'm trying to fix it— I still feel lost.

The love you had for me was stronger than what I deserve. I feel like I've failed you more every day, and I'm not sure how to start over— but the thought of you thinking about me and what I could be inspires me to strive to reach the potential your love so often dreamt of for me. I may have lost love for myself along the way, but I know I haven't lost your love… because of that, I'm going to keep trying to be what you deserve. Spring is a new beginning, and this spring, I'll be starting fresh and it'll all be for the little girl you are. I may not deserve a new beginning, but you sure do. This is the greatest *I love you* I can give to you.. a chance to love yourself again.

> You in 15 years
> *United States*

P.S. A letter from a young adult to herself as a child.

Lovely people,
This love, may it always reach you,
may you always feel it.
When the wind softly touches your skin,
think of it as love
that hugs you gently.
When you see a rainbow after the rain,
think of it as love
that brings color to your day.
After all the loneliness and sadness that you have felt,
when you hear the birds chirping in the early morning
and quiet afternoon,
think of it as love
that sings it's perfect melody to you.

> Blue Sky
> *Philippines*

P.S. A letter to the people that I love. To the people that find joy in simple things. To the people that need comfort and pure happiness.

To a fantasy,
One day, I'll be able to love without you being a part of it, but I fear, on this April day, I have yet to stop falling. Maybe I'll be falling forever, maybe not. So, until I do stop falling in love with you, I hope this reaches you. You with the blue eyes I've never seen, the hands I've never held— you— the

feel of a ghost whenever I take walks.

When there's a breath of woodsmoke on the still-cold wind, I hope it carries your cologne. I've looked into your eyes in my dreams and every time I wake up without you next to me. I meet your gaze everywhere I go: blue, twilight suburban clouds, my denim jacket worn with weather, the way the sky looks before a storm.

I've collapsed into free fall for someone whose eyes were always too brown— and never enough green.

I found you, dear fantasy, in all the boys I thought I loved, and hated what I found in the creeps that loved me back. To look for someone so perfect is a nightmare in itself— standards suck, because you keep mine so high. There's something so romantic about not being able to love a ghost outside of a fantasy.

I fell in love with you, dear fantasy, and though you did somewhat fall with me into reality, I could only ever find pieces of you here: the scent of laundry mixed with nicotine on rare, golden evenings, the color of your shirt in the twilight, the warmth of your heart in glowing windows, riverbeds full of the brown depths of reality`s eyes— and in the shades of the trees, the green I could never see there. So many shades of eyes, I couldn't choose between the ocean and the lake.

I found you in the blue July twilights where everything was warm, where everything was cast in the same shade, like your eyes would be when looking at me. Your face was in so many things, yet it was never the face I wanted to kiss. Veiny hands and flannel shirts, a tender word from a caring friend when I was upset, a softened voice, a song I couldn`t stop playing because I knew it was about you. Cotton candy-colored sunsets, nicotine in the night air, the sleepy feeling in my bones when I think of your kiss that I will never receive. So many pieces, yet never a complete picture.

I was full of letters I never sent to you (and letters to the one I can't make mine, even in reality); they make it seem like you're easier than they are to keep in my life. Why is that? Do I prefer what is artificial, because it seems safer? Would there be more adventure, given what reality can give me?

You were there when they weren't. You made me feel something I couldn`t catch with them. You made my mind a whirlwind of pictures, not pieces. If I could ever choose you over who I fell for in reality, I would in a heartbeat. At least you would be as quiet as my thoughts were to everyone else.

If I could meet you in a dream, I pray that it is by this letter I can reach you. I carry it with me to bed like a text that was left on read. If, unknown-and-yet-to-be-met-fantasy, you happen to read it, give it to the one I love in this life. Then write me back from the next life that I will meet you in, be it transported to me in the self-love poems I tell myself, the poems I write about you (which are really about me), or those little things of life that I can't explain. I fear I will only meet you in death, when I myself become fantasy, and reality breaks its crush on me.

Love,

M. C. Flora - someone who is stuck in reality.
United States

P.S. This letter is to the perfect person we all wish for and can only be found in fantasies. It's hard when reality strives for your attention, as fantasy beckons with every call. It's for the man I've loved in my head, my fantasy, and wishing for him to be found in reality— and one, day perhaps, I will find him.

Dear L.,

It's been a while since I wrote you a letter. Even months since we last talked about it, my love for you still lingers. If I'm completely honest, it still grows. I've always been one to go all-in and put my claws into anything I find worthy of holding onto, however that makes letting go all the more difficult. None of that changes the fact that you don't feel the same. No amount of love nor time will change the way you feel about me, I know. Just the same, though, no amount of time will make me love you any less.

I know I am supposed to let go, move on, but darling, how can I when all you do is make me love you more? How can I move on when the second I feel like I've set a step in the right direction, you put in the effort, say something that makes my heart skip a beat or do something unexpected? Winter was meant for letting go, for grieving the loss of something that wasn't ever truly there. There's a word for it: anemoia. It means 'nostalgia for a time you've never known'.

In the past year, I have been allowed to witness your growth both as a human and a soul, and it has been a true honour to have been standing next to you. You have grown more into yourself, more confident in who you are and aspire to be, more kind but simultaneously more firm in standing your ground and standing up for yourself. Like the flowers bloom in spring, I've seen you blossom and I loved it.

For the longest time, I thought love was simply not destined to be mine. I've always been a hopeless romantic, however, no such relationship has ever been mine. Yet, I was at peace, content with staying on my own... at least until I met you. You made love feel possible, you made connecting seem so easy. Nearly a year has passed since we first met, and as I now write this letter, I think back to the year we've had. Over two decades of living, yet I have never met anyone who made me feel as safe as you do. Someone with whom I can talk effortlessly, regardless of the topic. Someone who doesn't make me feel 'too much', someone who laughs at my silliness and my weird, at times, random questions. Someone who isn't scared of exploring deep thoughts and complex topics with me. Someone who approaches everyone with the same kindness. Someone with a soul as beautiful, a mind as marvellous, or a smile as radiant as yours. You made me hope again, feel again, believe again. No mutual feelings were needed for you to make a lasting impact on me.

All this is to say, I love you still and I know I always will. For now, I have returned to a point where I will be content staying on my own. This is for the simple reason that I don't want anyone to share my life with, but you. Maybe in time, I will feel different, but as I write this letter, that is where things are at. I love you with all that I am, and letting go of you will take all that I am, for we only love as deeply as we grieve and suffer when that love has no place to go, but to be let go.

Friends are what we will be, as there is no way I'm living my life without you in it. I just need some time first.

>   EVER YOURS,
>   L.W.
>   *Belgium*

P.S. A letter to a love that never was.

ELIZABETH,
  My darling wildflower,
  you've dealt with so much.
  The wind pushing you down,
  the sun burning you dry,
  people crushing you harshly,
  and yet you stand tall
  for the world to see.
  Petals blooming
  to the fullest of your beauty.
  My darling wildflower,
  Could I pick you?

>   F. WOLF
>   *United States*

P.S. Elizabeth is my best friend and I just want her to know she is loved. She is my wildflower and I love her so much. We've gone through a lot so I wanted to create something to remind her that she is loved.

To My Beloved Jasmine,
    You may not recognize me.
    You may not, yet, be able to grasp the immensity
    of my love for you.
    But I love you gently.
    Graciously and godly.
    With a love prone to grandiosity
    and filled with goodness and gratitude.
    My love for you is as full as the sun in all it's glory.
    Big, burning, and bright.
    Birthing all we see and know to life.
    I love your absolutely pure, profound, and peculiar joy.
    I see you bursting forth into a dance.
    Feet cha-cha-chaing.
    Arms embracing the heavens.
    Swaying in the rhythm laughter.
    Stepping in the name hope.
    Exploding in vigor and raining celebration.
    Soothing the terrors of disability and dejection.
    You don't wait for your savior or your oasis,
    you dance it into being.
    I have never seen something more beautiful.
    It is marvelous in my sight.
    If I had one request it would be this:
    Cling desperately to this joy.
    Hold tight to this love.
    For I am soon to come.
    And you will adore all you have been, are to be, and
    What you and our Father will become for eternity.

    Love always,
    The Me I am To Be
    United States

P.S. A letter from future me.

A LETTER TO THE BOY FROM SCHOOL:

Well, first off, let me start by saying we all know we would be together if it wasn't for my lack to see love, when it was right in front of my eyes. I was young. And I know it wasn't from your lack of trying. I didn't see the difference between lust and love. Which is why I chased him. Over and over. I'm sorry you had to chase me while I kept running after someone else. Someone I knew could never hold my heart. I've never been very good at being comfortable. At thinking I deserve to be happy in love. And that's what it would have been with you.

I try to look back and see how differently things would have turned out if I was brave enough to let you in. But instead I pushed you away. I see that now. And I hope you know I never ever tried to use you. You know you spat that out at me the other night. 8 years later. And I was left wondering for the rest of the night if you resented me for not liking you back. I think the one thing you can't control in this life is your feelings. Your true, deep, gut-pulling emotions. And at that point of my life I wasn't ready to meet myself where I needed to— to be ready for you. And I know I could never have asked you to wait till I was. Is it selfish that I wish you did?

You know, you did make me nervous. And laugh. And feel safe. And liked. And beautiful. Thank you for that. I liked being around you and I miss that. I sometimes wonder why we don't really talk any more. And I hope it is not because you still feel burned by me. It is time to let that go. Which is maybe why I'm writing you this letter. It's time for me to let go of any possibility of a future where we share this lifetime together. Where you realise, again, we would work out. Friendship on fire. It's funny. I've never even kissed you, but that doesn't stop me from romanticising how perfect we would be together. But you have moved on and changed. You seem to have turned into someone I don't recognise anymore. I see us tangled together, but the version of you I see is your past self and that makes me angry. Then I realise maybe I'm not angry at you for changing. Maybe I'm angry at myself for not being by your side while you did.

I also want you to know it picks at my brain often. As I'm sure it did yours many years ago. Why? Why didn't I listen to all of my friends? My family? You? That we could be great together. And you would treat me like a princess. But no matter how many times I try to answer this, all I can hear my mind saying is *you were afraid*. I was afraid because, yes, you were perfect. I was afraid everyone else would have been right, I was wasting my time on anyone other than you. I was afraid of getting hurt. I was afraid we would ruin our friendship. I was afraid to be loved. I was afraid to love. Maybe these all just sound like meaningless excuses to you. But how can they be if I am here writing, hurting, by finally saying the words out loud.

I was afraid of breaking your heart. When in reality, all these years later, whenever I see you— I break my own. I'm never going to send you this letter but I want you to know that you're the person that clouds my mind with every what-if.

> P.O.W.
> *New Zealand*

LOVE LETTERS TO YOU, THROUGH TIME:
>   This letter is to tell you
>   how I feel when you're not here.
>   I sit in my bed all day,
>   wishing you were near
>   It's like a string of love
>   is entwined between our hearts,
>   It tugs at my chest
>   whenever you're far.
>   Your smile lights up this
>   feeling of ecstasy in me
>   And whenever you're happy
>   I feel like I'm finally free.
>   ~ love confession

>   I offer you this red rose,
>   one made out of love
>   from the shrub I planted
>   many years ago.
>   I watered it with affection
>   and showered it with my warmth,
>   but in the blindness of love
>   it grew white roses instead.
>   I made an incision
>   in my heart
>   droplets of scarlet fell
>   on the soft petals
>   and turned them red.
>   ~ my love is scarlet red

I'd never been in a relationship before
but when we met,
I knew it was going to be you.
We laughed and talked on our first day,
a few weeks later you asked me out
and we planned some exciting stuff
for the next couple of dates.
Now it's been two years,
something is amiss.
The sparks have gone,
the love has flown away.
Where did we go wrong?
No, it won't end this way.
Let's pack our bags
and find those sparks,
bring the love back home
and start afresh again.
~ those lost sparks

The time we spent together
stargazing from the Ferris Wheel;
a part of me wished we could stay there
talking non-stop about our dreams.
You looked at me sideways,
a smile spread from your lips,
and grasping the romantic moment,
stole away a kiss.
You laughed at my surprised look,
but my chest had burst with bliss
and we sat holding hands.
~ a memory I wish I could relive.

Little did we know
what we were going to miss
when we went our separate ways
and gave each other a goodbye kiss.
Now I miss your laughter
the jokes, the memories
I will always cherish our friendship
I hope I meet you again someday.
~ goodbye

You're the desert wind
echoing my name
You're as radiant as the sun's rays
when you smile
You are the heartbeat in me
that makes me feel alive.
~ but I miss your place by my side

I've done my best
to get us back in touch
but my efforts are in vain
so don't you say I never tried.
You stopped answering
and seeing my letters
unaware that I was patiently
waiting for your reply.
I suppose this is life
we're growing apart
you've gone your way
and I've gone mine.
Should I have tried harder,
perhaps something different?
Or maybe I've tried too much
and pushed you away altogether.
~ I have lost you

Your promises I believed
the feelings that drowned me
I let your love consume me
hence, 'lovers' they labelled us.
But they didn't know about our fight
or the moment I was left behind
I let the dagger pierce my heart
And death did us apart.
~ a broken lover

Those unwritten letters
you promised you'd send
The unspoken affection
you tried to suppress
The sparks of love
are on the funeral pyre

breathing their last
like the glowing embers
of a dying bonfire.
Accept this as my eulogy
as it's the end of you and me.
~ eulogy

SAMYUKTA
India

DEAR HONEY BEAR,

I still see pieces of you in my car where your laughter still rings in my ears; your presence lingers where I lay my head to rest, blurry memories still live on behind my closed eyes. Little did I know that your memories would scatter themselves around me, encroaching on the edges of my world, begging to be let in again. Your fingers clasp mine when I place my hand on the passenger seat, your face still follows me in my dreams; those I have loved and all the ones after you still haunt me, despite my best efforts to leave them behind.

Sometimes, all I can feel is your body pressed upon mine and I cannot help but wonder what beauty I have missed out on, the twinkle behind your eyes still making me ache in all the ways I wish it would not. My hands tremble softly when I see the spring flowers bloom as I whisper your name, wishing peace and growth upon them as if they were you. My heart has found a home in every chest but my own, as if my own body will not contain me; perhaps I was already born half empty, with all the loves that I have shared blooming within me to take up the abyss that resides within.

You are all I love and all I have ever loved, you are all the things I wish to cast away and everything I never wanted; a piece of me so sacred yet so damned, I wonder if I will ever rid myself of your beautiful, tragic memory.

FOREVER YOURS AND EVER MORE,
INSEPHRIEL
Canada

P.S. A letter to my first love, the one who changed my life in every way. I live my life through the love you gave me, I hold your name in my mouth in fear of losing you too soon; you were my stars, my moon, my very heart and soul. Until you were not.

Dearest you,

Before you, I accepted the thought that I was damaged goods and wasn't capable of knowing a healthy love, but when you kiss every curve, stretch mark, and freckle of my body, you show me the way my body should be loved. I feel beautiful with you clothed or naked. I am a whole garden blooming in bold delicate colors when you hold me. I feel like this is forever.

I talk a lot but you sit and listen with grace and try to understand. You ask about my family and friends, loving them as if they're your own. We disagree and I'm comforted in knowing a small disagreement won't push you away. You tell me not to worry, but all I've ever known is someone leaving, but my faith is in you and in us and the passion we have to make this work. We drive down back roads with our windows down and music up. We talk to the stars the same way we talk to God. It's the simple things in life with you that bring me so much happiness.

You protect the parts of me that have been abused and shield me from the people and things that try to bring harm to me now. I am better because of you. I'm given space to be me, but you're close enough to pull me in if the waves of my decisions become too rough. I picture all the things we can do and how we can be and I want to be patient with you, with us, because I know this is a once-in-a-lifetime kind of love.

> Devotedly yours
> *United States*

P.S. I think it's a beautiful thing to write a letter to your future spouse often. Everyone in their lifetime deserves a love that sets their soul on fire. A love where they can be themselves and still be loved.

To the one I'll never see again,

You were in my dream last night— looking exactly how you did the night we met. White sleeves rolled up, tattoos peeking out from under every hem, your blonde hair was still longer then— you were wearing your rose colored glasses— this is before they broke in the trunk of your car. This was back when your vision of the world still veiled in pink— before it got cloudy from all the drugs. Before that night, months later, when you looked into my eyes and couldn't even recognize me. I told myself it was nighttime and hard to see, but I'm scared to admit that maybe I really was just that insignificant in your eyes.

I promised myself years ago— I would never write to you again. But here I am. I can't get you out of my head. That damned dream— the way you looked at me— the way you smiled at me— it was all so real it almost feels cruel.

I asked if you still wrote poems about me— you told me you did. I still write about you too, from time to time.

Neither of us knew why we were so affected by each other— so instantaneously— how we fell in love so hard and so fast. When people talk about love at first sight, they don't talk about how you don't really have a choice in the matter. How it sweeps you up in a riptide of emotion and confusion and ecstasy, how you never stood a chance against it. How it isn't always a good thing. I still wonder how it was possible at all, and my only explanation would be the idea that we had loved each other— fiercely— in another lifetime long before this one.

You were my great love. Knowing us— we probably promised each other that we would find one another in every lifetime after— I guess we didn't realize how much trouble we would have to go through once we did. People always romanticize and talk about finding their lovers again in the next lifetime, but they never think about what happens when you actually do— and all goes to hell. How am I supposed to love again after that?

I think I have loved you for a long, long time— maybe in our next life we will try again and have better luck. Maybe not. Either way, I really don't know what to do when I wake up from a dream with you. I wonder— do you dream of me? What does it feel like? If you do see me in your dreams— do you even recognize me?

My last words in the dream were, *you know I have to go.* As if we had met there before. As if we knew this had to happen. As if maybe we were only ever meant to exist in dreams. I was standing right in front of you, holding your hands, looking up— I waited for a response— you said something— I woke up. I don't remember what you said.

It was the same, our last night together years ago, when I told you I had to go. As I ran off into the crowds of people and echoing music— I heard you yell out, "I love you."

I don't know how— but deep down— I knew you meant it.

Then I kept running and I didn't look back.

Elara
United States

P.S. Like most fairytale loves, our book had to end far too soon.

To my younger self:
    take that chance, dear one
    you may find
    joy
    take the leap, my love
    you may find
    strength
    take the first step, child
    you may find
    ambition
    take the first fall
    you will see how you will
    rise above
    you will see how you are
    more than just a
    wallflower
    how you are
    so much more than your
    appearance
    you will learn how to be
    comfortable
    on your own
    you will learn the
    armor
    you have
    does not mean
    you cannot get
    hurt
    you will see hearts
    break
    but will be put together
    again
    you will see that
    dreams
    are attainable
    if you keep reaching for those
    stars
    you will learn that taking
    risks

may be worth it
you will make
mistakes
and have
heartbreaks
but you will always have
me
friends will come and go in life
but me?
I will be where I always am
reflected on the mirror
looking at a
beautiful soul
for I am you and
I love you

take a chance
take the leap
take the first step
take the first fall
and see how
you will rise above

>   Love,
>   Me
>   *United States*

P.S. For when I was growing up. Learning to take chances and not to be afraid.

T.,
    I give you pieces of my heart
while my whole being is in love with you—
I love each part of you,
I love everything about you.
I love how every time the sun kisses your cheeks,
they turn red, and your face stays as radiant
as the ever-glow of morning light.
Lips as red as a cherry,
singing such a sweet,
enchanting melody.

And your eyes—
those captivating eyes of yours,
they are always the last thing on my mind
before I close my eyes to sleep and dream of you.
It was your eyes, made of galaxies,
that romanced my heart
at the very beginning.

R.
Philippines

P.S. A letter to the one who captivates my heart.

HEY POPS,

It's been a while since we last spoke. First and foremost, I'd like to say that I miss you. I think of you often and wonder if I'm still making you proud.

The last thing you said to me was that you loved me and you were proud of the person I was becoming. It was the perfect thing to remember you by, almost as if you planned those to be your last words to me.

And maybe that's exactly what you were doing. What makes me look back at our last moments together— is if there was anything I could have done to make you stay. If you were proud of me, if you really loved me, then why did you leave?

The question that will always remain unanswered:
Why?

LOVE YOUR KIDDO,
A.K. BAY
United States

P.S. A letter to my father who passed away.

DEAR STRANGER,

I don't know any other way to address you than that, although we weren't even strangers were we? Where do we draw the line between not complete strangers and acquaintance? I wish I could ask you one more time.

You know, I never really talked to anyone about what our relationship meant. Did you ever talk about me? If so, what did you tell them about who

I am? Because I have always hidden you away from people. Ironic, isn't it? How we hide the parts that feel so raw and vulnerable from the rest of the world.

Because there were a lot of things that felt raw between us. The unnamed relationship we had, the always vulnerable 3AM discussions, the undivided attention to another's poetry, and a whole lot of things we didn't define. Never even tried to because it was easy with you. Always.

But maybe I only saw it from my perspective. Maybe I took things for granted more often than you. Maybe it was different for you. Maybe you always knew how short your life would have been. Maybe that is why you saw beauty in everything. Maybe that is why you lived everyday owning it. Maybe that is why you never defined anything between us. Maybe that is why this is even harder because you're no longer here.

I wish I had talked to people about our relationship. Maybe then it wouldn't be so hard right now. Maybe I could have talked about you now. But I can only write about you. I can never tell you in person what I feel. So I'll write about you. I'll immortalise you within these pages. So you'll live on in here.

Sometimes, on my most selfish days, I am glad I never got to say goodbye, because then it would really mean that you are gone. And how do I move past that feeling? Who do I share my grief with? Some days I wonder how someone I never met could have such a deep impact on me. But it's never about seeing each others face, is it? It's about the feelings we shared.

I miss our 3 AM conversations. I miss hearing you read your poems to me through our phone calls. I miss reading my poems to you. I even miss the static sound it makes when the line connection isn't good. I miss you sending a recorded audio of you reading your poems. I miss your out of the blue, random text messages. I miss sending you a random text message. I miss talking to you about anything and everything. About our dreams of writing a book together. About our dreams of making a YouTube channel together. About meeting up someday. About travelling. About what this could have possibly been.

I'm not writing this in replacement of the goodbye we never shared. I'm writing this so that when I try to talk about you the next time maybe it will be much easier. Maybe the feeling of loneliness will dissipate. Maybe if I talk about you then I won't feel like you're someone I crafted out from my imagination. Maybe you will feel more real. More you.

Always,
Ally. A
India

[TW: SA, R*PE]

How do you write a letter to someone you don't know anymore— or never really did? Someone you swore to love and protect with all your heart, until you look back and question everything right from the start.

I wish I could look you in the eyes and show you the pain you passed onto me. But sadly, I already know the blame, the guilt and the sorrow, is only for me. Our relationship started fast at fifteen, I think I'd known you all of two weeks before you told me you loved me. I remember just saying it back, knowing one day I'd feel it, it was just too soon. That became a regular thing I'd say in my head. I think I still do.

Our breakup was bitter, random as it seemed. You did something that bothered me and I saw that as my opportunity to leave. It had been on my mind for a while but I wasn't sure why. I'd asked you to give me space, but you'd still call and text and ask to see me— it was always hard to say no to you.

Eventually, I grew irritated with your attempts to get me back, so I called you boring, unpleasant, anything to get you off my back. Sadly, that's the one thing I regret most in life, by calling you boring, I unlocked the most evil side of a family I've ever seen.

I felt suffocated for months after your parents forced me into telling my parents we'd had sex. I was accused of crying rape and sent threats so fearsome that I was physically sick everytime I thought of running into your mum. I felt a distance between my own mother as I kept secrets, pain and thoughts all to myself. I guess your family had turned on me so fast and played with my innocent mind, that I forgot to remember that their was some truth to their find.

Three years later and I'm learning about such matters; consent, sexual assault, rape, etc. They were matters I found so easy to speak of before, as if their definitions were so simple. But then I heard myself saying no, no and no to your requests at sex. But then you changing my mind, telling me to get undressed, 'playfully' slapping at me if I didn't. I cried for four days straight. I'd been raped.

I don't know if you know, I don't think you'd be aware. And that makes it worse in my mind, that somewhere out there, you still think I'm the evil one. Your parents and their friends, sitting there, laughing at me. I honestly wish I had the evidence to prove you guilty. You still appear in my dreams, you still ruin my thoughts, everything I thought you were— it turns out you're not.

My heart breaks for young me who was scared into silence, and my heart breaks for older me who still fears your violence— in every man, woman, or person they see.

    L.G.
    Scotland

X.D.V.,
    The ship and crew were tired.
    I was there too.
    At the start it was exciting,
    the world was ours.
    Oh, nothing could stop this—
    but how naive a thought.
    As we rocked back and forth,
    the storm swarmed in and waves crashed against us.
    The ship split apart.
    We all tried to fight against the pounding sea.
    Tried to hold on—
    but the outside forces were stronger.
    The fight against the water made us weary,
    so, we let it win.
    And would you look at that?
    As we drifted apart, the storm ceased.
    The waters turned kind,
    the sun bathed us in warmth and light.
    Feeling my body pulled against a shore—
    how safe I felt.
    I still had thoughts of the departure—
    We'll never come together again.
    Slim possibility.
    So I'll choose safety—
    I choose these shores.

    A.J.X.
    United States

SHIV,

I am writing to tell you that you will survive. These cold bruises that you are carrying will fade away and then you will, once again, be in touch with the sense of your being. I am still so proud of you and the fact that you stick to your faith. This is how you have made it so far. I am here to remind you that faith is not only a strong feeling— it is more than a feeling. It can be a cure for many of your struggles. It may seem difficult to come out of that deep well of sorrows when you have lingered upon it for so long, but you have to trust that it will end soon. All your worries. All your sadness. All your concerns. They ought to end soon and it will happen.

Stay here a little bit longer. Grow your wings around the deep waters and learn to swim through them. Acknowledge the fact that you can't stay at the same place forever . You've got to move. You have the power to change your course.

There are times when your patience is tested and the best you can do is practice. Whatever the external forces may be, you must be true to yourself. You have to learn to follow your instinct and remember what you are made of. From the days of childhood, you have been the strongest. Days, months, and even years have changed. But I want you to promise yourself never to change.

They may have taught you, *Change is the Law of Nature*. Now, it's your time to relearn and respond back. Change is necessary, but not for you. You have to move on, so you will grow— but not *change*. Your roots are beautiful. They made you who you are today.

You may have forgotten yourself, but I don't wish you to be changed. Maybe I wish you to unlearn a few things if required. Maybe I wish you to relearn a few things on your own. But never to change.

One day, you will be surprised to see the shining of that first ray of light. That day is not far away when you will bloom. That day is not far away when you will finally become the true *you*.

I BELIEVE MY WORDS
India

P.S. A letter to acknowledge my struggle to find myself. A reminder.

J.S.,

It's hard for me to accept this new *us*. Actually, I think we're back to *you*… and *me*. You're still around, which I love, but my want-to-be-happy-to-see-you heart feels hollow when it's near you. My smile gets flimsy. It's weak and shaky from holding back tears. I move too fast in hopes you won't see the pain I'm dragging around with me. I know I've told you I miss your incessant "hi"... twice every time. I miss your midnight words when I wake in the middle of the night. Your sunrise and bedtime words too. The x's and o's that got me through.

The few times I surprised you are still my favorite memories. I can't seem to stop myself from remembering the way you held me. Your hugs were my favorite... the tighter they got when I refused to let go. Nowadays, I just have your hoodie. I still wear it and wrap those arms around myself and imagine they're yours.

I'm sorry if I hurt you somehow. I still don't understand what happened. There are days I tell myself the reason I'm hurting is because you didn't want to take the risk. Was I not worth the chance? I know someone else hurt you, but that wasn't me.

I know that's what led you to me. I remember meeting you before you cared. The moment you held my hand, though, something was different. It was only for a second, but I felt it. A year later, you reached out. It made me happy even though I kind of figured I was just a stepping stone. That I'd be your sidekick to get you through the dark days. I told myself it would be an honor; to be your friend and confidante while deep down, I knew in helping you, I'd be the one to get hurt.

My heart believed you were worth it. I just never expected it to hurt this much. If given the chance, I'd do it all over again, just the same. Because you'll always be worth it... the joy and the pain. I still want the best for you. I pray for you every day, Jack. You deserve all the happiness in the world. I just wish it was with me.

C.C.
United States

P.S. A letter to my other half, who came and went too quickly.

DEAREST TANA,

If you were a flower, you would be a Roselette peony. Like the ones you brought to hospital all those years. Back then, I would rest them against my cheeks and the cells I thought had died would start waking back to life. I could feel it. I could feel their scent filtering through my skin. And I like to think it was you; your touch, your empathy, your joy.

At the time, I was buried beneath so many layers of soil I could not hear myself breathing. So arrived the bouquets of Roselette peonies. Those peonies— the scent of them flooded the hospital room so that we almost forgot why we were there. And your laugh, your silliness, filled the rooms with springtime you brought in from the outside. I bathed in it then— it was a wonder.

When I woke from surgery, you were there. Beside my bed, you held my hand, massaged my feet with your soft hands. And we were only kids. But you knew— you knew that I could not survive without your love— that love that exists between sisters. I would never have made it without you all.

It seems for you, it was not even a conscious choice, to remain by my side those months when the rest of our world crumbled. For that I will always be grateful.

Now we live continents apart. Space seems to have condensed. We seem to miss each other— as we glide down different rivers. I am still hoping to meet you again— in a space of open vulnerability. In that safe space where we can both be entirely free— to just be & accept each other fully. In a space where we both let ourselves be as delicate & vulnerable as those peonies. The ones you brought with all your love and heart to the hospital all those years ago. I will never give up hope that one day we will meet again, with that complete sense of trust— knowing nothing can break this— because we are sisters. To stand again on the same shoreline, as open hearted to the world as peonies in bloom.

Love,
Zerzura
Sweden & Kenya

R.,

There she is, still— front and centre in the spotlight of your stage. And there I am, still— backstage behind the curtains, in darkness.

Has she done her part? Is it my turn to debut in the spotlight and finally be front and centre on your stage? Will you finally showcase me?

I patiently yet painfully await my turn… but you never draw the curtains to reveal me. Sure, sometimes you hastily come back to check on me and have me practice my piece every now and then; to which you make some excuse to her as why you need to repeatedly return back there.

The days, weeks and months are passing by. I pop my head out to try to get a glimpse and sense of what is going on out there and what's next. You spot me but only to put your hand up, motioning me to retreat further into more darkness.

Don't you see me??? Don't you hear me??? Don't you feel me??? What else do I have to do for you to notice me??? Don't you care about my love? Or do you only care about hers? Aren't you aware of all the pain you're causing me? Or are you only aware of hers?

I still wait and hold on for so long through all the past and present torment, but you stopped coming. You forgot what I meant to you. You forgot about me. You forgot about us. I finally realize that she'll always be front and centre on your stage, because of your guilt, and you'll never show me off for my debut. I'll never get to dance my piece that I want to so badly. Maybe it was always your intention to only have me as a supporting dancer, never the main who receives all of your attention.

I am a ghost. I am invisible. And yet I still gave you everything.

I ask myself, what's more painful than walking away??? Staying.

And now it's been over a year of your agony, neglect, avoidance and running. How many times are you going to turn your back on me? How many times are you going to leave me? I force myself to walk off your stage when instead, you should of told her to walk off a long time ago. I walk off with my head held high as devastation burns me alive. But a diamond who has worked so hard at becoming one doesn't deserve to be hidden away and kept a secret. A diamond deserves to be revealed to the world… to be proud of, cherished, and held up for all to see.

I am tormented knowing everything about you and her, and she is comforted knowing nothing about you and I. Little does she know that it was meeting me that ignited the changes within you. Don't you understand that lessening her pain just increases mine??? I go to sleep countless nights wondering how you even feel about me, when I am all about you. You make me feel more alone with you than I ever did being single. But I'm the kind of woman who knows what she brings to the table and isn't afraid to eat alone.

I'm the kind of woman you go to war beside, not against. I want my relationship to be a safe haven and a happy place, not another battle I have to fight. I deserve the world and when it happens for me, that someone is going to take such good care of me. They're going to be the rock that I was for you, for so long. They're going to treasure my deep soul, my intelligent mind, and my pure heart. Everything that makes me, me.

By leaving me for the last time, you set me free. Thank you.

She can have your stage, I'm building my own.

C.
Canada

P.S. When the timing is wrong, and wondering if it'll ever be right.

Dear M.,

You've been there for me for a very long time. You still are. When you used to get triggered, I would tell you how the fear you're feeling was just a perceived threat, and you would listen. Sometimes, you were stubborn and only wanted to believe you were right, what you thought was right, and that I was weak. But I have forgiven you for that. And we both moved on.

Then we met again on good terms. You were more accepting, as I inspired you to be. Even if you expected the worst, you accepted these feelings, whatever fears you felt, and henceforth— it didn't affect us.

J.H.

Lebanon

P.S. The initial 'M' stands for my Mind. This is how we became friends. I no longer am afraid of my own thoughts.

To: April

It is said that after 7 years,
you know if a friendship will last.
Well, that's not right, is it?

You wanted to have space,
you had your reasons.
You promised things would change—
in time.
They would heal,
be better,
"Just give it time."

I held on.
For years.
Hope—
turned false.

The promise of
"Always."
I'd always be there.
I had to keep my promise—
even if you had not.

I can't do it anymore.
I can't hold on.

D. JUANITA
United States

P.S. Relationships end. I've learned this the hard way. The hardest ends have been those of friends. April is not the person, rather the month they were born, as I am unsure how to refer to them. Brother? Friend? Bestfriend? Past-friend? Past-best friend? Regardless, every April belongs to them.

TO THE BOY I COULDN'T SAVE,

I like to tell myself that we tried– but did we? Not hard enough, not in those last days– but at first? I was pulled to you like a magnet– and you know I tried to fight it. I don't know how many times we tried on the words 'just friends'— but they never quite fit. Two people who look at each other like that could never be just friends. We met by absolute chance, it was you that reached out, asking around until you found someone who knew me. I was always told 'never get involved with a co-worker'— but wasn't it thrilling? I could have lived without the workplace gossip, but at least we turned some heads. I always liked making people wonder. And boy, did we give them something to talk about. I still remember walking into that party behind you and all those eyes on me. I felt like a zoo animal behind glass– that's when the rumors really took off. You knew everyone and I was the new girl— they couldn't resist turning us into front page news.

Is that what drove you to be so cold? Or was it because you knew I'd have to leave soon? My time there was always temporary– you knew that– so why did you turn into someone unrecognizable? You shattered me to pieces with your silence. Cursed with the recent memory of your kiss, your touch, the way you understood my body more than anyone before. How you held my hand in the car, how you drove me to the coast that day just so I could touch the ocean one last time. The boy who smiled while I collected every broken seashell. The boy who held me in the morning. Five more minutes.

You were a forest fire and I was gasoline.

I wasn't what you needed. We didn't help each other heal. All we did was burn. How I burned for you. How you burned for me. It felt good. Too good. Like we were addicted to one another. It didn't end well. The withdrawals from you we're killer. To this day I wonder, if you walked into the same room as me now– would I relapse completely?

I wish I could have been your calm place to rest. I wish I could have saved you, but at the time I knew you, you didn't want to be saved– you only wanted to keep burning.

It turns out, ice cold silence burns in a way that leaves more of a lasting impression than the fiery touch of a lover. With you, I've felt both— I've given both. In the end, all that was left was ashes and soot and a kind of pain that's indescribable.

I'm sorry I didn't know how to love you. I'm sorry you never learned how to love me.

THE GIRL MADE OF SMOKE
Jupiter Island, United States

P.S. If you don't understand the kind of pain I'm talking about, I hope you never do.

LAKE SHINE,

It's me again, but it's spring now, the season I met your waters in. I remember how full of sunlight they were, how I never knew brown eyes could be filled with anything, and yours proved me wrong.

But I miss you, and your waters don't run through the garden of my heart that much anymore. I see the moon and think of you, when we sat on the roof for hours, gazing at stars until we shivered, as cold as space itself. I was shivering for different reasons.

I miss when the grass would be emerald-new, and we would lie in the creeping charlie vines, myself being ignorant of what was creeping onto me. There were days in spring where the green in your eyes would be that of the leaves moving around our heads. When summer's heat was filling my veins with warmth at the thought of your presence.

Maybe this is too personal. Or maybe it won't ever come across, and maybe you won't read this and know it's you. It shouldn't be hard to figure out, but a part of me hopes it would be, so I don't cut you loose with the paper's sharp edges.

The woods I could write books on, the fields about poetry, I could write a few lines about the sky and stars, maybe a sentence about the bugs and birds. But your rivers I could write on and on for, as flowing freely as the water, for they are the color of your eyes, cologne ever at my throat, sound forever a lullaby.

With spring's newness comes winter's afterthought of loneliness, and that's what crept to me when your waters turned to slow stillness in the garden of my heart, of which you once helped to water my soul. What will my soul do, if your river runs dry, if your eyes turn bronze like its bed so the sun never shines upon its surface?

I hope by then the moon will keep watch over me instead.

> Forever To Never Be Yours,
> McCartney
> *United States*

P.S. This is to the same Lake Shine from my winter letter, only now it's spring, the season I met them in. I am afraid to lose them, and wonder what I will do if that happens, if they drift away from me. In this letter is the fear of loss, and the wish to get lost inside them. Spring brings about many memories, and many wishes.

Dear lover,
> could you give me a break
> so I can see whether or not this is safe?
> What I had before sure took a toll
> so it's hard to tell what I really know.
> Lover, let's take this slow
> so love isn't blocking what I feel in my soul.
> You're stealing my heart away,
> but I want to feel like it was given
> I know you understand,
> because you've lost yourself in love too.

So dear lover,
be good to me,
and I'll be good to you.

> Amy B.
> *United States*

P.S. This is a poem I wrote after a date where I realized I was falling very quickly for a new love interest of mine. The rush of feelings I had were catching me off guard and after leaving a very difficult relationship prior, it was hard for me to trust the love I was experiencing. So, I wrote this in my car right after that date.

Dear E.,

You deserve more words than the ones I have for you today. You deserve every word in the world. As a writer, I create life in the words I write and I pray with every fiber of my soul that all the words I write could create some world with you in it. But my words don't hold the magic I need to save you.

These are the days when the world begins to blossom again. I see life anew with each passing day. The blooms on the trees grow, the grass turns green again, the wind whistles and dances across my skin. Moments like these remind me, all too well, of the void in my heart. My heart bangs on the cages of my soul, wishing to be released from this grief I carry with me every day of my life.

As the times continue to fly by, it's as if I can't catch my breath. Holding onto some faint hope that tomorrow will bring some kind of relief to this madness I feel. I wish to be renewed like these springtime flowers, but I remain as dead inside as I was the day before.

Elle R.
United States

P.S. A spring letter to my heavenly daughter.

Hey there stranger,

It's a fact.

We've never met. Before this at least.

Well, maybe we have and either, A) We've only crossed paths, B) I didn't have to nerve to speak to you or, C) I already know you by another name. All three are entirely possible, given my recent streak of mishaps, but please know that I'm not hopeless.

Maybe you are also waiting for someone like I am, fed up of dating, or currently in a relationship with someone you love, or in the process of getting over someone— but you can't help but hold on to hope that your soulmate is out there somewhere waiting for you too.

Although sometimes I'm not even sure what I'm looking for, I sometimes get a deja vu like feeling that you were thinking of me— maybe that same special moment belongs to the two of us— if not now, maybe in our near future.

But I'll know it, when I meet you. That cliche snap: that instant connection: that feeling like a warm butter beer down your throat: *so this is what it feels like.*

I'll know it when you rap every word to a cliche pop song, confess you also wanted to go to Hogwarts one day, quote a soul stirring few words from your favourite book that keeps you going on bad days, share your opinion on the last piece of news you've seen, or tell me I have a piece of spinach stuck in my teeth, without an ounce of judgement. Or just maybe we will just happen to bump into each other in a coffee shop or sit next to each other at the movies and I'll just know it's you.

The details don't matter, but here's what does: you'll be totally, honestly, unquestionably, unabashedly and enthusiastically *you*, whatever style that comes in. And when that day comes, you better believe I'll fall in love much quicker than you ever will, as— for all the bravado and strong front that I've been putting up— I really wish you were next to me.

So, until that day comes, I'll be here, doin' my thing. Maybe we'll meet through our group of friends—you'll get dragged along by your bestfriends and there I'll be, or maybe someone at work may casually introduce you to me and we'll look into a familiar set of eyes and hit it off immediately— somehow finding ourselves talking like we had never stopped our unspoken conversation. I'll do my best to play it cool and you'll be perfect, or not, it's okay if you come along in a form I just haven't recognised so far.

Maybe we'll meet on the bus and you'll be sitting there, listening to your favourite music and I'll be sitting behind you, oblivious, probably, listening to the same song. Maybe you'll decide to up your game by gazing over your shoulder with a gentle smile— hoping that's enough to crack my radar, like it always has with folks you know. Until finally, maybe you'll cut straight to the chase—spin around, point out the tune I'm humming and tell me how much you love it— and I'll do my best not to fumble, and talk back confidently with you.

I'm not perfect— I'm far from it— and I don't expect you to be either. I don't want you to tell me what you think I'd like to hear and I promise to treat you the same, right from the start. The worst thing we can do in meeting someone is to project onto them who we'd like them to be. So if we meet, please be *you*, and I promise I'll be *me*.

If you want to know my feelings on late 90's songs, rom-coms like *Serendipity*, please ask. Whatever pops up, ask. If you want to tell me about your exhausting day at work, I'll listen, your favourite part of the day, I'll be there to reassure you. Even if I may have no idea what you are talking about, I'll still adoringly take in your face while you talk on. I'd be happy to share my favourite cup of coffee, go on a long drive to watch the sunset together, even watch a match, which you seem to enjoy, all to just keep you company and cheer along with you. I'm happy to just sit next to you if you don't want to talk, and share uncomfortable silences with you, and if need be, give you time until you are ready to find the language to speak. You don't know it yet, but I'm already here, falling for you, and I'm fighting like hell to keep my

patience from wearing away— all in an effort to find out who you may be.
 We've never met, but I'd like to.
 Now hurry up and get here.

> Sincerely,
> Hopeful in love
> *India*

P.S. I'm still hopeful one day I will meet you and everything will just seem right, until then this letter is a manifestation to form and protect you until our paths cross. Here's to wishing true love exists.

April 26th, 2022

Myself,
 As the leaves change once again,
 I am reminded of how quickly
 the things around us change
 before our eyes—
 again and again.
 Just like the leaves,
 people usually don't notice the changes until it's too late
 and we're already different,
 left craving the next season,
 the next version of what's been—
 of what's to come.
 Once again,
 I am surrounded
 by beautiful, blooming flowers,
 singing birds,
 running water,
 chirping crickets,
 colorful skies,
 spontaneous adventures,
 and Sunday's spent on the lake.
 I will cherish these moments,
 for they go by too quickly,
 becoming distant memories
 sooner than you'd think.
 I will do my best
 to be present,

to make the most
of the time I've been given
and the time I have left.

I know I will miss this person—
this version of myself,
when the seasons change
once again.

> Desiree M.
> *United States*

P.S. I feel like we change just as much as the seasons do and we are constantly learning about ourselves.

To Ely,

I'm not sure where you'd be right now. Perhaps in your bed, perhaps out of the house, perhaps with your siblings. Perhaps you're not okay. I miss you. I missed you last night too. I think I'm forgetting you. I think I'm moving on. Well, I think I have moved on and it hurts. Of course we could never be together. Or maybe if things even could have gone that far, we wouldn't have wanted to— but still— leaving you in time feels like I'm leaving myself. I miss you everyday. Somedays I feel it. Somedays I don't. Somedays I question this whole thing that happened. I say to myself it was some petty infatuation. Perhaps it was nothing more than that for both of us, because we were so lonely in our worlds. We thought with this, with whatever we had, at least we wouldn't be as lonely.

So maybe we found a little peace in each other, in talking to each other— or maybe, in reality, we were just saving ourselves from dwelling in a void. Although, now that I think about it, I remember that even when you were there— I still felt that void. Right there. I often felt it getting bigger, so I wouldn't be this unrealistic love-struck girl who's like, *Oh! I finally found a boy to take away my feelings of emptiness.*

The void was there and so were we and perhaps that's all we needed. Not some unrealistic dream or illusion to come fix our empty souls— but to see otherwise, to be okay with both. So perhaps, it was love? That's the real question here. That's why, at 10:32 in the morning, I'm thinking through all this and writing a letter to you. I miss you, even though you never filled that void. You were everything. Or maybe just an illusion of hormones. Just a mere infatuation. I don't know. God, I don't know.

Someday I'll find somebody to love, Ely. A part of me is more than happy about that and a part of me doesn't want to. I don't want to leave you or your ideas behind. Yes, you're gone. You were gone the moment you cut the last call and that's what I am reminding myself of for the past two months. I have accepted it. I keep telling myself this, I have accepted it. Yes, I will forget you– despite not wanting to forget you. I don't want to. Please. Can we just stop this moment in time? Sometimes I think I might send you all these letters someday. I want to. I want you to know, if I ever loved you, my love for you really did go from selfish to selfless. And if, somehow, these letters bring you any kind of pain– even just a split second of uncertainty or dwelling over the past– I don't want that. I don't think I want that. But I do want that because I want you to miss me. I want you to be in the same pain as me because we're together– and we'll never be. What toxic love!

I am not ready to picture you with somebody else– I would hate it. Maybe these are just mere words, you know? Words are sweet. Words can change you. Oh, well– you know me– what a contradictory personality I have!

I just miss you. So much. If these letters bring even a minute of feeling loved and wanted– I hope you read them someday. Someday when we're less broken. Someday when we'll care less about this teenage illusion. So then, even if we break– we wouldn't shatter. At least not so much that we wouldn't be able to pick ourselves back up.

I lost you, Ely– and I hate it.

Every minute of my life I hate that I lost you.

I don't know if it's just me dwelling over the loss of a person who could make me feel less alone or if is me actually in love. In grief. I love you in every minute this heart beats. It's so painful– to endure this loss.

Zahru
Pakistan

Our spring walks of memories,

As the weather begins to warm up and spring is upon us I think about all the joyful memories of me and you sitting outside. Of us basking in the cool breeze and the warm sunshine hitting our skin. Walking through the grass– seeing all the beautiful tall trees– enjoying nature. Feeling so at home with you…

I always enjoyed our walks outside surrounded by nature, surrounded by your love and kindness.

I miss our walks together, and even though you're no longer with me– I will always have the memories in my heart. Now I take walks alone and you are always right there with me— in my thoughts. I still see you everywhere.

I love you, Hero.

>   ALWAYS AND FOREVER,
>   KRISTAL
>   *United States*

TO MY ELOHIM, WITH MIGHTY LOVE,
Dawn is a myriad of color & sound
that we never hear elsewhere.
I wait in dawn,
in fields of rolling gold,
for my Love, My Echad.
He comes to me through shadows.
He is light, no darkness touches Him.
I cannot see His face.
His form comes to me in dreams.
I know Him, My Elohim.
We dance through dawn and into day,
there is no part to us—
We are one.
We are Echad.
Elohim is my Love.
You cannot take us apart.
Though we are separated by many miles through looks,
We are together in Spirit— forever.
Always.
Elohim and I.
My eyes shine forever in His light.
There is no end to His gentle touches,
His graceful speeches and soft words.
You may wage war,
you may take out your guns—
you will not split my heart in two,
or four
or seven
because long ago I chose Love over Hate.
There is no war that has not been won in my favor,
for Elohim is my Love— always.

Forever.
Mine.
Just as I am His.
There is no greater Love than this.

> ARYREJIN EL
> *United States*

P.S. I pray everyone knows a love as strong, and deep and heartfelt and truly, truly wonderful in their life time as I have known with my Elohim. I pray you are open and willing to search and fight for such a love, and will do anything to attain it. May you be blessed in your journey.

WINTER BEAR,

I want to love you like how the summer sun beams itself across the glory of a sunflower. Or how beautifully it reflects itself upon the ocean.

I want to love you like how the ocean waves gently hug the sandy shores.

I want to love you like how the spring brings about the most gorgeous flowers in the month of May.

I will still love you in the season of autumn, as the leaves on the trees start to rest themselves upon the ground.

And as the winter season comes, I will love you warmly, like how your favorite sweater wraps itself around you.

This is how I'll love you,

in every season of this lifetime.

> SUNFLOWER
> *Philippines*

P.S. To the one that I love in every season of my entire lifetime.

HEY B.,

I have such a hard time getting out my feelings for you, I figured I'd write them down and go from there. Like we mentioned while walking, being vulnerable is so scary, due to the fear of losing someone because they don't get a certain side of you. You are one of my best friends, with unrivaled joy and strength, piercing ocean blue eyes, and an innate passion that impacts every soul you touch. When you talk, you get so excited over what most people overlook. I have temporary lenses, where I can see things in this light and think it's something profound, but you don't need contacts to see the world this way, you just do.

You chase your Sunday school kids with the joy and power that God chases you with. If you define someone by how they react to pain, you cry, freak out, but then you know it's going to be ok, and choose to care for others with radiating joy despite your own world falling out from under you.

You really get going when you speak, and will talk with no filter, but somehow you're still utterly intentional and compassionate.

You are more forgiving than most, especially in the way you've forgiven and love your step brother and biological father so fluently.

You are loyal to the end, I mean to the friends you have, that have been a part of your for life so long, those you continue to love tirelessly.

You know how to love the people and things that most overlook, or deem too difficult to love, and do it with a faith like a child's.

Your eyes brighten up when you see the color yellow, or a giraffe, a fun sunset, or while on a simple walk. More specifically, you get excited at the sound of shoes on pavement or just going on a walk. Remember that bike ride when you told me of all your pain and news of your dad? I hated the pain, but loved how those fireflies danced seemingly on their copper wires.

What about in your new town when we went to that event? I think about that night a lot. Mostly with regret that my car had manual locks that made it hard for me to open your door for you. When we left you wondered why I turned left (the way we came from) and mentioned how it normally takes 25 minutes to drive home but this way would take just 10!! I drove so slow. I then convinced you to drive back over the bridge and "got lost." I just wanted to BE with you. Like, I didn't care what we said or did, I just really liked being with you. Never felt that before. When we were "turning around," we decided to walk the pier.

As we walked, we could see the backdrop of the bridge and the city colored in a deep crisp Carolina sunset, outlined by the beautiful darkness. I looked at it for several split seconds to collect my thoughts, to try to respond with wisdom. The rest was me tripping over my feet, thinking of kissing you. But there I was, like when I saw the rocky mountains for the first time, with the most beautiful sunset imaginable. But it could not hold my focus. There was something, someone new before me that I hadn't yet realized would be my favorite. No matter how scary or rather beautiful my life was, I was intoxicated with this instance of you.

Or what about that hike, I was so set on getting to the river, I lost the euphoria of just sitting on that log with you. It's weird how you remember some parts more than others, like how beautiful your eyes looked as we were just sitting and transcribing, a moment so simple, yet it is etched into my brain. I want to talk, listen and just have the chance to see the world through your eyes, through your thoughts.

I wish I had made sequels to these memories, rather than getting drunk on the one that had already passed. Miss ya. I don't know how to talk to you anymore. I want to solve and take away your anxiety, but I don't want to be annoying.

My mind tends to trace the way we once talked. When we talked you heard me, and may have forgotten some things I said, but you made me feel like I could say anything and for that, thank you. But then when I didn't hear from you for so long I felt as though the wings you gave me were just a part of my imagination. I always I wanted the girl of my dreams. Until I realized too late, you were the girl of every waking moment.

B.
United States

P.S. It feels good to get out the last of my thoughts I never sent. Now, I choose to live in a space where I share my thoughts more freely with less fear of what might be lost.

May 8th, 2022

Momma,

Happy Mother's Day. I know someday, somewhere– you'll read this. A letter never sent– but you somehow always manage to read everything I write. I suppose these are the words I don't know how to say aloud. I know, I'm a turmoil of emotions, late twenties and yet still– I am an ocean. It's funny how 26 doesn't feel all that different from 16. I thought I'd feel more sure of things, more steady, less afraid. I just feel like one of those nesting dolls, with all of my past selves still inside me— living and breathing and worrying. You always used to call me 'your little worrier'. I'm not sure what a seven-year-old had to worry about, but I remember not being able to sleep. I remember crawling into bed and laying between you and Dad and barely being able to turn over because I was so small and both of you were like giants to me. I don't remember if being there really helped me sleep but I do remember not wanting to leave.

The thing is, Mom, I'm afraid of a life without you in it. I don't think I could bear it. I don't think I could handle it. Do you know? Can you hear how scared I am every time I say, "Goodnight, I love you too."?

I don't know how to leave you behind like so many people my age seem to be able to do so well. I don't know how to be okay with only seeing you on holidays. You created me. I am alive because you never gave up on trying even when the doctors told you it was impossible. Why does society pressure me to leave you behind? I'm worried you'll get lonely.

I look at you and I see a mirror of my own loneliness and worry. I see my apathy and bitterness. I see my resilience and cleverness. I see all that has made me and all I could become and I wonder what you see when your own reflection stares back in the walnut brown of my eyes. Do you see your hope for the future, your ambition, your anger, your ache for something more?

Do you see your exhaustion and confusion and compassion?

I watch as you carry your own pain and I wish I could take it away. Being a daughter, at times, is unbearable. Being a mother, I imagine, feels impossible. And yet, we make coffee every morning, sit at our round wooden table, and look out the window— watching the birds. You always tell me if the cardinals or blue jays or hummingbirds show up. I always tell you when I see a new bird and finally identify it, like that goldfinch or the grackle. And we welcome our new neighbors. Those are the moments that are etched into my soul. Those are the moments I refuse to give up.

I love you more than words could ever possibly express. And I will continue to do so— beyond this existence, just as you have loved me. It's getting late now, I'll see you in the morning. Good night. I love you.

>   Roo
>   *United States*

Dear J.J.,
>   You were once my dream boy—
>   the one to take me away and
>   lead me to my fairytale ending.
>   My prince of light.
>   Then you became my prince of darkness—
>   stealing away the joy I had for you
>   questioning my every move
>   draining my hope into nothingness,
>   haunting my dreams
>   leaving them to be only nightmares.
>   You were my fairytale that turned into my misery.

>   Love,
>   F. Wolf
>   *United States*

P.S. He was a old fling that I thought would be the one. He checked all the boxes that I wanted in a future husband, but once I started to date him, I found out he wasn't right. He was a right guy/wrong time situation that I needed to let go of.

To the woman I cannot name,

I've never purposely hurt another human. Never sought to cut someone down or take their pride. I don't believe in violence, I would never condone it— or shouldn't, anyways. I had heard your name before, coming out of his lips. I never liked the way your name sounded, nor the words that soon followed after. I could tell you were trouble from the start, I just wish that's where the story ended.

You soon abused your power with him, you were the one that sought to cause damage. In fact, I'm pretty sure you're alarmed at just how much you've managed to tear from him— It's hard to think of consequences when you're too busy reporting lies. It's weird to say, but did you think of him at all? His family being left to question his innocence, his children hearing of sins so evil that their minds physically cannot cope with the thought of it.

I have never met you, never seen a picture, or gotten a second opinion on your nature. But I already know you to be the ugliest soul there is. My heart breaks at the thought of you walking with your head held high, knowing your stories are full of nothing but lies. I have never met you, and you have attacked me. Threatened my family, my father. My everything. How am I supposed to react?

You are the reason I cannot sleep at night, the reason he has stopped eating, the reason my brother can't stop asking questions about what will happen to us. You are the reason we sit in fear, in our own home, what is meant to be our safety. You have ruined my peace. And for that, I wish you nothing but pain.

L.G.
Scotland

Dear S.,

You may never truly learn about the nature of your soul— how much it's able to give and handle— until it faces the unwanted demands of life.

Until it goes up against the undesired wants of people, from you and your soul's own absurd miseries and waves, its greediness— when you never thought you'd see the day when you'd choose to not be generous. Its rage in situations when you thought you'd forever be a calm giver. And its astray, when you forever thought you were on the right path. But you'll learn to feel the depth of who you are, you'll find the real you, you'll find the self.

> J.H.
> *Lebanon*

P.S. The 'S' initial is me speaking to the Self. I'm offering these words to you. To your journey of Self discovery.

Kisses sweet like strawberries
tea in a forgotten cup—
light breaks over mountains.
A field full of flowers,
curtains blow softly.
They are carrying memories through the windows.
A shadow who loves me.
A shadow who loved me
in another life
walked across the floor
to hold me in the only way a ghost could.
Through spilled sugar and kitten kisses,
glances outside the café,
still nights by the fjord.
Golden hour mead,
pieces of lace who are holding pages
in favorite children's books,
letters in a desk drawer.
Used candles in melted wax
stains from honey on tablecloths—
recipes waiting for tomorrow.
My love is a library—
quiet and outlasting history.
And you, dear one,
are written on every page
of my life.

> FREYDIS LOVA
> *United States*

May 10th, 2020

Love,

The rains come with force, painting the river in a dark and foreboding shade. I see hurried water rush with quickened pace pounding more and more by the second. It is quite unstoppable, washing everything away in its hungry current. I stand alone, watching the water rise and fall. Autumn left the river dry and wanting, but now, approaching spring, it cannot wait one moment longer to touch the parts of its path that have been just beyond reach for so long. Its mouth longing to rise up onto her shore, and it keeps climbing higher without end— like a hand on a thigh daring to push limits until it spills to boundaries unknown.

Then, there is a summit and a settling, a slow drop as stream meets river, and river meets something larger than itself, draining itself of its fullness. And here I am to watch it fall like a lover's heart, roaring and seeking eagerly until it peaks and slowly falls. Just like arms and legs wild and twisting beneath sheets in a wanting embrace. Lips hungry for another kiss. Eyes wild until their pleasure peaks and gently settles, taking the moment. Arms and legs are strewn lazy, and hearts slowly fall to a much softer, steadier beat. And then it's normal again. Normal, but never the same— because just as the river etches a path in earth and carries away pieces along its course, it changes it, reshapes it into something the same, but somehow different.

You do the same to me. The feel of your body is etched into my mind. The feel of your hips against mine, the taste of your kiss lingering so that even when you're gone, I know you were here. And you take pieces of me away with you. My smile, the pleasure of companionship in my eyes, the feel of my skin, sweat-slicked with yours. A moment. Even if the water should never rise again, the banks would never forget its touch— because it has carried a part of her away with it.

So I will tell you, even if you should leave, never to return, I shall never forget your touch.

R. DESHEA
West Virginia - Hills of Appalachia, United States

P.S. An old flame whom I had no promise would stay. When I penned the words, I knew somewhere inside me that he was already gone, that he was no longer mine. Our bodies came together for a time, but that's all it was. He changed me in so many ways. I can't say they were all good. We both loved the water, so I see this as a goodbye to something that never should have been.

J.C.,

Dreams singing a lullaby, soft tunes pressing deeper and deeper into my soul, and I feel the eye of someone watching me sleep, so peacefully, that it hurts them to watch. Something beckons to get me out of this bottomless slumber.

Am I awake?

I am unaware, because the stars are bright today, and the moon is slightly hidden. The leaves are moving, yet the calm is unsettling. The roads are empty but my heart is full. I am amazed at the beauty of leaving, because the one who leaves never realizes it, and the one that stays is immersed completely in the absence. Today I believe, because I am soaked to the brim, and the reason is purely illusional.

My words are pouring now because I am right here, and you are away, you are always away! Until now, I have never felt nerves so acutely, the sound of you so loud in my mind, I can feel it. We've never met, you don't even know me, but you are my hope. Wherever you are, near or far, you deepen this ink of hope, because you make me wish to follow what I dream of.

All the birds speak, the leaves weave,
the shelter of my hope,
amidst the dark sky of your departure,
I shall also soon arrive at my destination.
My tears are my memory of crying for you,
because one shall only waste them on someone precious.
If fate permits, we will meet soon!
Under the full moon,
they will celebrate,
the whole of constellations,
the hope reunited,
the dull shine,
but the never fading one!
The happiest journey is not what I wish for you,
but a path of self-exploration, with lots of laughter!

    S.S.K.
    United Arab Emirates

P.S. We never met.

L.,

I knew from the beginning that I wanted to protect that heart of yours, and make sure it never had to go through anymore heartbreak or pain. You were always so important to me. Even when you pushed me away, even when we didn't talk. I never stopped caring about you.

I wanted to show you that there were still good people out there, ones that make you laugh, give you the world, and be there for you all the time, every time. I'd be lying if I said I wasn't in pain, because I am. It still hurts. But instead of becoming angry, I want to understand.

I knew we had crossed paths for a reason. I had nothing but absolute love for you. Maybe I was the only one who felt it, who knows, but it was there for me. Maybe I'm stupid, and that's okay, because I'd rather bring my wall down one last time and tell you the truth, than regret not ever telling you how I truly felt.

Please promise me something though… find someone who never makes you question yourself. Who respects you all of the time, even when you're not around. Someone who is honest and loyal. Who lets you be 100% yourself, and doesn't judge you for it. Someone who looks at you like they can't imagine their life without you. Who is proud to be yours, and reminds you why. Someone who is excited to spend the rest of their life with you, wants the best for you, and finds you too rare to lose. Someone who knows exactly what they have, when they have you. Who will try and lift your spirits up when times are hard. Who gets butterflies around you, and can't help but smile when your name is mentioned. Someone who loves you unconditionally, all the time, no matter what, and tells you how much they truly adore you.

C.L.P.
United States

P.S. A lost love letter.

Dearest E.,

The wind whispers your name as it swirls the star dust that is yours. I trust you twinkle above me now. Undoubtedly, you're more than a mere star, you're the sun. Drawing in those most unsuspecting and burning them when they get too close to your core. I'm married now and have a son of my own. I almost named him in your honor, but with all we've been through it would be much too painful. I feel as though I'm nothing more than a mere twig tossed to and fro in the wind of a thunderstorm— and that storm is *life*.

Does it surprise you to know that I nearly got a music note tattooed behind my ear? Not just because it reminds me of you, but because it would be concealed— unlike you. You visit me not only in my dreams, but also awaken me in my present. Don't we all have burning questions for you? How were you able to remain so mysterious, yet give such vulnerable parts of you away?? I suppose that's the talent of artistry, which by now I am sure you have mastered.

After the pain you caused me I could have easily turned bitter, and it was really hard to not be triggered for quite sometime. This marks 6 years and I feel lately I've been releasing a lot of anger upon those who don't rightfully deserve it. But they don't know me like you do. I told you everything. I thought you were my sweet escape. You released something in me that made me feel like I was home with you. You were a once in a lifetime lifeline and you're gone away from me now.

How does one surface to breathe when they're constantly being shoved underwater by the waves that weigh me down like anchors? I have PTSD and it rears it's overarching reach in the forms of overwhelm, stress, anxiety, and a depression cycle. You never would have wanted me to linger in this abyss of sadness. You would tell me to pull myself above water and find a log or a raft to cling to. You would tell me to find ways to be present with my son and my husband in the here and now and release my memories in the past of and from you.

I know you would encourage me to be the best mom I knew how and to give my husband the love, affection, and support he deserves. What I tried to give myself amidst my abuse, but alas, could not. Eventually your vice became too strong and I'm a "fixer," who thought I was stronger. I didn't think I knew everything, but I thought I knew what I needed to.

You showed me the dark side of the moon, if you will— those things and places I never knew existed before. I engrained myself more deeply into my convictions, in the end, because you caused me to dig in my heels and contemplate why I thought and the viewed the world the way that I did— I still try to help and love others and just be optimistic.

Deep down I know sober you wouldn't have hurt me in that way; in any way for that matter. It was a true Jekyll and Hyde experience for me at times. But ultimately, you weren't loving and caring for yourself right, so how could you have loved me properly and truly? I have to be honest with myself and know that there were points in time when you manipulated and used me, but the truth is, I continued on with you at times and ignored blatant red flags. Yes, I was still vulnerable from my past trauma, and that was taken advantage of. But I must pick up my own cross and bear it as well. I thought you would like to know that I talked with your mom after your death. I finally got to officially meet her. We talked about all things you and she truly helped me decompress. It turns out we have a lot in common. She has been through what I have and tries to find ways you would have agreed with to cope with her own grief.

We both turn to the great outdoors— whether it be walking, hiking, camping, kayaking, + reading, writing, and therapy. Please know that you weren't a burden, and you're much more than a statistic. You're my sun spot and I know now that I will always love you. And I cling to the one time you told me along the very same lines that you had love for me too. Ultimately, you were destined for an other worldly place and I'm stuck here living out those fragments and paths in your life you had yet to take. I hope I make you proud, E. I mourn all of you; even the messy chaos and the life we never got the chance to create or for you to really begin.

> Love always,
> A.
> *United States*

P.S. A letter of healing from a once best friend.

My younger self,
My darling,
I remember when you used to cry for Mum and Dad
after they'd dropped you off at the school gates—
your anxious soul not yet ready to be separated.

My darling,
The quiet one, the shy one.
Who kept herself to herself,
only a handful of friends—
not counting the fairies, of course.

My darling,
Always so sensitive to the world outside,
preferring those in your imagination instead.
Worlds of magic and fairytales,
like the ones painted on your bedroom walls.

My darling,
If only you could see yourself now,
so strong and ready to take on that outside world,
clutching life with both hands and running towards your dreams.
Little darling, you would be so proud
of the woman you have become today.

The one who still believes in magic,
in each and every way…

>   Magic & Musings
>   *England*

Dear what could never have been,
    When I close my eyes I can still hear the street lamps as they hummed out into the darkness, illuminating all the glittering-gold lies.
    That warm spring evening came along so easily full of first wild promises.
    I can feel the pull of my heart as it navigates towards this unexpected kaleidoscope of emotions, that spill out to form life's new normal on the sidewalk between us. The lights grow more lustrous as the earth falters away from the sun. I was always pursuing you in eternal graceless circles against these delphinium-blue skies.
    Face to face we stood silent as five years struggled on my lips and that first opal kiss dissolved until we formed the same breath.
    These long held perceptions of endearment cascade down quickly and fade right back into warm obscurity, like an uninvited guest. How quickly you retreated from them.

>   A.
>   *United States*

My Queen,
    I may forget many things,
    but I will never forget you.
    For your joy is calcified in my bones.
    Your kindness, knit into the fibers of my beating heart.
    Your peace, a reservoir deep in the belly of my soul.
    Your laughter, echoes on the walls of my ear drums.

Your forgiveness, closer to me than my own skin.
Your love, etched in the neuronal pathways of my brain.
Your connection to Christ, forever before my eyes.
Your humility, forever on my lips.
Your words, wisdom, and wit,
have become woven into the fabric of my spirit.
I could never forget you.
For as long as there is life in me,
you will be.
But it is I that worries,
you will forget me.
For what whitewashed memories will remain,
when you become immersed in the glory of the Holy of Holies?

If I had not known a greater love,
I might despair.
But the truth is,
the greatest news is that we will see Our Father there.
Take joy, my queen.

JASMINE
United States

DEAR J.M.,

I wonder if all this time spent apart equates to extra jewels in our heavenly crowns. Oh, my darling, these days are arduous; there's no denying. Despite the longer, warmer days, a chill settles over me in your continued absence. Even still, as the moon waxes and wanes, as the wind accompanies the waves, so too does my love for you remain an ever-fixed mark. Can I ask you a question – are you looking at the same star-studded sky on these lonely nights, wishing you were here with me?

YOURS,
S.J.
Canada

P.S. This was from a season when my husband and I were separated by an ocean for a time. We were able to talk on the phone/facetime and the like, but the romantic in me wanted more. So, I wrote many love poems (and posted them on IG) in that way, this is an unsent love letter, a compilation of those love poems. xx

E.S.

"If the world were to end today, what would you miss most?"

Her head tilting inquisitively.

"The rain. The way it washes over your skin like heaven's hands. The way it smells of dirt and earth and the tenderness of spring."

I smile and laugh gently, but with vigor, "Oooo. Springtime. The color yellow. The sound of birds awakening with the day.

Love..

Oh.. love. I think I'll miss love the most.

Your smile.

The warmth in your laughter. The way the Sun gently caresses its feet across mountaintops and makes a home in your hair. The rushed greeting of waves at your toes; the way they are hurried, but patient… the way they never stop doing what they love. The way it feels, when midnight has passed into memory, and the only present I know is the gentle beat of your heart against the starlight.

The feeling of saltwater welling in your eyes, that moment before you cry, when you feel universes but also the nothingness in between them, when you are gasping for breath and the world is trying its hardest to remind you how brave it is to simply be alive.

… You.

If I'll miss anything, it will be the way I feel when I'm with you."

M. RYAN
United States

P.S. The letter I will never send to the person I will always love.

TO THE BOY AT THE BOOKSHOP,

You look happy, really happy. I still wonder about you from time to time— wonder if you knew my heart raced when I saw you for the first time.

Did you notice me by the counter, debating on whether or not to say hello, that day at the cafe? I walked in and you were sitting there and I couldn't believe it. I thought maybe I was in some movie and we were meeting again by fate, I was meant to be there and so were you. It had to have been fate, right? Were you happy or annoyed that I sat down to talk to you? I was never sure. You were too sweet to be annoyed, I think. I hope. I wonder what would have happened if I had met you a little earlier— when

I still believed in sharing a life with someone and long before you met her. I am glad though– that you did end up marrying her. By the time you met me– I guess she was all you thought about anyway.

So now, it feels silly to think how nervous I was– but at the time I didn't know. I should have– she worked at the bookshop too– and my god, she was beautiful. She was kind, too. You would have been a fool not to fall in love with her. So I'm glad you did.

And me? How ridiculous. I was nothing compared to her, a blip on your radar, just another customer in the store. Sometimes I sat outside to read, write, dream. Never really working up the courage to be more than just a passing thought in your eyes.

And still– years later– when I walk by that bookshop (though neither of you work there anymore) – I think of you, I wonder what life would be like if you would have seen me first. Then I convince myself that I'm better off and push the thought of you far away, where you have always been and forever will remain– just out of reach.

AMARIS
Ireland

NANA,

How do I begin to put into words the loss you left when I was a little girl? A loss that young hearts don't comprehend. I only have fond snippets of you when I wish I knew you whole. I remember dressing myself up in layers of your favourite hard-earned jewels, the scent of the pink porcelain Avon perfume you gave to me, and how I felt its beautiful smooth surface in my small hands. The taste of your favourite mango ice cream you always treated me to and the little tiny bows you tied to your Millie dog.

Nana, I wish we had had more time. I wish I had known you as I grew old, learned womanhood with your wise soul, but Alzheimer's had other plans. Plans that took you too young and robbed you of your truth, of your knowing, of your self. A cruel end to your vivacious lived youth. An injustice to all who knew you. You were the mother of my father and I thank you, for I like to think some of how he shaped me was how you would have, too. While memories fought you, know that your memory is ever held, ever vibrantly alive and beautifully loved.

GREY
Australia

P.S. From a little girl to the Nana she loves.

MY LOVE,
   Your face is my kind of sunset.
   You are my meadow of greenfields
   that I would love to lay myself on to.
   Your vibe is my kind of melody, resonating within me,
   and just like the ocean— I love you deeply.
   My love for you is like a rage of waves,
   I love you madly,
   and also, my love is as calming as the sea on the days
   when it dances with the wind so softly.

   MEADOW
   Philippines

R.M.,
   It took me a while to be brave enough to undress my sorrows in the form of poetry. First I had to pour out all the happiness you gave me in the form of tears. Because by your side happiness fulfilled me, but away from you, it was draining from me. I've been loving you in silence, and yet, I've been telling the whole world about you with all these many words left unsaid, because no one I know is worthy of my words except for you. So, I'll continue to throw my words to the wind and hope it'll bring you back to me.

   MAYARA K.
   Brazil & Japan

P.S. The accepting phase of loosing someone.

DEAR E.,
   We don't talk much anymore, but you used to be the first person I'd tell everything to. You were my best friend, and not really an ex, but a lover in many different ways. What started as a silly schoolgirl crush grew over the years. From friends to lovers to never anything more than that. But always the craving for it to grow more. Like I said, we don't talk much now. Some-

thing has changed between the dynamic of our relationship. From always speaking to never. It's paralyzing in a way, to know someone so well and then go back to basically being strangers.

Now, I wouldn't say we were lovers that just met at the wrong time, I just think we were scared. Scared of being wrong, scared of pushing for more. Scared of ruining the good things we had going. But I think in the end, we did.

I used to think back and be sad about the what-ifs and possible maybes, but now sometimes, I just get angry. The hurt I went through. Realizing now how manipulative you were with the entire relationship we had somewhat forged. I felt like a toy you'd put away when something shinier came along, coming back when that something shiny would dull and break. I never really saw my worth in the pseudo relationship we had.

And while I'm angry, it's at myself as well. I let myself be treated that way. I've thankfully grown from that. Met someone who didn't see me as the backup plan, but the plan. The future. And I'm marrying him. I love him to the moon and back.

So while I may be angry with you, may still wish that we were as close as we once were (friend-wise at least), this unsent love and hate letter is kind of more like a thank you.

I feel like I couldn't say my vows to him while still feeling so hurt and angry over you.

Thank you for showing me I'm worth more. That I deserve to be the first and only choice. That I am worthy of the love I am receiving now. Thank you for not choosing me, because now I get to choose him— and I couldn't ask for anyone better.

WITH A FIERY HEART,
K.
United States

P.S. Growing from heartbreak.

R.B.,
Thoughts I try to hide—
the endless doubts and worries
that keep on spinning inside my head,
trying to decipher your messages
and what it was you really meant;
the question if I lost my mind,

if so it must have been a while ago,
and whether your awareness even
includes my existence—
sometimes, I can't tell truth from fiction
and I really don't know;
the fact that I feel invisible
compared to your entourage
while simultaneously wondering
whether your social picture is real
or just camouflage;
the things I've wanted to ask you
since day one:

Does it matter?
Do you feel it too?
Is this love real?
Or has it been nothing
and this was just
some grand mirage?

    K.J.
    Germany

Baby H.,

You would have been 8 in May. My little Taurus. (or Gemini if you were late.) I wonder what theme your birthday party would have been. Spiderman? Babysitter's Club? Sting rays because you got to pet one at the aquarium?

I wonder how many nights you would have asked me to read to you. I wonder how many arguments we would have had because you didn't want to clean your room.

I wonder how many long stories or weird facts I missed out on at dinner. I wonder if you would have been a momma's boy or a daddy's girl. Or maybe you would have been too cool for either of us.

Life would be so different that it's honestly hard for me to imagine. I feel a sadness for not getting the chance to live out the timeline you are in. I feel a sadness for all the I love you's never heard or spoken.

But if you had lived, I wouldn't be where I am now;
And most days,
I love where I am.

But every once in a while, I wonder.
What would life have been?

> STEPHY H.
> *United States*

P.S. Miscarriage at 10 weeks.

TO THE ONE WHO CHOSE TO WANDER WITH ME,
   I long to disappear
   into the garden where nothing grows drear.
   Although I'm happy you came along
   it was only in spirit— in my heart
   you remained invisible, but strong.
   I head to a blue tinged mirror
   in that garden where nothing could be drear
   and wonder how I only see lakes—
   the same as your eyes reflecting my heart's only breaks.
   And in that broken glass are the fractures of a love once lost,
   never found and never having any cost.
   Unless I reached for them, searching with dirt stained fingers,
   then wished with all my soul for something that never lingers,
   something that can only be found
   in the memories I had drowned.
   In a fountain of a garden only found in my dream
   that you accompanied me to,
   every denim-washed night,
   under the moon gleam.

> LOVE,
> THE ONE WHO WANDERED ALONE ANYWAY
> *United States*

P.S. I go on walks a lot, sometimes just to dream or be alone. Yet, I always wish for someone to accompany me, but I often walk alone anyways despite that desire. This letter is for the person who would choose to wander with me, out of their own wishing, but who I would never have the courage to ask.

To my almost,

You could never be anything other than gentle, soft-touch, vulnerable and innocence. I believe that's why I attached myself to your gaze in beach waves, finding myself walking the path of unsung memories. Each time feeling as if there was another piece to our story, lost and confused as I.

Your eyes will always be my safe place, my ease of breath, my confidence, soft blow to the knees as you held me and smiled across the gearbox. You attract it, this warmth encompassing my wintry life, and beyond the curtains I always wondered if it was all a facade of foolery, if you really are a ball of negativity, what lies beyond your veins?

Though I am convinced even beyond this breaking away, you are a petal soft soul, beholding a heart so delicate, the kind I wish for. I think part of the struggle is admitting this gift was never in the cards for me, but perhaps I can linger on what could have been, remembering you as you were. As you once were to me.

With love, your almost.
S. Wallace
Australia

P.S. I wrote this letter to the person I loved so deeply, in the way of fearlessness, confidence, and safety. It was easy with him, as if we were meant to be. And then just as soon as he arrived, he went away. He was my almost.

My love,

You may have doubts, but you're truly perfect. I can't even put into words how wonderfully perfect you are… but I'll try!

The way your heart shines when you smile makes me weak in the knees.

When your eyes meet mine, I know that you see me for who I truly am.

No matter where I am, no matter what time of day, I know I can depend on you to be there for me; and I hope you know I'll be there for you, too.

I can't imagine my life without you.

Can I keep you?

Yours unconditionally,
A.K. Bay
United States

P.S. To my greatest love.

Dear Rue,

You are not alone. You are loved and remembered. Memories may haunt you. You may feel helpless and pointless, but you are not. You are a thousand times stronger and I know it. You just need a bit of time—we all do. We grow at our own pace, for life isn't a race.

Storms come and go, and *you* will be the rainbow to triumph after the rain. You are brimming with so much hope and healing that flowers themselves crave your light and warmth. It's okay to feel lonely sometimes and it's okay to be alone for a while. There is nothing to be ashamed of in feeling grey in a time of sunshine, in trying to find a lighthouse— despite having reached the shore. It is not an act of cowardice to ask for help, to hold someone's hand.

Healing is a long process, but it is so, so worth it. It is a cycle of rebirth and renewal, of restoration and respite as you break the chains and grow your own hope to be wilder and wilder. Love yourself— because you are worth your love. Only then, will you find yourself.

I know you will— and then, you will find everyone and everything else.

You are a wildflower. You will bloom, soon. I know you will.

SENDING TIDES OF LOVE,
MAL
Pakistan

P.S. A letter to a broken soul, who needs to find love inside themselves.

Dear Dad,
I love that you gave me
your appetite for food.
Your eagerness to try everything
at least once—
surprising everyone at the table
who aren't brave enough to even try.
I love that you gave me
your passion for classical music.
A deep appreciation of how
the right melody can move you
to tears or to smiling

and stir feelings deep within
that can only be explained as magic.
I love that you gave me
your light-hearted nature.
The courage to find the good in things
no matter how small
and to find the humor in life
when it all feels too heavy
to carry all at once.
I love that you gave me
your devotion to Notre Dame football.
Saturday game days were the best memories
from my childhood
and cheering on The Irish in the fall
is what I look forward to most
all year long.
I wish I could say
I love that you gave me
a great father-daughter relationship.
So today, I choose to remember
all the tangible things
I love that I got from you instead.

Happy Father's Day.

JULIETTE
United States

P.S. I've never been one to connect with the traditional Father's Day cards you find in stores. They all feel too sentimental to be true. So, today, I wrote this letter. It's not everything I wish I could tell my dad— but these are the things that make me grateful to be his daughter. They are the things I hope will never fade as the years wear on. I hope they overtake all the bad memories, and I can simply be grateful for all the little things I got from him.

L.V.,
    this garden blooms of thorns
    flourishing from years of care
    I hide myself
    I'm afraid... you will leave me once again

I give you an upgraded version
I can't show you the real me
no, I'll bloom as the me you know
but I still love you

if I had the courage to stand before you
with my broken mask in my hand
outside my garden of thorns
and let them wilt for all I care
would you accept me?

BONNIE FAY
United States

NOVA,

The night I met you, I still felt like a void masquerading as a star. I was afraid— if I opened up, you'd find a vacuum— a black hole of a girl— not the burning flame of compassion and bravery I always longed to be. That warm spring evening, every word that passed through my lips was second-guessed— except for those first words I spoke to you. I don't even remember what they were, I just remember they were honest.

It was risky, being so direct to a perfect stranger. I don't know what caused me to do so, to drop my act. Maybe it's because I'd never seen you before, the thrill of a stranger— or maybe it's because it had been such a long time since I'd met a pair of eyes that could see right through me. You made me reckless. Maybe you were what terrified me the most, so I reacted out of impulse. Was I trying to scare you away? Or was I trying to draw you in?

I wasn't as afraid of the prospect of being full of nothingness, but more so, the prospect of you so quickly discovering it. If you saw emptiness inside me, then my greatest fears would've finally been confirmed. I knew in an instant I could not lie to you. I could not show you a mask or tell you all of my well-rehearsed pleasentries— for you're the kind of rare creature that is not satisfied with seeing only what is shown to them. Your gaze pierces deeper than that. You'd see right through any facade I could ever try to show you. The crazy thing is, when you looked at me— I didn't want to show you a false, tempered down, manageable version of myself. I wanted you to see me. All of me. My stubbornness, my trust issues, my short temper, my pride, my desire, my selfishness, my intensity, my grief.

Usually, I keep my real thoughts to myself, but that night— I remember taking a chance— revealing my observations aloud in order to do what nobody else has done in quite some time— *catch your attention*. I remember feeling your energy, your scattered energy, come to a halt— shift— and point solely at me. There was nowhere to hide when you looked in my eyes.

What does he see? I wondered. *Can he tell I'm a liability, an abyss, an imposter?*

And it's true— what you saw did astonish me. But not in the way I feared.

You saw something alluring, something worthy, something soft and kind and intricate and courageous. You told me so again and again. You still do, to this very day.

You tell me how it is always better to be too much than not enough. How people often fear not having something they're fundamentally made of. Like love, or decency, or patience, or inspiration. That they're so close to this notion of something that they still *need* to obtain— they find themselves on the other side of it.

I was like a little fish searching for water in the ocean. I didn't realize I was surrounded and made of all these wonderful things. I couldn't believe it myself until you saw them within me. I needed someone to tell me to look closer— I've had a burning flame inside me all along. I simply couldn't see it because the glow was coming from within. It wasn't made for me to see, it was made for others to be drawn to.

Since I met you, I've felt like a source of light. With those blue eyes, you looked at me like I was a bright, shining supernova, a lighthouse guiding you closer to shore, a warm fireplace beckoning you home, a buzzing streetlamp just around the darkest corner, the morning sun peeking over a cold horizon. A safe place to rest. A comforting presence.

You looked at me as if you had never known darkness and smiled in a way that made me believe I've known you for a long, long time. And from whatever ancient star our souls were fashioned from— it's been a while since we've crossed paths and I'm so happy to see you again. I must admit— I think a part of me was waiting for you to find me once more, as you must have in every lifetime before. After three years lost in the dark— a part of me was waiting for you to awaken this belief that maybe, I really can be the kind of girl that makes those around her feel alive. I catch a glimpse of myself in the reflection of your eyes and I'm starting to believe it's true— that maybe, I really can inspire people to live, to have courage, to be kind, and to believe in themselves, too.

Thank you, for finding me again. For being unique in all the world.

Vega
United States

Summer

My light,

As the darker seasons change, so do my moods. The cold eventually becomes suffocating as I yearn for warm weather, lake days with the family, sitting on the porch swing as I watch my children play, calm fires and cold beers, camping, sipping coffee while watching thunderstorms pass by, back road drives with the windows down, your hand on my thigh, and the wind blowing gently across my skin, and taking adventures as often as possible.

After feelings are pushed away, I will someday quit returning to the place that doesn't bring me peace— to the place that steals it, rather than comforts me. Love should be a home— a safe haven.

Through the darkness, I will find light. In my weakest moments, I will fight for the strength hiding in the shadows. Through the storms, I will become a better version of myself— stronger, more certain of myself and my place in this dark yet beautiful world.

As I pull myself from the darkness once again, I watch another storm pass through our small town, and I remember as the warm weather soothes my soul and my mind, that I am loved, blessed, and so grateful to be here with you. Wherever we may go, you will always be my home.

Desiree M.
United States

My dearest Nanny,

A love letter to the summer blue of you. You are not a stranger, that is for sure, but is the image of your soul slipping? No, it could never, because I have all the memories of you wrapped in the neat blanket of my mind. The house you grew old, accompanied by stories to your great-grandchildren told. The soft glow of your aura lies in the crabapple trees.

Oh dear summer, let me explore that backyard once more. Where the mountain is visible to our childish giggles. Give me board games to play at her rounded table. A seat where I can stare at her gallery wall. Let me chat near the fireplace, before the hearth I stood tall.

Before summer turns to fall, I love you sweet Nanny. I love you most of all. To love you and the 7 decades you've lived more than I. I feel like I've been there, your years now rest in me.

I wish to leave my visit, with a cup full of jelly beans. Cherry is our favorite, perfect like the fruits of this season. The juices of these fruits I eat, roll alongside my tears, down my arms, and you float in the river of my dreams.

I must soak in this unsent love letter, to the summer blue of you. I know you cannot come back to this physical earth, but please just stay. Stay in my memory, do not go away. I am only getting older and only have more to say. I want more than just playing in your yard on a summer's day.

>Sincerely,
>Your Kendall Hope
>*United States*

P.S. A love letter to a great-grandmother, that will forever be unsent, with an address no longer to exist.

B.,

If I was to write you a letter, it would say that I have never felt so at home in another person's arms. I would say that some words you have thrown at me have hurt me more than I knew was possible for a love like ours. But then I would want to remind ourselves that love isn't always easy and we should not pretend it will be. That you are the one I want to forgive. Fight for. Fall for, over and over and over. I would like to grow beside you while we never stop reminding each other of every little good thing that we bring to each other's world.

Would you like to hold my hand and do the same? I would say I know things got tough but I think if we both tried a bit harder, then this little thing we call love, could be the biggest adventure of our lifetime. That every time I hear a love song, thoughts of you cloud my mind. Or every time something funny happens you are the first person I want to tell. I am not sure this holds true for you, anymore? But as I look out to where the sky meets the ocean, I send a silent prayer it still is. That in the little heat of the moments you have not forgotten the hills we have climbed. The views we have conquered together. Every single moment we never took for granted of finding each other.

As you read this letter I want you to also know that the months we spent falling in love were the best of my entire life. And Hunny, I know they were for you, too. Because we were lucky enough to experience a love some never will. I understand now when people talk about the magic of falling in love because we experienced it.

A rare love. A wild love. An epic love.

And as we learn what buttons not to push and how to love each other even more fiercely, with time, we will only become stronger. With time we will learn the ins and outs. With time we will create a bond so strong even the heavens could not break it. And I am not here promising it will be easy. There will be times when the old ruts reappear and we will have to do everything in our power not to let them ruin us. There will be times when we will agree to disagree and it will be so worth it because that night we will still have each other. We will still be in love at each sunrise, as a team.

If I was to write you a letter, it would ask you to please not throw this all away. That I wish you were better at saying sorry. I want to know that you would rather work on the things we'd have to in any relationship, in this one. We are perfect for each other in so many ways. Are you willing to accept our differences? Because I am. I have travelled enough of this world to realise no one is perfect. That every relationship has its extreme complexities, but the people your heart always comes back to, they are the ones you should fight to keep. (and we both know our souls have never truly let go of one another's) So here I am fighting within the only realm I know how, a love letter.

My babe, can you close your eyes and remember the nights we would lie next to each other and you would say to me *this is rare, our love*. We are the lucky ones. Can we stop focusing on what makes us different and rather focus on what our love story is all about?

Which is laughter. Passion. Dancing and music. It's travel and adventure. Projects and problem-solving. It's Japanese restaurants and holding hands. It's keeping our flatmates up while we laugh too loud.

It's hiding love notes in each other's cars. And middle-of-the-day I can't stop thinking about you. It's helping others. It's ocean swims and sunset picnics. It's cuddling our dog in bed.

It's looking into each other's eyes and saying *I love you* before we turn the light out. And running into each other's arms after only being separated for 24 hours, with the whispers of *I had a good weekend but it would have been better with you there*.

It's warm showers and koala hugs. French kisses and love songs. The windows down and your hand on my thigh. To the moon and back. Doc Martens and poetry. Sunflowers and Eddie Vedder. Playfulness. Desire. Trust. Commitment.

I only recently learnt that love is not always about the grand gestures. That maybe it is in the quietness of falling asleep next to the one who chooses to come home to you each and every night.

That was you. That was us. I am sorry I did not realise this sooner. But you also know you are the man that made me believe in love again. Unequivocally. (which feels a little ironic now) I trusted you with my whole heart and more.

If I was to write you a letter it would shamelessly say that every time I think of home, it is you.

It is you.

It is you that I always see.

So this is me asking one last time, please fight. Don't let go of the love we have spent our whole life searching for.

P.
New Zealand

To my person,
 the moment I knew it was *you*
 I listened to your entire playlist
 without skipping a beat
 finding deeper self-reflection
 in the unknown lyrics
 singing every word
 of those so familiar
 4 hours and 4 minutes
 I feel completely at peace
 the life I have created
 building the foundation
 for our home—
 within your playlist
 is the story
 I have been writing in
 my search for everything
 I have been patiently
 waiting for today
 awake in the morning light
 sun of summer solstice
 I can hear the message of
 what the birds are singing
 the notion you are the one
 waiting for me too
 the answer is always
 in the music

J.M.C.
United States

Dear Rose,

I want you to know that I am always with you, no matter how far apart we might be. Leaving isn't easy for you. It isn't for anyone. Fate has peculiar ways of changing our lives, and we have to mold around them sometimes. I know it's hard, but believe me: you are stronger than you think and we will get through this together.

Even though I am helpless at finding the strength to hold myself together, there is always hope that ignites— like the June sun inside me, and with that fire, I remember your name in every lick of my flames.

Hold that summer moon in your hands, and see how it wanes and regrows. Just like that, souls do this too. Life is a cycle of waning and growing, a masterpiece that is never complete.

True souls are never apart from one another. You will always remain in the heart of my hearts, in those deepest chambers of love. You have my word. Somewhere in the future, our stars will align, and our souls will meet again. When? I do not know, but fate will decide that.

> If you ever remember me,
> just wish upon a star
> and I'll love you back
> from afar.
>
> Know that a thousand miles
> can't keep us apart,
> for you will always stay
> in my heart.

> Always,
> Mal
> *Pakistan*

P.S. A letter to a parted friend.

Dear unborn child,

I miss you.

I know I never got to know you and we didn't have much time together, but I do miss you.

Mama is sorry. She really is. For not being able to protect you. For not being enough. I spend every waking moment questioning what I could have done differently. Questioning why it had to be you.

And no matter what anyone says, you were more than just a foetus. You were a bundle of hopes and dreams entangled with love and joy. You were a dream.

My dream.

I had dreams of us smiling, laughing, crying, having heart-to-heart talks. I had hopes for us travelling and seeing the world. I loved you even before I knew you and dreamt and hoped someone would love me, just because I am. And that someone would have always been you.

But life is cruel. And you, my Baby, you were so pure and innocent and untainted, I almost feel glad you never got to know this cruelty. Almost.

Hope really is a heartache, Baby. I miss you, dearest one. I know you would have been amazing because you left such a mess out of me when you were gone. Just like that.

I know I'll search for you in every one of my children to come. Think about the could-have-been and the would-have-been and all the things we could never be.

I am sorry, my Baby. You were never for this cruel world. This longing. I wish I could cut it out. I only know now how the pain of something I never had is so much worse. The regrets and the thoughts of "what-if".

I love you, my heart. I always will.

Always,
Your would-have-been Mama
India

Carefree Darling,

You run barefoot through wet grass and tell everyone it's the best feeling. You hunt for treasures, like rocks, leaves, and other things people would normally walk right past. You gather stories from the people you pass by on your walks and make them into your own.

The wind blows, the grass dries, and the treasures become lost. Those stories are forgotten and never returned. You run, you hunt, you gather, but those bright days in the sun still turned to night.

When the summer sun sets and the cool night sinks in, you think about what you lost instead of what you gained. You become overwhelmed with what lies ahead instead of looking forward to what will come next.

My carefree darling, you are overly careful now, and I miss the old you.

As I stare into the mirror and remember those summer days, I can almost see the me I once was. Almost.

Always thinking of you,
Overly Careful
United States

Dear future wife,
 I want you to have a life outside me
 and outside our relationship.
 Go enroll yourself in a yoga class.
 Be a gym member.
 Try pole dancing.
 Go out with your friends.
 Have time with your extended family.
 Go book a flight to a place
 where you want to go alone,
 or with your other best friends.
 Fall in love with any animal you like.
 Buy a fish, a cat, or a dog.
 Read your favorite book if you have free time.
 Fall in love with literature, paintings, and illustrations.
 Go buy that dress, shoes, bags,
 accessories you've been eyeing for weeks.
 Try to bungee jump or paraglide.
 Be lazy on Sunday afternoon.
 Don't take showers on Saturday mornings.
 I want you to do things alone, with yourself.
 I want you to have a life outside me.
 I want you to have a life outside our relationship.
 I want you to have a life outside us.
 Have a life because I know, at the end of the day,
 we would always have a life together.
 We have a life together,
 but I want you to enjoy your life without me.
 I want to share your magic,
 your warmth,
 your beauty,
 your kindness,
 your craziness,
 your immaturity,
 your flaws,
 your imperfections,

and your heart with the world
outside our world.
Because you don't just deserve a life in us, but also a life in you.

IRISH V.
Philippines

P.S. A letter from a yearning soul to her soulmate.

ELIJAH,

You were my first. My first love. The first person I made love with. We moved to the city. You were the first man I lived with. We were just kids… I had just graduated high school and it was the first time either of us had lived away from our parents.

Sometimes, my love for you felt so big I didn't think I could contain it all. I would tell you *I love you I love you I love you.*

You would tell me: *you already told me that.*

You took me for granted the majority of the time.

You were so young. Maybe you didn't know how to love someone the right way yet.

When I left, you brought flowers to that coffee shop I worked at and came by every day to check if they were still there. I let them die there—unmoved. The staff told me you sank in your shoes the day you stopped by and they were dead. I'm sorry I did that instead of having a conversation with you. I hadn't yet learned how to be gentle with others' hearts.

You brought cookies to my apartment with a note telling me: *I love you I love you I love you.*

You went to my dad's office and gave him a letter to deliver to me. At the end it said: *I love you I love you I love you.*

But I didn't budge. I was hurt. Where was this person when we were dating? The one who saw me? Who valued me.

I heard from friends about the cancer diagnosis. I assumed you would be fine. You were so young! How could you not be? Young people don't die from cancer. I heard you went out of state to get your treatments. I saw on Facebook that you lost your hair. I heard from my sister that you were trying to contact me. To make amends.

The man I was seeing at the time said it would make him uncomfortable for me to meet up with a past lover. So I didn't. I thought I was being respectful to him.

I was in shock when I heard that you passed. I felt so guilty that I didn't give you an opportunity to talk to me. What is wrong with me that I can't give a dying man his wish to make things right?

I didn't go to your funeral.

I thought your friends might be mad at me. Would seeing me make their pain worse? I was so nervous to see your grieving mother. Would seeing me make her pain worse? Can there be a deeper pain than losing your child? Did they know I had ignored your attempts to reach out during your final days? I think of her often, how painful it must be… I hope she is finding some joy. I messaged her my condolences.

I saw the posts other people made about your passing and it made me upset. They hardly even knew him! I didn't realize I was also grieving. I didn't let myself finish the thought… they didn't even know him as I knew him. I was the one in pain.

Now I'm living in New York and I think of you often. We used to talk about this city, about moving here someday. I walk home from work and I think of you sometimes. You would have loved it here. It isn't fair that I get to go on living and you don't. How does God decide who gets to live and who doesn't? I wonder what you would have become. You were so young. I think of all the things I've done with my life and I'm angry that you didn't get to have that.

I go to little basement jazz bars in Greenwich Village and I think of us in your dad's Subaru… listening to smooth jazz on NPR. You would have loved it here.

I think of you and your guitar and your songwriting. You always wanted to be like Thom Yorke. I think of the songs you played for me that you had written about other girls. It stung to hear them, but they were beautiful.

I'm a nurse now. When I was studying in school we learned that the cancer you had mainly affects young men and the mortality rates are very high. I didn't know that before. I wish I had known that. I thought we had years to patch things up… that someday we would come back to each other. I was so young I didn't yet know how fragile life really is. How there are no guarantees on how much time we have left.

As I walk these busy streets I think about how much I wish I had just let you say what you needed to say. I wish we had made up before you died. I'm so sorry I didn't give you the chance to do that. It's been 6 years since you died and this is still my deepest regret.

I'm sorry.

L.S.R.
United States

My dearest Ry,

I have bared my soul to your eyes of amber in hopes of you realizing what is in my heart for you. You are a song of the prideful sun, gleaming in all its searing glory; a melody that soars through the heavens, you have left me humming in memory of your smile. You ignite something so reverent within me that I wish I could cup it in my hands forever. But beauty is not a thing to behold, so I admire you as you continue to show yourself to me, in all your fragments and stitches you have so carefully pieced together.

Take my hand please, my love?

Show me your world that shines with golden flames; my tired heart cannot take any more breakage, in fear of myself never returning again. Every time I see you, I feel as though these shadows have been put behind me. There is something so tangible about the radiance you exude, I wish for nothing more than to hold you till it floods me too. There is more beauty in you than you know, and I hope one day I can show you just how much of it I see. Your touch feels like a kiss of summer rays, your arms around me— an embrace of sunlight; things seem to have fallen into place when your presence made its home beside mine and I would be damned if I threw this all away.

Ever yours,
x Adrian
Canada

P.S. To a love that shines with golden flames, wait for me at the crossroads between my heart and yours.

Dear Jack,

It's funny how time moves on, yet emotions stick around forever. We say they don't, that emotions eventually just evaporate and disappear, but that's only the common lie we repeat to ourselves over and over and over again in attempts to convince our minds that we are okay. Or at least that's what I do.

It's funny how you made me feel loved. Oh so loved. It's funny how you cared so deeply about me, how you cared for me, how you loved me so dearly. You made me laugh like I never have before and the funny thing is— I still haven't laughed like I did with you. Jack, you made the most miserable time of my life happy, fun, cheerful. I thought that it would last forever, that the happiness we had for each other would last until our last days. But the only thing that has lasted is the constant heartbreak you gave me.

It's funny how your dark brown eyes, curly black hair, and innocent smile make me want to cry out in love and wail in hate all at the same time. I fell in love before you, and I knew that when I met you, when you hugged me so tightly and I only made it up to your chest, when you touched all over my body and when you would cry with me, I knew that this love would be different. I knew that this was going to be the best decision of my life. Yet it turns out to be the one that haunts me the most.

It's vile that I can hate myself so much because of you. I hate that I loved you and for adoring every single thing about you. I saw no wrong and still have a hard time finding any. The only thing that comes to my mind is the small detail of that day you left and married a few months later. The fact that still to this day— five years later— I do not have any answers as to why you did that. Why did you leave? What went wrong because I have zero clues as to where I messed up. Was I not enough? Was I wrong for loving you? Was I not pretty enough? Was I not funny enough or not boring enough? Was I not smart enough? Did you not approve of my career? Did I not wear enough makeup or dress the way you liked? Was I not what you wanted even though you told me I was? Was I just quick, reliable entertainment until you asked her to marry you?

And now, five years have passed and I should be over it. I should just stop thinking about it and your new wife. I just feel like if I knew why, I could feel better about myself. But no. No, I will never know why because it's too late. You've moved on five years deep into marriage and I'm happy for you. But then again, I want to be happy for myself. I want to be happy for me. For me.

I am not a bad person. I am not boring. I am not just entertainment. I am not ugly. I am pretty. I am fun. I am happy. I am here. I am present. I am capable of being loved and able to love back.

It's funny how someone can make you feel alive and kill you at the same time. How you can feel whole and empty. It's funny how I feel like I should be apologizing when you're the one that left. When you're the one that hurt me so deeply. I feel like I'm the one that should say sorry. But Jack, I just wish I knew more. I just wish you had told me or just explained why. I just hope you know how much you damaged me but most importantly, I hope you're happy. Because it's obvious that I was unable to do that for you.

MOLLY
United States

P.S. A forever unfinished closing to what I thought was the love of my life.

Dear Jen,

I am writing you this letter to let you know that your heart will one day be safe to feel every beat.

Unfortunately, you'll first have to go through years of confusion and pain. And for too many years it will be hard for you to receive the love you need.

There are a few things I need you to know...

You are a soft and sensitive soul in a world that has a hard exterior.

It is not your fault those who raised you never asked you what you needed.

It is not your fault that no one taught you how to process your own emotions.

It is not your fault that no one taught you how brave it is to cry.

It is not your fault that no one ever offered to hug you when you felt lost and couldn't understand it.

It is not your fault that you feared asking for help when the world around you got too heavy to hold.

So, over the years, you'll acquire armor to protect your heart, and then there will come a day it will be ready to be stripped. You might not believe it right now, but one day you'll find refuge deep down within yourself to shine and be seen. And you won't shine in just one color, you'll shine to be seen for every color of that damn rainbow.

I wish someone would tell you today that you are an energetic vision holder of the future, a creative, an artist, an alchemist of emotions, and that it's safe to bare your heart deeply and offer it to others.

But have no fear, you'll go inward into your heartspace to find this all out for yourself. And your soft sensitivity that was once left unnurtured will become your superpower. The funny thing is, you'll use all these lessons on your journey back to wholeness to step forward and empower others.

Dear Jen,

I am writing you this letter to let you know that your heart will one day be safe to feel every beat.

JENNIE LUCCI
United States

P.S. A letter to my younger self.

I'm disappointed in how deeply I fell for him.
How much I tolerated when I knew things weren't right.
The issues I overlooked just to have him 'one more night'.
I fell for him so deeply that I lost sight of myself.
I fell for him so deeply, I simply can't love anyone else.

L.G.
Scotland

M.,
I presumed it was limerence, but still, I believe you actually loved me.
Do I blame the chemicals in my brain?
I never knew it would be this way.
Through all this good there was a silent strain.
You said forever & I felt the same.
I never thought that I'd see the day you'd leave me.
I've been waiting for one more sign, another message, for you to change your mind. I promise that all I need is a little more time with you, but I know that it won't happen anytime soon.
Even though I am the "love of your life", not even love can hold us together anymore, but I still have hope for one day— be it another time, another life, another universe, or in my head— we're still feeling the comfort & contentment provoked just by simply waking up next to each other in your bed.
Where you still never let go of me when there's a pillar between us when we walk because you believe it's bad luck & I still kiss your bumps & bruises to soothe your pain and we still talk endlessly.
Endless is my love for you, as if it were to be the same.

A.V.G.
PA, United States

P.S. To my self-proclaimed twin flame, a.k.a the love of my life, things I wish I can express/feel again. We separated under unfortunate circumstances over 1,000 miles apart. He will forever take vacancy in my heart.

Apate,

You broke me. You betrayed me. My ability to trust shattered in your careless hands. How could you leave me alone with those horrible strangers to chase some boy you just met? And while I was half out of my mind too– do you realise the danger you put me in? I was so scared. You were supposed to be one of my best friends– but friends don't treat each other like that– they don't *leave*.

And the worst part is? You'll never even realise what you did was wrong. How you demolished our friendship with one childish antic at a time. I never thought you'd be the one to teach me what toxicity feels like. I never wanted you to be that lesson. I wanted to be your friend, to save you from the demons you confided with me– but I had to learn the hard way– I can't save someone who picks their own vices above their friends time and time and time again. I couldn't give any more chances, and that's why we haven't spoken in almost four years– why we likely never will again. I see old photos of us smiling or dancing or laughing and it makes me want to scream– it makes me want to cry.

Why couldn't you have chosen your friends? Why couldn't you have chosen me over him? I was there for you– every step of the way– so why did you betray me? Do you even realise what you did? Do you know the damage you caused? Years worth of trauma to sort through. It was hell. Why did you do that to me? Why did I let you do that to me?

Aletheia
United Kingdom

P.S. A once best friend I thought I could trust completely who shattered my heart when I least expected it. Our friendship didn't recover, and in truth— I never want it to.

My Dear R.,

I have never confessed my love to you, not for the 5 years I've held it in my heart. For the longest time, I was content with adoring you from afar. I was happy to do so forever. But here, I want to try to put it into words, even if you'll never read them.

I remember seeing you first through fleeting moments: my best friend's older brother. I remember stealing glances at you in middle school at book club; watching your nervous hand on the gear while driving me and your sister back home from tennis practice (you always hated driving); listening to stories about you from friends and family while you were away at college.

All these tiny moments, a different brush painting a beautiful portrait of the sweetest boy. It's like I had these mismatched puzzle pieces before I actually met you. One from your sister about how you're so soft, the kind of person who gets disappointed with their friends for gossiping while saying, "Hey guys, let's not talk about people who aren't here." One from your best friend about how your room is still decorated with frames of stock photos you've never removed. Another from a friend about how you leave your homework until the last minute, but you still received the National Merit Scholarship while taking the Pre-SATs. They painted someone with a good heart. Someone a little weird. Someone smart. Someone I could fall in love with.

And then I met you.

And you were just as lovely and silly as all the stories.

At your sister's graduation party, I could finally step back and see the painting. I could put all the puzzle pieces together. It was the first time I got to hang out with you. And I fell. I fell hard. You were kind. Kind without wanting anything in return. You were wholesome and endearing and sweet and soft and quirky and nerdy and overly apologetic and I was so in awe of you. In awe of how a boy could be so darling. I remember playing *Headbandz* at the end of the night. Every time it was my card's turn to be guessed, you called this person beautiful. You called them kind. You said you haven't known this person for long, but you really really like them. I wanted so badly to know who you liked, until the end, when I looked at the card and saw my own name. My heart was bursting. That night, I wanted to hug you goodbye. I felt it burning in my chest, this need to give you a hug. It could have been the last time I'd see you before you left for school again. I remember leaving for my car and noticing you with your friends. I ran up with my arms wide open and you accepted me so quickly. Like this was familiar. Like holding me was the most natural thing in the world.

And then I did nothing. I was too afraid to say anything. I was afraid of losing my best friend. I was afraid you wouldn't feel the same. I kept quiet about this feeling. I didn't really know what it was. All I knew was that I was safe as long as I kept it to myself. For the next couple of years, I let boys use my body. I wanted someone like you, but most guys aren't like you - genuinely innocent, while most guys feigned innocence to get what they really wanted. So I let them have my body while I hid away my heart. I told myself I was okay with this. I wasn't lowering my standards if I knew these boys were using me. If I was in control and I knew the stakes, they couldn't hurt me. But they did. They used me. Then they threw me away. Pretty enough to play with, but too dirty to keep. I got so used to boys saying, "I love you" in between heavy breaths and pillow talk that I grew tired of the word. The L-word. It didn't feel honest. It didn't feel like it mattered anymore. It was just a word boys used when they were high off my body. And after those heartbreaks, I would write to you. Tell you about them. Tell you how much my heart ached. Tell you how much I missed your kindness. Tell you how much I missed your wholesomeness. Tell you how much I missed that pure feeling I had for you, like kids in love. And then I would lock those letters away and hide them in a drawer.

> I still think about you.
> I still cry about you.
> I still love you.

> Yours Eternally,
> J.
> *NY, United States*

P.S. A love letter to the most darling boy I know. I found out you shared the same feelings a little too late. I go back to that summer's night after every heartbreak, the one where you looked at me as if I hung the moon. They may have taken my body, but you will always have my heart.

B.U.B.,

Hi to the first girl I've ever loved. Since the day I met you, I've known that you are worthy of every opportunity in life. You show me a different side of me, the romantic me. On June 28th, I confessed my feelings to you— that day was my first confession and my first rejection. After that day, I vowed to stop liking you, but every time our eyes meet, I feel that tension and that pain in my heart.

I just thought there was a chance that "us" could exist. I am wrong, but I can't stop myself from hoping.

I still like you, and someday I hope it'll change.

> Pocky-Pepero
> *Philippines*

L.,

You might think that it's all over and I did let you go a long time ago, but it's not true. I've changed a lot since you walked away from me. I've been hurt, deceived, heartbroken, and broken as a person. I dyed my hair black,

I love it this way. I've spent time with lots of guys after you, but none of them feel the same as you did. You absolutely broke me as a person. I can't even express my love to the people I love the most. It was my ability, my superpower to express everything I felt, to cherish and love people genuinely, to give them a world, to understand and comfort them but you took it away from me. You took everything I was and now, none of them are left. You broke me in pieces but most importantly you took those pieces with you. There's no *me* no more. I am the coldest, most distant, diminished person anyone can meet. You took the ability to believe in people from me, it's devastating. I can't feel anything no more but the thing I realize is that you're the only one I wanted to express my love towards, I would give you the damn world but you took it from me and walked away with it. The thing I hate the most is that I still love you, damn it, I LOVE YOU. I understand that we can never be together because my pride said so but that doesn't change the fact that I'm head over heels in love with you.

I'm sorry, I truly am for being someone so stuck on you, for believing in you, seeing your progress, and being nothing but happy for you. I hate everything about you but still, I love you. I can't even explain what it feels like. You would burn me for the sake of the world but I would never hesitate on burning the whole world for you. Let me be a queen of ashes if you'll be my king.

What it would take from you to reach out to me, to realize that I'm the one for you and you're the one for me.

Let me breathe because I can't feel the air no more…

Anon
Georgia

Lake Shine,
Have you ever known to love someone,
even after time has gone,
that the love is stronger, though muted— as if in a whisper?
That's how I felt with you.

Your eyes were beautiful to me the moment we met. The shouting we did to my river, the skies, the songs we sang to golden summer grasses and air, they filled a flower bed I hadn't known existed inside me with stardust and rich sunlight, richer than I had ever drunk upon my tongue.

Even when I thought I had swallowed the richest of all, you made it as smooth as butter. I wish to feel that way again and not frown at the memory of thinking I loved you, but I realize now I never knew what that meant.

Only when you left the garden of my heart, did I realize how much it needed your river - your eyes the color of a lake shining under trees, nurturing whatever veins of dirt I had forgotten inside of me.

Forever to never be yours,
M. C. Flora
United States

P.S. Letters to Lake Shine always come up whenever I thought I had written enough. This is one from me trying to accept that what I had loved I had not, in turn, understood what love meant.

And the voice said, "Velkommen,"
and I don't think I've ever
heard anything so beautiful before—

except for, maybe, the first time you said my name.

Freydis Lova
United States

Dear Bittersweet Déjà Vu,

As I write this, it's 2022. Last year, when I met you, I was captured and free, lost in you, lost in insanity. I fell for you deeper than I ever knew I could fall. It hurt, but it was worth it all.

What hurt was not being able to feel your touch, because I wanted you so much, and I still do, oh, if only you knew.

The cruel rule is what kept us apart. I knew that my heart was doomed from the start, 'cause how could I ever be loved so much that someone would break it for me? A patient and a nurse just cannot be. But honestly, I have a feeling that the rule was just an excuse, that I'm not someone that you would ever choose, but what do I know? What did you want me to know?

The reason it was worth it all, even losing you, was all the things you made me do.

You made me write, you made me sing, I wouldn't trade my art for anything, because it's a part of you, it's a part of me, the only place we can be together for eternity.

I feel like there's not much left to say, at least not in this letter, and maybe that's for the better, because you know what they say, less is more, but trust me, I have so much more in store, but that will have to wait.

I just hope that it's not too late, for us to change our destiny, I'm still hoping for you and me to become a reality, but even if we never will, I still want to thank you for everything, so thank you, Bittersweet Déjà Vu, and remember, I will always love you.

FOREVER,
FOREVER OR ALONE
Norway

MY LOVE,

I hope one day you look back at our love and realize what a beautiful life we would have had together if only you had stayed. We could have walked the beaches, sand between our toes, holding hands as we tried to make it through the undertow. Dancing beneath the moonlight as the stars twinkle within the night. Camping alongside a waterfall with only the sound of the water cascading down.

Darling, the fears you hold do not exist. They are a figment of your mind. We are the same, inside and out. I wish you had given us more time.

If you had, you could have been here with me. And you could have seen with your own eyes, the life I live is beautiful, happy, and healthy. With no worries beneath my heart. The sun always shines where I am and my dreams always come true.

I believe it is because I always pray to God to help me carry through. He gives me the light I need to overcome and allows me to live in his Grace. I hope one day you open your mind, my love. And see the life you could have had if you had stayed with me.

All your dreams would have come true, every wish you ever made. With me by your side, you would always be within the light. Living life beautifully.

I hope one day you come back, love. In the light, I will wait. For your heart is unlike any other I will ever come to meet. I will wait a lifetime for you, if that is what it takes. Because darling, I am hopelessly in love with you, and that is how I will always be.

C.
United States

P.S. A letter to my soulmate, may he find his way back to me.

Dear July,

You hold my hopes for the future in one hand, and my regrets of the past in the other. You craft every wish I have in the promise of the coming seasons. And in the ocean of summers past, you keep every person I've ever lost or let fade away. Now, it seems I've let too many suns fall between me and the people I loved to say what I wish I had.

But to you, my past Julys, the memories will belong.

I adored your salty, airy laugh. The great blue sea that scared me, but not when you were there. I would've explored the world with you, and we'd made a good start, before the autumns and winters got in the way. I wish I'd told you how much you really meant to me. How much you inspired me to find who I am. To fall in love with places and languages first. To find humor in the most trying times. I wouldn't change a thing now, because I know you're happier in the present than you were in the past. But, our July on the sea belongs to you, and I will always adore that scruffy, foolish, perfect version of us that I knew so well.

Our friendship was built on the promise of July. A time with no sixty-hour work weeks or anxiety about what came next- just that little house in the south of a dreamy place far away. We'd paint and pick lavender and laugh about the time we both cried on the kitchen floor. I'd teach English and you'd make breakfast for travelers. *We'll travel and make better memories*, you'd promised. But that shiny July never came, you left before spring, and I still think about the dreams we crafted after all this time. I wonder if you ever do.

You never felt like a stranger. You were an unexpected comfort against the harsh winds of an unfamiliar coast. I didn't realize how much I would miss your heart, your dry jokes, and how much you cared for your friends. To tell you the truth, I wanted to go on knowing you, finding more reasons to cross your path- but a summer storm came and washed them all away. I regret that evening, when I suppose I could've told you this or said goodbye in the same breath, but I never said anything at all. I doubt we'll ever see another July— but maybe, if some star aligns, I'll meet your eyes, and laugh, and say *It feels like only yesterday, the last time we met.*

When a car speeds past, or leaves sizzle in the wind, or a setting sun sends oranges across the waves— I think of you. I've been drawn to you since we met because you're someone I don't understand. You trust so easily and believe the best will come. I met you in one of my bleakest months and you gave me sunshine, with no expectations, like you had more than enough. You inspire me to assume joy. I'm so grateful to know you, and despite the time between us, I hope we meet again, one bright July.

You're the reason I believe in July. That each one will bring me the greatest wishes and heartbreaks of my life. That I will get through the worst to greet the next challenge. You're every *hello* to a stranger and attempt to reach out again, even if too much time has passed. You're the happiness found in experiences, not possessions. The call to explore, to discover why I've been given my one chance. I've let our July haunt me, guide me, and now I'm letting the tides go. May the seas be kind, and may angels lead you in.

And to you, my future Julys-
I look forward to our inevitable meeting, however many I am promised. I will cherish you like memories.

> ALL MY LOVE,
> YOUR TRAVELER
> *United States*

P.S. A letter to the Julys of my past and the people who filled the days with memories.

Un amante de la luna
A LOVER OF THE MOON -
> When you asked me to dance
> in the dimly lit bar,
> my heart skipped along
> to the merengue beat.
> A holiday romance,
> turned to long-distance laughter.
> You told me you loved me,
> thought I was 'mad' cute.
> I fell for your charm,
> and the magic in your eyes.
> How naive I was, to see past all your lies.
> My first crush and heartbreak is all rolled into one ball
> of late-night video chats.

You were the one who was simply not meant to be.

> J.N.S.
> *England*

You,

By the time the cicadas faded out, you'd long since decided you were done. The timing was almost uncanny, as if you were in collusion with one another. The eerie resemblance of the simultaneous surge and then wane was startling. In every way.

I felt it most in how you, too, rose up from below. Earsplitting was how my world screamed of you, for you— you, you, you, you. Nothing could drown out your presence, try as I did.

I ran 'til the soles of my feet ached as much as my bleeding heart. I ran through swaths of you and them diving headfirst into my skin. I ran to escape the haunting of your voice, only to be surrounded by their incessant cicada songs constantly reminding me— I ran and ran and ran. I writhed my way out of dreams turned nightmares turned the ultimate terror-filled reality I couldn't pinch myself out of. Until one day, I looked around at the ground littered with sun-shriveled casings, and realized they were really gone.

And so were you.

S.K.
United States

Dear Amanda,

I read what you wrote in the journal I bought you for your 40th birthday. It reminded me of when I would sneak into your room to read your journal when we were younger. That's how I learned about some of your parties, and your boyfriends, and how you thought you might be pregnant at 15 or 16 years old.

You were all grown up this time, but still writing about a boy you loved. It made me sad that you spent most of your life searching for the love of your life and for 19 years, he was right in front of you. Your son Jalen was and is everything those men could never be. He has character, integrity, sensitivity, humor, and love—and I do believe some of your light-hearted, do-not-give-a-crap spirit will carry on with him.

It also made me sad that you were trying to quit drinking and doing drugs. I don't think you wanted to die that night, but I couldn't help thinking it was your final selfish act. A lot of people have hurt you, including yourself. But you were wrong when you wrote in your journal that Mom and Dad would someday stop thinking of you as a loser if you could just get it together— you were wrong because they never thought of you that way in the first place. You may have driven them crazy, yes, but they loved you fiercely and their hearts shattered into a million pieces when you died.

We all thought you were a badass, *more wildfire than woman* (R. Clift). You had a lot to give, and I wish you would've let people in more when you were alive. It's interesting that we all spend so much of our time worrying about what other people will think of our mistakes— especially family— and then when we die, our family goes through our personal belongings and learns most of it anyways. I mean, why even hide anything in the first place?

Amanda, I'm sorry I distanced myself from you so many times throughout our lives, times when you probably needed someone the most. But I never fully went away. I read a letter that I wrote to you when I was in high school and you were in college that basically said, "you can try to push me away, but I'm not going anywhere." Like our parents, I loved you fiercely, cared about you, wanted the best things for you, and wished you were happy. I hope you know that I am still here. That our relationship doesn't have to end here. And even if I'm mad at you, I'll never think you're a loser.

You were so talented—I loved being your DJ groupie and dancing the night away with you in NYC, Boston, Providence, and Cleveland. I will miss spending every Christmas with you, watching SVU marathons and Hallmark movies for hours and hours, visiting each other wherever we lived, and messaging each other funny stuff on social media. I'll miss your incredibly contagious laughter the most. And somehow, I'll also miss your bitchy attitude and terrible advice.

I wish you would've had the chance to live the second half of your life. Especially because I thought we would have each other after Mom and Dad pass.

But I hope I can make you proud in the second half of my life. I'm leaning toward taking a few risks (only with your strength), and I just want to fill my life with passion like you did. You were a powerhouse, an inspiration. I miss you every single day, but I'll always carry you with me. Thank you for being a part of my life then and continuing to be a part of it now. I love you.

"Love does not give up and neither will I." – R. Clift

> Love,
> Ali
> *United States*

P.S. This is a letter I wrote to my sister two months after she died unexpectedly in 2020.

Dear Niona,

As I write this, you are miles away. So many I couldn't count. If I drew a line straight across the Atlantic from Amsterdam to the far North West, I might reach you. Even then, the Yukon seems so wild, only my imagination can reach it.

And you, wandering amongst the snow caps and firs and singing at night with aurora borealis. Perhaps you can hear me then. When all is silent. When all that has gone astray is briefly blanketed by the night. And we remember, even just for a few hours, how it felt to stand close. To know each other without walls. To feel your heart beat beside mine.

There is a silent longing in the crevices of my heart. A longing that stretches over ridges to find you. To sleep beside you beneath the stars. A longing to dive into the ocean of all we have been through and hardly spoken of. Barely touched upon. Parts of you I would like to get to know once again. Out of reach. For now. For the time being.

It seems you have more mountains to cross, to reach those parts of yourself that are willing to reach me. To let me in. To walk beside each other and gaze bravely. The way you do with snow. And the wild valleys and glaciers you wander through.

I admire how you do not fear them. And wish you were as comfortable with emotions as I am. As willing to wade with me through trauma and grief and all that we lost along the way.

I wait here. In the landscape of the soul. This inner wild. This space I wish to walk with you. A place we once roamed and then let be. When I walked with death and you left me.

But I am here. I am here. Perhaps I will always be waiting for you. Here. Between my lungs and burning. Perhaps I will always be leaping between our heartbeats. Waiting.

Waiting for you.

Love,
Zerzura
Kenya & Sweden

To the boy with brown eyes,

I hope you're somewhere that makes you feel as alive as the night we met. Do you remember? When we were simple, when we were just two travellers crossing paths by absolute chance.

Down by the coast, in a town unfamiliar to us both. Outside that bar, I'm getting some air, you're with your mates. Someone says hello and the next thing I know I'm looking at you as if you hung the moon and you're holding me like a missing piece. We break away from the noise, the crowds, and run, remember— we ran to the shore.

I wanted to see the ocean and you weren't sure why, but you'd have followed me anywhere. The sea had swallowed the night sky, too dark to see my hand in front of my face, but I could see you— outlined in stars. You carried me through the changing tides, I held your neck, you kissed me like I was the only woman in the world— and maybe I was.

For a moment.

I hope you're somewhere that makes you feel alive and I hope you still smile at strangers and say hello to the ones that look lonely and I hope you have forgotten me. I think, years ago, I did a foolish thing. I loved you. I left.

I'm sorry, it wasn't my decision. I think of you often and wonder what would have been if I had stayed, but god, I hope you don't think of me. I'm sorry I kissed you like you were mine. I'm sorry I never called. I'm sorry if I ever caused you any pain. If I had a choice, I would have chosen you.

With remorse,
THE GIRL WHO ALWAYS LEAVES
United Kingdom

My dearest, Ares,

You always expressed how fascinated you were by my reading habits; how I could get lost in a book no matter what was going on around me. I think you should know that I read even more often now.

For years I searched for words to describe how I was feeling in libraries, cafés, and bookstores alike, leaving no page left unturned and no spine left uncracked. I searched and searched until finally, I decided that if I could not find the words, I must create them myself.

We were both growing and I realize now that there was no way for the two of us to grow as individuals if we did not grow apart. Since then, I have grown to understand that I am beyond lucky to have spent each moment sharing a love as innocent as ours. Most do not get to fall in love like we did, I just didn't know that back then. I am so lucky to have loved you, even though your love still burns my tongue, like a much too hot coffee that cannot fully be enjoyed.

The love we shared was not tragic nor was it catastrophic; the love we shared appears in our favorite movies, poems, songs, and fanciful daydreams we created when we could not be bothered to be anywhere else; but the feeling of loss is present too. It is present in the way your soul aches as you get closer to flipping the final page of the trilogy you have spent weeks reading or as the credits begin to roll after watching a much-anticipated film. Having read the book or watched the movie, one gains an excessive amount of happiness, but in that same breath, the individual is left with an ache as the moment has come to an end. An ache that reminds them they'll never be able to experience this moment for the first time again.

Your love still stings, but I am forever grateful for the hurt because it reminds me of how alive I once was. I still trace the shelves of our favorite bookstore, wondering aimlessly, attempting to find my next new read, all the while sipping on our favorite coffee from the café below. Sometimes I see the ghost of you walking beside me. Most of the time it hurts, but even through the tear-stained glass my eyes produce, I get to look back on the fond moments and realize how much love was once there.

Leaving any type of love behind is hard, especially one as epic as ours, but the age-old story of someone having to pack their bags and leave so the other could thrive is very real and there is no other way it can be done. The painful irony of meeting the right person at the wrong time is a timeless tale that will continue to repeat as each generation progresses. Our ancestors did it before us and our kids will have to do the same, but that doesn't make it any less hard. It also doesn't make our love any less real.

So as I have told you before: I packed my bags and headed for the train to start a new chapter, but before boarding, I left my bags just outside of the door and snapped a quick picture. With me, I carry images as light as a feather, but speak for a love that could have lasted a lifetime, if only we had met in the right one. Maybe I will catch you in the next, but then again, maybe not. All that I know is that I am better for having loved you, but it hurts to know I will never be able to experience it for the first time ever again. You are still my comfort book with a severely worn spine, my all-time favorite movie that I can quote in my sleep, and you always end up on my top-played Spotify recap as the year comes to a close. Long story short, there is no me without you, but that's the thing about memories meant to serve for a lifetime, I never have to be without.

XOXO,
COLLINS
United States

P.S. Old souls and young love bring a lot to the table. But when you love someone this much, you'd do anything for them; even if it means walking away and shattering your heart in the process. Not all love has to be ugly when it ends, but it comes with consequences when you love someone this much. Their ghost haunts you every step of the way and somehow, that's the most comforting factor of it all.

Dear Grandpa Dave,

I know I was the only one to never hear your last words to me, or really even remember them. You were rushed out so fast, and out of my life so fast that I never got the chance to say goodbye really. Maybe by this letter, somehow, it could reach you. I didn't know the last time I'd see you alive and well was watching westerns. I know I was the only grandchild who couldn't be there, no matter how much I asked, I knew deep down it wasn't possible. I feel like I should've tried harder to see you before you left, but then again, none of us knew.

To be honest, I found a lot of ways to move on, my life feels guided almost by your hand, now able to move beyond your arthritis. You put in a good word for me once in a while, didn't you? I saw you a lot in more ways than before, I think. I met Andrew just before you got sick, I met another boy with eyes that made electricity jump inside my chest and actually, maybe, even replace those hazel ones I'd fallen for so hard. Brown eyes got me good for a while, I knew that was you putting in a word for me, because he had become a mystery to me after the first time we met last spring. I didn't know he would want to solve the mystery for both of us later on by becoming one of my only friends.

After you left, I entered a new chapter. My friends became quality rather than quantity, I received my new bedroom, I turned 21, I started to have the adventures I needed and fantasized about for so long. I know you had a hand in all of this somehow, somewhere - wherever you go. You sent so many little signs and wonders to everyone to say goodbye. I'm sorry I couldn't give you the same thing, but I think you're forgiving me by helping me get to chapter four in my life. I didn't know I had to say goodbye so soon. Part of me maybe knew, but then again none of us did.

You may feel like there's a little anger here in my letter, in the way my sentences write out. I learned that grief is a weird little spell. I'm a little mad at myself for not being there, for being distant. If I ever had the sense that something was ending, I would have done better. But I was numb for days. My feelings didn't know where to put themselves, my hands had thrown themselves into work that wasn't connected to them. My brain liked to think everything was normal. But my heart told me it wasn't. I don't really know where this little shred of anger resides, but it's buried pretty deep. I'm hoping maybe also by writing this, others would read it and be able to find some consolation in what I'm feeling. I tried to make it sound like a love letter, but to be honest, it's me being honest with you for once.

I used to talk about boys with you on the phone, and now it's like you're sending me them too. My mood ring turned the same color as the violets on your shiny casket, basking in the afternoon sun, even if I didn't know what mood I was feeling. I felt like I didn't need much else from you except an old flannel you used to wear, the same color as your tractor I rode in as a child. One day, I'll step up to that tall step again and we can go feed your cattle in another world where mornings don't end.

I loved working one more time on the farm with you. That was all I could've asked for, it was a dream I felt like I didn't get yet, and for some reason, the sun shone through those leaves, the feeling of crisp fall days was in the air of apples and cinnamon and sunlight on warm wooden walls. You asked me that day if I wanted to go to work when I was sitting on your porch. I don't remember what scripture I was reading, but I'm happy you interrupted me. Forever happy you did. There's a lot I can put into this letter, but it might get too long. I guess that, though you may become a distant memory for me in my younger days, I'll always have you around. You're not a grave to me. You're not a ghost. You're Grandpa, gone for now and will be back later like you were when you went to do chores. One day I'll get back in that field with you and step back into the tractor, and we can drink coffee and talk about the cattle again.

I love you, I know I was quiet about it a lot, but please know I do.

McCartney
United States

P.S. My grandpa passed away this summer, and I was the only grandchild who couldn't say goodbye. I felt really bad about it, and I was hoping my little letter could get past all that and reach him to help me.

Anu,
On the 15th of July I heard a love song,
It was you singing for me— my Mr. Wrong.
The smile on your face brightened the whole town
as if a queen had given you her crown.

That shine attracted me— in search of you,

I roamed and roamed the entire west view.
I was hoping to find you straight away,
You were just behind me by terrace gate.
Candles, music, the whole lovely scene
made me forget my pain– all I could do was gleam,
We both smiled at each other,
as if it was the first and last time–
never realizing we were falling too fast.
A few months back I was Mrs. Right,
but now I am a queen and you, my knight,
a knight that I called Mr. Wrong
who sang a song that was unfinished as the night went on

The 17th of July the lovers met again,
Mrs. Right on her knee to propose at end.
Yes, Mr. Wrong– it was me–
I love you, will you love me?
This is how the song was finished at last,
the singers were Mr. and Mrs. Wrong – together til the end…
Or perhaps, this was just my dream and nothing else
as the reality of our relationship was a threat
I used to join pieces,
I used to join me,
Every time when I call us "we".

The next day I find myself broken apart,
with nothing special inside if you are not in my heart.
Love is approaching me,
and knocking my door.
do I have the courage to open up and let it in?
I tell myself I will do this, yet every time I'm too shy,
in front of you, your friends and partners passing by.

I hate this feeling and I think, honestly, you too,
but I can't say this out loud even if I knew.
One day I will run to you,
and kiss you hard
not because I love you anymore,
but because we are apart.

I don't think you'll realise this poem is yours,
as you are not so incredibly smart.

But remember, it's just because we are impending apart.
Just because we are impending apart.
I don't know if I can ever tell this to you, maybe
one day I will send this letter to you in Westview.
One day, one day it will come.
That day my dream will come true
As you finally read the words *I love you*...

QUEENIE BELL
India

P.S. In many relationships, one has a dominant partner. Maybe they love you but you feel incomplete, feel suffocated in that kind of relationship— where you love them but want them to change a little. You want them to give you direction, but also some freedom. This letter is written by a girl who is suffering a lot in a relationship, but can't tell her partner about it for fear to lose him.

DEAR M.,

I am writing you a love letter because I know no one else will ever write you one. I need you to know how much you are loved and how beautiful you are, even if no one else tells you. But I know people say you are beautiful. I wish you could believe them. Because you are beautiful and in your own way. God created you and He made you look the way you do because He thinks you're beautiful and He loves the way you look.

To Him, you are perfect just the way you are. So please believe Him and everyone else who tells you that you are beautiful. Who cares if you have moles and freckles? Who cares if you're slightly overweight? None of that matters. We are all beautiful in our own ways. You are beautiful in your own way. If someone can't see that you are, then you don't need them in your life. Ignore them. Please know you are beautiful and if no guys think you're beautiful, then they're just dumb and don't know what they are missing. Besides, you don't need a guy to be happy.

Because as I have been saying all through this letter, *you are beautiful*. Never forget it. Don't be hard on yourself and beat yourself up, thinking you're not good enough, not pretty enough, because you are. You're smart, funny, beautiful, kind, and loyal. Anyone would be lucky enough to know you and love you. Please love yourself and be kind to yourself. Know you are beautiful. You are perfect just the way you are. I'll always be here to help you learn self-love.

LOVE,

M.J.
United States

P.S. I always get told that I am pretty or beautiful and I always have trouble believing them. I don't think I am. So I figured I'd write to myself to help me learn that I am pretty, even if I don't believe it. To learn self-love.

Society,

    can't believe I tricked myself
    into wishing the shoe would fit,
    when the raging fire in my chest
    demanded that I smash the glass slipper.

    Flair
    Ireland

July 21, 2022

Dear No One,

I don't know how to write a love letter. I don't know if I want to.

I'm too young for a lover, nor have I ever wanted one.

I could write to myself, but what fun is that? It's true, however. I do love myself—I'm modest… and wonderful. I would write to my family— my mom, dad, brother, and sister— if I were more talented, but I don't want to risk confining these people to a few heartfelt sentences.

They mean more to me than that.

I don't want to write about the love I dream of having. Or the thing inside me. Or my family's kindness, wit, and warmth. Some things are too important to talk about. If I were smarter, perhaps it would be easier.

I once wrote a poem that started like this:

among the things i hate
are the things i love.

And that, within itself, is as human as I get.

I can't write a love letter without thinking about the things I don't love. Everyone is always saying choose love, but it's not that simple. It's a choice we must make over and over again.

It's difficult. And brutal.

Choose love, but don't be ashamed for not loving everything. That's what I would say, instead. People are amalgamations. Our experiences mold our person. To say that love is the only emotion or feeling worthy of guiding us is to erase half of who we are.

Love is boundless, which is why I can't write a good love letter. Love isn't a piece of foil I can crush into a ball. It's not something singular. Why do we write about love so often if not to understand its magnitude?

Love is bright. It's so bright.
We would be fools not to reach for it.

MY OWN,
STELLA
United States

July 21, 2022

DEAR SIMON,

I wanted to write you a letter that I will give you someday, when the time is right. You said once that you liked my messy handwriting, so you're in luck! I just want to say a few things that can be stamped by time. Sometimes it's more powerful to look back and see just how early you felt things— like when we read through your poetry from your younger days. I really do enjoy that by the way.

More than anything, what I thought you should know is that you're the most important person I've ever met. You came to me at exactly the right moment (sometimes I can't believe just how lucky I was) and helped me along when I felt the most lost I've ever been in my life. Your kindness and care is something I will truly keep with me forever— no matter what. And you can be sure that no amount of time or change is gonna take that from me.

We met exactly 112 days ago. That's how long you've been ruining my life in the best way. I told you weeks ago about this unforgettable experience of leaving your studio the first time I saw it. It had just rained, we watched an old couple outside of the flower store, and when I came outside, the most beautiful rainbow filled the sky. I was overwhelmed in that moment with the first dose of hope I'd felt in a long time, long time. Hope that there were good people out there after all. That it was possible to dream bigger than yourself and still take care of those you love. You were shining to me then, and you haven't stopped for a single day.

I know it can be easy to chalk my affection up to artistry, muse, infatuation, or just a passing phase, but Simon, it's much deeper and wilder than all of that. I know what it feels like to latch on to greatness or follow a desire to be seen, but you should know I really, truly, and deeply love you. And I have no reservations about saying that to you. "You are what you love, not what loves you." is a quote that changed my life dramatically. I think I've loved you from the day we met— I'm almost certain. And although the reciprocation (if only) may not look the same, I am damn proud to feel this way for you.

You are kind, and gentle, and a fierce protector. You are considerate of all, still you know how to put yourself first. Your perseverance is admirable, and the way you keep kicking down the door of every obstacle is something I have learned an unmeasurable amount from. You are a badass, Simon. In all the true ways.

And this wouldn't be a proper love letter without important things like— how your eyes make me lose my breath even now. The way you belly laugh when things are extra funny. How your head feels in my hands when I'm scratching your neck, or the way you put your arms around me by the window. I dream about the delicate rings on your fingers and how the veins look going up your arms. These are just a few out of a million more I could tell you about. But the point is that somehow you've gotten under my skin.

I don't know where our roads will take us. And I do my best daily to hold you close, but keep my palms open. I am delighted to be near you, but you always have my blessing to fly. I will love you probably more than I will ever love anyone, but I will never depend on the return of that love. It's mine, and I will give it to you freely. It's stupid that I was so young when I met the person who would change my life forever. Raise my standards and make me— me again. But I'm so happy I did, Simon. Thank you for everything, always.

ALYSSE
Denmark

P.S. I met the most important person I will ever meet in my life. I knew I loved him the minute we said hello. For various reasons I'm not sure I'll ever be able to tell him how I feel, so it will live in this letter instead.

K.,

I miss you most on Sundays. Whether it's a song or a piece of a poem, there's so much I want to share with you. Have you heard "Almost To The Moon" by Daisy Gray? That's one of many I wanted to share with you. It reminds me of your music. I hope you're still listening and enjoying it.

I hope you have friends to support you in everything you do, and that there's somebody you send those late-night thoughts to. It isn't me. But I knew that, didn't I?

Back in January, I dreamed the two of us were at a festival celebrating life and death. You were with your friends, I was alone in a crowd. Like always. It was enough to be seen by one person, to be seen by you. Our phones kept cutting in and out. There were too many people, too many different directions to go, too many sights to see.

We committed the little details to memory. So many experiences we wanted to share with each other, but we were never in the same place at the same time. I wrote it down to ask what you thought it meant, but by then we were strangers. What could I say? How could it ever be enough? Are you working on something new? Have you learned to play the guitar? What songs are you listening to what books have you read i'm sorry i miss you i hope you're ok

C.J.
United states

Dear Expe fam,

I never would have expected the closeness that would be formed when I first met every single one of you. It was truly God's doing, one of the things I am deeply grateful for.

You are all a blessing. The love I felt and the freedom to be fun and young were wonderful emotions that I am forever going to cherish. The memories I had with you all in a few days are for a lifetime. I don't think mere words or even poems can truly capture the beauty and happiness I felt with you all. The food was a bonus!

I learned to be happy in the moment. To live life unexpectedly and to be flexible. To pack at a moment's notice and treasure the conversations made. To build stronger connections with every person and to go on adventures more often. You have all inspired me, especially in serving our Abba Father.

> And to you, the person I talked with on a certain beach...
> I am grateful for you as well.
> Wherever we find ourselves,
> whatever our story is,
> I am grateful
> for every moment I had with you.
> I may not be able to send you a letter,
> but know that this is for the better.
> Emotions did flutter

and I wish our time together
was longer—
Yet, we've been called to different paths,
for now.
I'll wait and so will you.
We'll journey our own ways
and we'll meet again someday.
Whatever our story becomes,
know that I'm grateful
to have met you…

RED TO RAVEN
Philippines

P.S. A letter of gratitude for a bunch of memories. ^_^

TO THE BOY WHO WOULD LIKE TO BE THE ONE,

I'd love you if I could. I'm sorry.

I see how you look at me. The little notes you deliver and hideaway in my books. The flower you chose just for me, yes, I know the meaning of it. I know you know that I know the meaning of it. You're clever and a romantic so of course you'd give me that one.

The thing is, you'd probably be good for me— and that's the worst part. You want someone you can hold close every night, who you can count on, face life's many problems with, who has eyes only for you, who you can dote on and give affection to.

Maybe I seem like that, maybe you look at me and see exactly what you want to see. A dream of a girl. A 'how could she possibly be real' girl. A 'makes me believe in magic' girl. An echo of a story I tell to the world— but what if I told you she's just a story? One small part of me and usually she doesn't win.

I'm a control freak, not in a cute way. I'm selfish. I want to be right. I want to have the room in the palm of my hand, but I don't want anyone to suspect me of being anything more than a wallflower. I want to be ignored. I want to be desired. I want to be adored. I want to be kissed for hours— but only kissed by someone who's inexplicable and probably a bad decision (and I want to be kissed well). I don't want to be held till morning, because I hate sharing a bed with anyone. I want to sleep alone.

I rarely want to be touched and when I do, I bite. I grip. I press. I'm entranced and demanding and after a few minutes, I want to be alone again.

I am part shadow and part star. The binary core of a nebula that is hot and cold and I could swallow you whole.

I can't stand when people belittle themselves in comparison to me (as if that could make me feel good) and I loathe being put on a pedestal. If you put me on a pedestal, I will jump off, I don't care how far the drop is. Don't you know? I fall in love every time I leave the house. I'm the last person you should want to be with, because I will always be enchanted by strangers. Intoxicated by the mystery, the challenge, the discovery of someone new and full of their own stories. I was never made to settle down.

You're looking at a woman who doesn't want children, doesn't want to get married, and doesn't dream of getting a promotion for the job I despise and finding herself trapped under mountains of debt to pay for a house in a town that I don't want to live in anyway. And no, I won't change my mind— so will people please stop telling me that? I was designed, handcrafted by the bad humor of god to be difficult, impossible, damn near untouchable.

Trust me when I say, you're better off giving your heart away to some other girl. The only thing I could ever do with a heart like yours– is break it.

THE GIRL WHO PREFERS TO BE ALONE
United States

NORTH CAROLINA,
   the taste of cherry lemon sundrop
   crushes on trumpet players and backstreet boys
   feather pens and bonne bell perfume based on a mood
   late nights on the trampoline
   soy sauce spilt on bedsheets
   melting crayons in the microwave
   laughing with nothing to say
   Carowinds and field trips into the city
   the Biltmore and the beach
   sleepovers that lasted all weekend
   the school newspaper and our first school dance
   I didn't realize I had a friend.
   I didn't realize I had a home.
   I said goodbye that summer because I was afraid
   you would see my scars bleed.
   I was too scared to be me.

   On summer nights, years later, when the crickets chirp

and the fireflies dance; I still find myself wondering...
what if I had stayed?
How different would life be?

STEPHIE H.
United States

T.,

Many times over the years, when I have not felt like enough, you've carried me, in your good and steady way. You have tenderly put me back together again when I have crumpled under the weight of the world. When I have felt like the very embodiment of disaster, you have shaken the earth to its core to make me smile again, to show me that I am not alone.

Soon it will be August, and I will be walking down the aisle in the blistering summer heat to your waiting arms. Only our closest family and friends will be in attendance. The birds will announce my entrance, the swallowtail butterflies dancing around my hair. My something blue. My something old will be the love for you that I have carried in my heart for nearly a decade now. I will borrow your smile, it will carry me through the hard days that inevitably come. Your name will be something new, something that I will bear proudly for all the days of my life. Perhaps an old-fashioned notion in this day and age, but I can't help myself. I can't wait to be your wife. These are the vows I make, to spend the rest of my years in your warmth and goodness. To do my utmost, reflecting them back to you.

To thank God and my lucky stars, the universe itself, for giving you to me.

A.
United states

P.S. A letter from a future bride, to her future husband.

DEAR TIFFY,

I hope this letter finds you above ground, and by that, I mean I hope you are not overburdened by stress or midterms, disease, or misfortune in general. I once had a nightmare, more of a waking dream, that you were buried underneath the site where Woodward used to be because you got left or trapped there. I never saw you a day after kindergarten and I wondered where you went, so often.

I would lay up at night, wondering if you were dreaming sweet dreams and if they included me, or if you even still thought of me. I hope that your habit of looking down at people's shoes has been put away indefinitely and that you are now looking up at the sky. Kindergarten seemed like a mystical sort of time, a place outside of time, where no matter what happened, it was filled with unconditional love, and this is a lot like most accounts of heaven.

There was one man who wrote *Proof of Heaven* that had to kind of go through trials, even after reaching parts of heaven. Like being in a dark place without light or sound until he found what limiting belief had held him there. It seems that God is always testing us. Although he is also always at our side, for after that ordeal, the man flew with an entity that was like a flying orb of light. He, I say *he* for clarity, though heavenly beings do not need a gender, was a friend to the man while he was soaring, for what in the human realm would have been hours, but the whole journey only took seven days. Where was this man's body you might ask? It was lying in a coma in an ICU.

It was quite the read and had been recommended to me by my friend Sarah, who was an aide to Michael, an autistic young man who was in my creative writing class as an undergraduate. Weird, how she had recommended that book when I had only just finished reading the book *Apprentice to Spirit* by David Spangler.

What does heaven look like for you, do you think? Me, I don't know, but I hear monkeys and see this house standing on the ocean. How you might ask, on stilts of wood, of course, and it's on a rather vacant beachfront. I also hear spinning and bells as if Mani wheels gave off this sound, though I know that they don't. I heard the wonderful cadence of tropical birds, though I don't think they were any bird that you would find on earth. It was ethereal, to say the least. I heard the ocean lapping against the shore once, the sound of ships and the horns from those ships.

It reminded me of when I was young and to help myself fall asleep, I would imagine— to the smallest detail— that my bed had become a raft on the open sea, strange, considering my fear of open water. But anyway, it was like my bed would rock back and forth of its own volition as I would be gently lulled to sleep.

Where in your dreams do you travel? I wonder where you would like to go? Would you sit at an outdoor table at some café, a stone's throw away from the Eiffel Tower? Perhaps, you are like me and wish to see London, and catch a tram, going up the narrow stone streets, surrounded by the world's literature. How would you take your coffee, two sugars, maybe three, if you have a sweet tooth like me.

The barista would pour a lovely leaf of foam on top of your coffee as you sit in Paris or London, taking in the sights. I could see you in an art gallery, looking over abstracts and Jackson Pollocks, maybe a Rothko here or there, like that time when I was in a restroom someplace and they had one of an orange square on top of a blue square. Sometimes, it is hard to imagine that that qualifies as art, but then again, I love Pollocks, and my dad only sees splatters of paint— or a big mess in other words. Whereas I see color scheme continuity transforming into connectivity, and bam, just like the big bang, creation is an explosion… or if you're my dad, a big mess… but don't tell him I said that, 'kay?

With love,
D.M.
United States

P.S. Letter to an old flame from kindergarten. She was my first kiss. She was how I found out I'm gay.

Dear Lily, dear me,

Summer has once again brought light and darkness close together, beckoning a period of reflection. This letter contains three parts. First I will write to little me, about the things I wish I had known before. Following I will put to words how I feel about things currently happening. Lastly, I will write to future me with the hopes I currently hold and the questions I hope to find answers to in my continuous journey of evolving.

Dear little Lily,

Looking back, I wish I could give you a big hug and tell you everything you are going through right now, will turn you into a beautiful human. I feel bad about the burden resting on your shoulders and all your were forced to face. You should have been given a safe space and the support to just be an innocent child and a reckless teenager. I know you're going through it, and at times you'll feel like you are getting handed more than you can deal with. Darling child, you are a sensitive soul in every meaning of the word. Your senses and perception are heightened and as are your emotions. You feel more, bigger, stronger which is also why things have a bigger impact on you and why you feel like the world rests on your shoulders.

Your parents are doing their best in the circumstances, with the knowledge they have, what they understand and the resources they have access to. Looking back, they did great in many ways, but in some ways they failed. Just like you, they are only human.

Darling Lily, your fear of doing something wrong and your need to be perfect have roots in how people have treated you and will treat you. It will both help you rise and be your downfall. If only someone would tell you that the image you are taught to live up to is idealistic at best and highly unrealistic. You are merely human, you are allowed to fail, to fall and to flop, as long as you get back up, learn and grow.

Dear little Lily, your heart is big, bold and beautiful. Your mind equally as magnificent, magical and ever mysterious. I know you have always felt a little different and out of place. This in part has to do with the fact that your mind just functions a little differently. As I have mentioned, you are sensitive, your senses, perception and emotions heightened. So yes, you are different. Sadly, people will make you think this is a bad thing. They will say you are too sensitive, they will try to fit you into what they need you to be, they will make you think you are the problem and that something is wrong with you. Trust me, you are different, but nothing is wrong. They simply aren't used to people challenging what is normal to them.

Because of this, you will be misunderstood often. Yet from time to time, there will be people willing to take the time to get to know you, and to learn to understand you.

Little me, just like everyone else, you will get hurt and get your heart broken, but you will rise, you will grow and you will find your light, always. From time to time you might be consumed by loneliness and darkness, but you will find your people, and they will help remind you of your light.

Dear little me, you are still learning and still finding your light, take your time. The darkness won't last forever, for the light resides inside you.

You are magical. You will be okay.
I love you.
X

Dear me,

As you are writing this, you are nearing the end of your twenty-fifth trip around the sun. You and I both know, on more than a few occasions we didn't think we'd make it this far. You have had your share of bumps in the road and people coming and going. However, you can be proud of the respect, grace and maturity you've shown in the ways you've been dealing with things lately. Even through the hurt, you try to stay true to who you are and wish to be. You are open to conversations and to learn from your mistakes. You are kind and caring, even to those that have hurt you. You stay respectful, and show integrity, even when the other person does not show the same candor. With the arrival of autumn, let that which no longer serves you, fall like the leaves do.

Let the light of summer illuminate you, so you can remember all of this through the darkness in winter until spring brings new hope. Just like Gaia, the earth, has her seasons, and Luna, the moon, has her phases, your life too, has different times. Remember this, for healing is never linear, neither is grief, nor growth.

You are both a work in progress, and a masterpiece, simultaneously. Shine your light, spread the joy, and stay kind, always.

You are a magnificent mind and a special soul in a beautiful body. Take care of yourself.

Keep evolving and always choose the light.
I love you.
X

Dear future me,

As I am writing this, I am nearing my twenty-fifth trip around the sun. I find it to be both exciting and daunting. Younger versions of us always thought that by now I would have a steady job, have a place to call my own, a partner and at least two children calling me 'mum'. However, life turned out differently and I went back to university, starting from scratch at twenty-two. Whilst many a soul has and might judge me upon learning this: I have yet to find love, experience a reciprocated romantic love and anything and everything that is linked to that. I hope you have found your equal. Your partner in life and love, your best friend to come home to. I hope you have found arms that bring you peace and walk with you in times of darkness.

As much as I hope the future holds love, I hope you find your calling, your way to feel fulfilled and your passion in life. For without passion, life is merely boring and mundane.

I hope you are ever as kind, caring, respectful and considerate. I hope the darkness never prevails in such a way either of those is diminished. I hope you look back on the next decade or so and are filled with pride because of the journey we have walked. I hope I get to evolve into a stronger, more fierce, beautiful soul unafraid to be true to herself.

Connected to every hope, as to every fear, is a question.
Will we find love, passion and pride?
Will we still take society in stride?
Will the Earth be livable for the long haul?
Will we survive society's downfall?
Will we still fight for what's right?
Will we still hold and spread our light?
So many questions whose answers have yet to be found.
As I grow, maybe in time I will know.

For now, I will keep evolving until someday when we will meet again. I will love you, until then!
X

LILY WOODS
Belgium

P.S. Things I wish I had known; things I'm proud of right now; hopes and questions for future me.

DEAR E.,

Summer is full now. The heat on my skin and the wind in my hair reminds me of everything I am and everything I am not; everything you are and everything you are not. Your leaving has taken so much of me away with you, I don't know who I am anymore. I am now as the folds in the waves, watch me as I break asunder.

Before you were here, I was blind to this desire. This desire that I would feel to the very core of me, making me question every single decision I had ever made and change the course of my life… all for you. I know too much now to ever go back to who I once was before your brief but overwhelming presence graced my life. And while you were only here for a short period of time, you have forever made your mark upon my heart.

I don't know where the seasons will take me, the chapters that are left to be written, but I know they will all lead me one day closer to you.

ELLE R.
United States

P.S. A summer letter to my heavenly daughter

August 5, 2022

DEAR T.S.I.,

I don't write on lined paper like this anymore— but I'm feeling nostalgic again. It's been a full decade since we've talked and I genuinely don't know what to do with this information. I do not know where to send the letters, why I keep up hope that your postcards will find me 10 years and a dozen moves later, or even how the words continue to bubble up from me so frequently and carelessly regarding you and things I'd like to say to you, when you've been away from me for so long.

I continued the countdown until it was 400 days past due because hope convinces us to do strange things— especially when love and friendship and artistry are ALL induced together. But I think you'd be proud of the things I've done— even if I couldn't find it in my will or heart to stay in school. And I know you'd be proud of how hard I've worked, even though you always said I shouldn't have to work so hard.

My birthdays still sting without you around to draw new things for me or to mindlessly play piano— because I never could learn. And I've tried to forget and ignore your birthdays, but I just can't. So I sing to no one and rewrap the same gift I've been waiting to give you since well before you left. Summer is too hot and nowhere near as magical without you around— but I still celebrate each new day burning at 100 degrees or more as a miracle— because it keeps me sane even when the weather cannot. And I miss you so so so much— you haunt orange juice and cinnamon and I'm sure there were other things in the beginning— there may even be more to come. But I still write and sing and paint and spread joy and kindness at any turn possible— because I know that is the contract of being an artist. I know you taught me so many wonderful things and I hope I was able to teach you some as well.

Anyway, this probably will not be the last letter, but I do believe this is the most important, because as I write this I am able to realize just how insanely proud I am of myself. Even if you aren't here to be wowed. Even if things did not go the way I planned. Even if my most frequent source of inspiration is indeed a ghost.

Sincerely,
BlueJay Baby
United States

P.S. Just a reminder that things don't have to go as planned to ensure success. And success looks different to everyone.

To The One Who Walked Away,
I can't tell you how many times I've sat down to write this letter, but I just couldn't. Maybe because it was too painful, or maybe because I was trying to run from the truth. When words are written down, they become memorialized, whether by ink or pixels on a screen. I think I thought if I didn't write it down, I could pretend it wasn't true and I could keep hoping for a

happy ending for us. But the truth is that's something you and I will never have. We're never going to walk down the street together, we're never going to have inside jokes, or share a cup of tea just to enjoy each other's company. I'll never know what it sounds like when you come home from work or how it feels to have you pick me up from school. No matter what I do, no matter how hard I try, you and I will never have that kind of relationship. All of my memories of you involve pain and disappointment. And that's not fair, but then life never is, I guess.

This letter is probably the only chance I'll ever have to speak my truth to you. So here it is. You did unspeakable things. Horrific, ugly heartbreaking things. You hurt me, you hurt our family and then you just left. I used to lie awake at night thinking about what I did to make you hate me, blaming myself for the evil things you did. Did you ever think about me? Did you ever wonder how I was doing? Did you even care? How was it so easy for you to walk away and not look back? When you did what you did and then just left, I was devastated. You didn't just break my heart, you destroyed me. You destroyed my character and my personality.

I became someone I didn't recognize when I looked in the mirror and worse, someone I hated. You destroyed my faith in love and trust and even myself. You made me think I was worthless and disposable. I let other men abuse me because I thought that was normal, because of you. Again and again, I found myself in abusive situations and I thought deserved it.

For so long, I let you hurt me, accepting apologies that died before the cheap daises you gave me wilted. As if that's what I was worth to you. Crappy flowers that died a week after you gave them to me. And then when you were gone, I blamed you for everything bad that happened to me. When I lost my job, it was because of you; when I was failing college courses it was because of you. When I gained weight, it was because of you, when I was afraid of a serious relationship, it was because of you. I used you as an excuse for not having a life. But that stops now. I can't believe I'm even about to write these words, but I'm sorry. I'm sorry I blamed you. You're not responsible for my failures. You were never the obstacle, I was.

I stood in my own way because I didn't think I was good enough; I didn't think I deserved true happiness. I've been punishing myself for something that was never my fault to begin with. But holding on to the anger I feel for you isn't helping me, it's holding me back. And I don't want to live like that anymore, I want that happiness, that carefree joy.

So, I'm going to let this all go. But I want you to understand something, I never hated you. I hated what you did and the way you acted. And I will always love you. I just can't have you in my life, it hurts too much.

Even so, I'm going- I'm going to forgive you. You have no idea how hard it is for me to write those words. I'm not even sure I believe them. But I'm hoping that if I see them written down and I read them enough times I'll start to feel them for real. And for now, that's all I can give you.

Hopefully, I can give myself more, something I never thought I could possibly have, freedom.

The One You Left Behind
Toronto, Canada

Dear S.,

I met you 10 years ago, and it was almost an immediate connection. I still care and will always care for you. Seeing you till now on a weekly basis still hurts and I always wonder if, like you said - we might have maybe made the wrong decision. It will never stop hurting. Maybe we are not good for each other, but I will always wonder what it would have been like if you chose me and if the timing was ever right. We never had more chances, but when we first did - you made the choice, and it wasn't me. You are gone now forever from me and the chapter has closed, I'm not sure if you ever still see me in that way, but I still do. You have spoken to me a while ago, and mentioned that we might be two people who are in love, but fate might never allow us to be. Do you really believe in fate?

I don't know if you seeing me and caring for me means anything special anymore. But I resent you for deciding not to choose me then. I resent you for not being truthful with yourself, but I still care about you. Do you? We have both supposedly moved on, but I am lying to myself. Are you? Am I happy? I see you and I think about all the things we could be. I can tell when you get close to me, when you lose your inhibitions here and there, but then you start distancing yourself again and I know why. You are now married. I'm not happy, I have too much baggage for you to handle too.

I don't think I might ever be able to get over you - I will never be able to tell you all this. You are lost from me forever, but I can only accept what we are now - supposed best friends.

Will you ever be honest with yourself? I will never know. But till then....

Love,
T.
Singapore

P.S. We met in 2012, we fell for each other and dated, but he went back to an ex. I got attached and then he went and got attached. Now he is married and I'm supposedly engaged, but going through depression and we work together as musicians.

To: the pieces of me,
   The pieces left on the side of the road
   for others to glimpse at.
   Perhaps a thought of caution for the commute,
   perhaps only simple debris,
   perhaps unnoticed.
   It is too common.
   The pieces hold a piece of me in them,
   a version of me is among the debris.

   Will I see her?

   D. Juanita
   United States

Rachel from Reading,
   Remember the time you laughed at all my bad jokes, you're terrible, so terribly good. Remember the time you laughed at me getting teased, you're terrible, so terribly good. Remember the time you always ended up next to me in the picture, you're terrible, so terribly good. Remember the time you shared your life story with me on the bus, you're terrible, so terribly good.
   Alas, it's time to end whatever this is or has tried to become. Since we couldn't be one, it's time to forever say goodbye and stumble our separate ways. While my tears are worthless, yours are priceless— so if you're ever truly feeling sad, give me a call and I will be there for you— as long as I'm not dead or being held hostage by beautiful Colombian women.

   Never yours,
   Loco Maulik
   United States

P.S. Two broken hearts that will forever remain broken

To the one,
   Streetlamp. Cherry trees. An angel who lost her wings.
   But what do I know of such things?

I am just a June day in an April summer.
Waiting for a love that never came, on a spring morn,
when snow still touched the ground. Winter loss.
Park bench. Shaded rivers. Leave me in a forest 'til dawn.
But do not hurt my heart.
For I am just a starless night with no clouds to shade my mood.
I wait still.
My love came, a July dame on his arm.
I saw her dark skin and flashing eyes.
The heat of her stare.
Are you truly? Or are you a fool?
I am a fool.
July came and went. My love is alone again.
How are you so sad? Rise and riser still.
Someday you will see
the white of my own eyes.
And you will know then that I have been waiting centuries to meet you.
Perhaps we met before?
London town. Empty floor. A babe who would not come.
Perhaps we met before… long ago.
Perhaps you are waiting too?
Gown of curling blue. Red hair that would not cut.
A fear. A smile.
Hope.
Streetlamp.
I am back again.
Light eyes. Dark crown. A smile to wash the worry—
is how I feel for you.
You are Green. Brown. White. Blue. Hazel. Cool.
You are water. Your eyes ever shifting in the sun.
Pink petals rain down on a winter night.
We stare at stars. Eat their light.
You are not a man prone to fright.
So why have we not met?
Streetlamp.
It grows dark and light.
I am in and out of dreams you and I share.
Come, love. Come.
I wait a while still.

Aryrejin El
United States

Rollno 68,

There are some people you can never forget in life and to me, you were one of them. One of the kindest, most chivalrous guys I've ever met.

I still remember the day you walked into our class as this neatly presented, polite new student with a clean uniform and well-combed hair— quite uncanny, yet unique for a teenager in my peers. And yet I knew you would be someone to make a mark, someday in the future— it was like you had it written on your face that one day the world would know you.

I don't think we ever interacted much more than colleagues in school, but you were impressed with my skills in math and I, with your quiet presence during math tuition class.

We both eventually went our separate ways, keeping in touch over social media and you and I both made our dreams come true. You continued to shine in your endeavours to reach the sky and I remained in awe of your ever-growing group of friends and the accolades you received in your life.

Alas, this year, when I suddenly thought I should look you up to ask how you have been, I was in for a shock when I found out you had passed away three years back. Such a silent exit, I'm unaware of how many people's lives you had impacted. I write this letter to you in the hope that you knew that I always admired you, looked up to you as a friend and such a great guy. I always hoped you would be the star you always were, you were like the warm sunshine which creeps up in the early morning and just makes you feel good, no matter how you felt before.

Maybe you were meant to be a star— one so precious— you were meant to shine, always. I regret not getting to tell you how I felt.

You weren't the guy who got away, maybe in another life. If we were great friends, I would have gotten to spend more time in your warm company. Your presence in this universe is very dearly missed.

I'm grateful if even for a bit, I knew someone as amazing as you and I just hope you always were happy like you made everyone feel around you. There's a favourite quote of mine from a favourite author, where we all tend to fear oblivion and yet sometimes we don't need the world to love us, we can be the world to someone and we can still be loved truly and deeply— even if it is by one person. I want you to know I think you were the world and I was one of your admirers.

I hope you are still shining, wherever you are.

Rollno 64
India

P.S. To the boy who I liked who quietly changed lives, yet when he disappeared, I never got to say goodbye.

To all the women I've loved before,

We weren't a fairytale, but I could've sworn we would be. I read every chapter front to back, but I always avoided the meaning between the lines, so I didn't know how the story would end. I find pleasure in knowing that I'm the one that cracked open your chest and showed you how to love again, even if it was only for a short time. I'm glad I could be your light in the darkness that you went through, but most importantly I'm glad you found your way out.

I thank God for sending me to you so I could be your temporary sanctuary for all the demons you fought against. I know it was hard, but I know you're stronger because of it. I'm proud of you for the generational curses you broke. I knew, eventually, you would. Sometimes I wish I could know the version of you now, but my heart is bigger than my body and that's my addiction love. What's meant to be let in, sometimes you have to keep it out.

So, I keep you at a distance, to keep the pieces of me that I have put back together as one. I don't resent you anymore. If anything, I'm thankful to have known you so I could know what love should be like. Maybe I'm the villain in your story, but in mine, I'm the hero. The woman that found herself after being lost in someone else for so long, in a fairytale gone wrong.

With Love,
Always
United States

P.S. Without the women that I've loved before, I would not be who I am today. Heartbreak led me to growth and for that I am thankful.

Lake Shine, my love,

Your eyes were beautiful to me the moment we first met. I know I'm breaking my own heart by pondering upon you, but somehow writing love letters is as healing as allowing myself to bleed out a fever.

Though I will love again, my heart may be forever tied to you, ever to be unbound, never to be unbroken. Though most days, when summer causes me more pain than winter, it remains inside me as the season of love is saturated in golden sunlight and put away with a sort of sadness at twilight's peak. Though my tears turn to summer storms, there's a weight upon my heart like the air before a storm hits, as if your eyes shall never lift themselves off my shoulders.

Be summer far from me or quite as near as you once were upon my presence, I hope to find a new love— but with your eyes like the river ever flowing before me, I fear the ink of my pen shall dry up with the length of me sitting by it, writing, ever writing…

Until this fever called summer love leaves me be, as dry as the sand we walked on once and may never step upon together again, in the days I now call nostalgia.

One day I'll put your name in my letters. One day I'll tell you for real, and not hide behind a vague ghost that people call a pen.

I still love you, as summer fades in and out, in the same way you seem to be within my life.

But somehow, I'll always love you.

> Forever to never be yours,
> McCartney
> *United States*

P.S. Yet another letter to Lake Shine. My hands needed to pen something for him once again, as they always seem to never tire from doing so.

Daniro,

Life didn't treat us kindly and now I miss you and your ocean blues. I still feel your pull on the string tethering our souls.

Oh, Another Place. Where our love wraps around us like Saturn's ring, where our timing is right and I can give you everything.

You are the greatest joy I have ever known. I know we'll meet again but oh, how my soul misses yours.

Space Pirates For Life.

> Your Nanmo
> X
> *England*

P.S. A letter to my best friend. We fell in love during a difficult time and had to part ways for a time. The Pam to my Jim. Space Pirates and Best Boos for life.

To you,
    It's like I've always known you.
    Catching me before I even fall.
    Somehow you saw me
    when I was lost in it all,
    the grief and feeling trapped.

The path to you,
it's like it was mapped.
The circles got smaller
and I could stand a little taller,
to be reminded of your light,
pushed in the direction that felt right.

Somehow I lost it,
the creativity I've always had.
I guess that's what happens
when you lose a dad.
But the way you encouraged me
helped me flourish.
I could owe it all to you,
but forgetting the universe is something I never do.

She led me to you,
no need to tell you.
You knew it too.
The feeling was mutual.
A magnetic, divine connection.

Somehow the universe knew I needed you
and you needed a bit of me too.
I will never not be grateful for you.

    KAYLYN MARIE
    Colorado, United States

P.S. To someone who helped me see the light inside me.

September 2nd, 2022

To someone who might listen,

My best friend's father died today, and in a way, so did she. The person I had coffee with last week no longer exists. She will never be the same girl that climbed trees with me and ran through the ocean waves. It's true, I know, people change every day– die every day— but don't you understand? She was her father's daughter, daddy's little girl, he was her best friend– her everything– and now he can't be at her wedding.

A certain kind of grief begins today, the kind that will never go away, more tethered to her than her own shadow.

I hope she knows, even if she can no longer hear his voice, or the notes from his hands dancing across the piano– every time she sings– his song, his memory, his love for her– will forever be remembered.

Callisto
United States

P.S. Words for a friend that I don't think I will ever be able to tell her out loud.

My Dearest Jay,

It's rumored that the human body completely replaces itself every 7 years. Whilst this is intriguing, it has been proven untrue. However, skin cells do completely regenerate themselves in 27 days and blood cells over 4 months; which means I have now undergone 51 cycles since you've touched my body and 11 cycles since my blood has pumped through a heart that was whole.

It's been 4 years and 71 days since we ended; and yet you still cross my mind almost daily. Even in moments of absolute nothingness, I find myself conjuring imagery of how you would have made the 'nothingness' memorable. I trust that over time this will fade; but for now, my thoughts of you are relentless. There's a saying: that *nothing lasts forever*, but I honestly think whoever says this is just scared it will last longer than they can love it. Because I know that you will never not be the one for me.

Our story isn't special. In fact, I'm sure the majority of love stories are a lot more mentionable and grand. But life isn't grand, it's a quick succession of busy nothings, filled with obligatory responsibilities and an array of tasks to complete in order to make the next orbital cycle run smoothly.

That's why I know this was love. Because our love existed outside the realm of shiny bells and whistles; impressive dates and expensive activities. In fact, most of our love existed in your two-bedroom apartment off of main street, at midnight on the beach, or in your car. It doesn't matter where we are or what we're doing, this unworldly and intangible 'thing' I feel, I know you feel it too. Every time I bump into you, it's straight back to 2018 and our unexplainable connection sparks right back up from where we left it.

When I first met you, it wasn't exactly love at first sight, it felt more like a soul recognition and a familiarity. Like, "Oh, it's you, it's going to be you." For me, it's still you. Two souls don't find each other by simple accident. I think our souls are cosmically entwined; there's no other explanation for what we have. If there's one thing I'm certain of, it's that we'd find a way to meet each other in another life, again and again. Never the same way, always the same outcome. In every life, we would find each other, every time; and I can only pray that in my next life I will do things differently.

I like to think that in another life we might have met under different circumstances. I would have been older and I would have learnt the thing I needed to learn before I met you. 1,531 days have passed and I can only dream of telling you about all of the things I've learnt and showing you all of the ways I have changed. I don't know what's happened to you in the meantime, but I can only assume you've grown and changed too; and as selfish as this is, I hope there's still a piece of your heart that has my name on it.

I always wanted a type of love that you'd read about or see on a big screen. The bold and beautiful type; both passionate and gentle, all-consuming. It took me a while to realise that these 'loves' always take a tragic turn first, and that's the precise reason they've become so beautiful and great. I'm still waiting for 'the turn'. Or perhaps, our story is just a tragedy, and no one will ever want to read about it. No happy ending. No ending at all in fact- for me anyways. But I will forever have hope.

How was I meant to know that my experience with you would be the most pivotal and shaping interaction of my life? I can't put my finger on any specific moment, but perhaps all 288 days combined amounted to this phenomenon. And that's all it took. 1 night to have me hooked and 288 days to change my perspective on life. About 10 days to truly feel and grow accustomed to being loved so purely by you. About 257 days for me to begin our end, and 288 days to ruin 'us' beyond repair.

You know when you walk into a coffee shop and immediately smell the beans roasting and perfusing into the air? Well, if you stay in that room long enough, your nose won't recognise that scent. I think that's what your love did to me. You were so consistent in loving me so fully, that I grew blind and accustomed to it. You were consistent, I grew utterly unaware and horribly ungrateful. Our type of love was the 'once in a lifetime' kind of love, and I was too young to know what to do with it. I was fighting my own battles and needed to be whole, before there could be an 'us'.

I'm sorry I gave up on us, and myself. I'm sorry for trying to love you before I knew what I was doing. With certainty, the next person I love is never going to touch the parts of me that you held onto.

I would never blame you for our downfall, and that's all that there is to it. You're not a saint and you're far from perfect, but the blame will forever lie with me.

On the glass-half-empty kind of days, I believe that karma has had its way with me, and I will forever sit in purgatory and be subjected to this insufferable longing for what could have been. On the glass-half-full kind of days, I like to think that it took losing you for me to grow and be ready for you in a future chapter of my life. That our parallel lines of lives have already taken a 1-degree shift in angle, and over the course of time, they will diverge and combust into one. On other days, I'm beyond content with where I am and believe that it all happened for a reason. You're where you're meant to be, and I'm where I'm meant to be. But I think on these days, I'm just lying to myself. I'd like to tell myself that I wasn't really in love with you; but on days I forgot to pay bills or brush my hair, I still remembered to check your horoscope and hope good things are coming your way.

There's a part that no one tells you about: even if you have supposedly let go, if you're convinced that you've fully moved on, there can still be incidents that will feel like a blow to the chest. Scenarios you couldn't have imagined in your wildest dreams that will make you lose faith in the process of healing. After months. After years. Sometimes a mere inconvenience is enough to tear our skin back open; whatever takes us back to that place doesn't have to be significant. It could be the most mundane thing, as simple as the first time I saw your car in town in months. Or seeing a look-a-like of you at the grocery store. Or when I heard another girl say your name. Healing isn't linear, mine most certainly isn't. I'd like to tell myself that I've healed and that I don't think of you at all; except for the times my nose remembers your cologne, or my ears prick up at the sound of your coffee order. I didn't think of you at all, except for the times that I do, and once I begin, I find it hard to ignore all of the ways that my body made a memory out of you. One of the hardest things you'll ever have to do is grieve the loss of a person who's still alive. I don't think this insufferable grieving for you will ever stop; these feelings will be ravaging my body for the rest of my life.

It feels rude to tell you that *I love you*, it feels like an injustice and a complete understatement. So, instead; I will plead with you to release me from this purgatory and allow me a chance to show you how great we could have been. I know you have a new life, and new commitments, and I know you're an honorable man; but your eyes have lost their shine and I can't help but think you're unhappy with where you've ended up. You have a choice, and I know every fiber in your being will tell you to stay, and do what's right; but what's right for you, Jay?

If this is all in my head I will understand, but if I speak even the slightest of truth, please, follow your heart and come to me.

We can run away like we used to speak about.

We'll flee to Europe and spend the summer frolicking by the seaside and eating romantic dinners while drinking wine as the sun goes down. We'd yacht through Croatia while smothering each other with affection and loving words, making up for all of the time that we had lost. We'd probably decide to stay because we fell in love with the country, and even more with each other. We'd pick up work in a cafe, bar, or boat and would work and live happily ever after, probably in a run-down country home in the south of France whilst our dog ran through the neighboring vineyard and our friends dined outdoors with us; and we'd all salute to love and life.

With you by my side, the opportunities of life seem endless, like anything is possible. I'd throw out my job, home, and any societal expectations in a heartbeat; it would just be you and me, and I know everything would be okay.

Consider it? Please.

You know where to find me.

>   WITH EXTRAORDINARY AMOUNTS OF LOVE,
>   R.
>   *Australia*

P.S. Let's runaway - a letter to an old flame.

BEN,
   My lightning rod,
   though the storm strikes all around me,
   you calm the chaos of the storm.
   Running effortlessly towards our love,
   leaving me breathless,
   lighting a path along the way
   to our never-ending love story.

>   F. WOLF
>   *United States*

P.S. This letter is for my now husband. I thought I would never find someone who would love me like he does, but he does. He loves The Flash so the lightning bolt was the inspiration for the poem.

To the dearest person I've ever met,

Since you are far away from me, I'm a little upset. It's the first time we are not together. When you left, I didn't know you were leaving forever, never to come back. You left without telling me. I could've come with you, but now time has only left ashes.

You left me alone in this world, among these fragrant vibrant flowers, but they do not smell good to me. I only whiff your memories from their bright colors.

You are gone. But tell me, how are you doing? Are the angels in heaven taking care of my angel?

Do you miss me?

If you do, don't worry. I'll come to you forever one day.

I still have our dreams to live for.

You remember, you wanted a big lavender field for us to spend our summer evenings. I have started growing lavenders and when they fully bloom, I'll come to your grave and place them on your chest. I know you will be over the moon after that.

It's raining here. The wind is cozy. Our room is relishing our moments. It's a little cold and I long for your warm hug. I'm sitting with your photograph, watching the rain dripping with our eternal love and writing this letter to you.

My eyes are dewy, not because I feel alone, it's because you can't make paper boats and I know how much you love playing with paper boats. Dear, I still go to our favorite beach and watch sunsets. They look a little drab without you beside me. I still make poetries and strum guitar at night. I still get nightmares, but I hug pillows now. When I wake up, the only thing I wish to see is your bright smile.

You know, the sparrows have come again and built their little nest in our backyard. They look so happy with their family. The library we always visited turns blue and yellow in spring. It still has your popular books on the front shelf. I visit it every day just to see you smiling through your books.

I know you are my most favorite author and poet. But now I read books by other writers, because you only wrote about me and now I don't like reading about me, without you.

You are now in the stars. You adorn the night sky. I'm so proud of you. Promise me to stay beside my moon, you know I love him, a little less than you, but still I love him. Our home is little weary. It had to bear a colossal grief, when it came to know you were leaving us behind alone.

I wish you come back home before I finish writing this letter.

It's been exactly one month since our hearts separated. I didn't cry at your funeral because I did not want all my grief to go away with my tears.

I want it to be with me until we meet again.

You told me my tears are rare, because you never let me cry. Sometimes I feel like ending this cruel, brutal life and then I trail in your memories just to remind myself, I have to live for you.

I have something written for you -

Even if you are gone
I'll call you standing
in the mist,
until the dusk and dawn
hurl me at the horizon,
I'll long for your love
even when the spring
turns into autumn...

It's me, your very own best friend.
I know, you'll never forget me.
because I was your rainbow you always adored. And I still am...

I love you and it's the 100,000th time I'm telling you.
Stay there until I come to you...

Your dearest best friend,
Ritika
India

R.M.,

I spent a year with you inside my heart and with tears in my eyes every day, waiting for you to come back. You didn't, but I'm writing all of this as a final letter, as a final thought, on everything that it all meant to me. To save for eternity how my heart and life changed with the seasons and how I'm thankful for your touch in my life.

It's because of you that I've learned there's light at the end of the tunnel. Because it was when I was surrounded by darkness and hopelessness that you fell from the sky like a shooting star, and I was struck by that light and fell in love instantly, and suddenly, I could see the brightest of futures ahead of me. That showed me that life can change in a minute, when you least expect it to, and that anything can happen even if I had no idea it could ever happen.

It's because of you that I've smiled some of my brightest smiles and cried the saddest, yet most hopeful tears, and held some of the strongest faith, because that's what you've brought to me since the first second I believed I could have you, and it was with me still, even when I waited for you day after day to be back after you'd left. Light, smile, a dream that comes true when you least expect it, even if I had to be in the darkness and cry for a while, I now had hope and faith.

It's because of you that I've grown so much as a woman and a person, because when I lost you I had to learn all the ways to be a better me so I could take better care of those I'd love in the future. It's because of you that my life took the course it did and two of the biggest blessings happened - I resumed my friendship with my all-time bestie, Nayara F., the girl that reads my thoughts and whose pure company gives me strength, whom I love and who is more than a friend, she's found family and I can't imagine my life without her, not at all. And while still searching for love I found it again, in one of its purest forms, in the friendship of this incredibly lovely and understanding American girl, Marina M., who become the honey to my bee, my best friend, who I love endlessly and who is and will forever be one of the most important people to have ever entered my life.

It's because of you that now I believe dreams do come true. Everything you meant and brought to my life through your presence was magical and all the tears and anxiety and suffering that your absence brought were equally magical. Waiting for you to be back, I had faith in God that things were happening as they should, and even though it all looked a mess back then, all the while, your absence was giving me one last gift. So here I am today, thanking you for making so many of my dreams come true. By showing up and leaving my life, you fueled me with the love and pain I needed to become a writer at last.

Someone on the other side of the screen talked to me when I needed a hand to hold and for that I thank you. Even if I have no idea who you are.

Mayara K.
Brazil & Japan

M.S.,

I knew it was never going to be love between us,

I promise I never tried to force it to be,
the same way you never forced me to understand your ways,
I knew we would end eventually, even if I didn't want to.
I saw you as the one that got away before you even left,
the one that would stick in my heart for years to come,
clogging up my lungs every time your name was sung,
I was prepared for those feelings to chew me up like gum.
but I didn't expect us to end in this way of guilt,
the mixed emotions of betrayal in the way you treated me,
the disregard of my feelings as you left me behind that last day,
only to be followed by an unpromising apology.
I knew it was never going to be love between us,
the only thing I had fallen for was your kindness,
right up until that very last moment when you said goodbye,
except now I fear my lust was led by my own blindness.

L.G.
Scotland

Dear Lucky,
I f*cked up. I didn't say goodbye. You didn't even know I was leaving.
You stand now in an empty house we never lived in.
But the truth is, you were never really there either. You were in a dream you created when I kept trying to click you back into reality,
saying *I'm right here. I'm right here and I love you.*
I stood as long as I could in this empty house, knowing we could fill it.
You deserve the world, you kind generous man.
I will miss you for all of time.
Find the house you are ready to live in,
I know now, it just couldn't be mine.
I'm sorry I didn't say goodbye.

M.
Australia

Dear Anam Cara,
The first time I met you, my body sang a song I had never heard before. Our eyes connected and I felt it instantly in my soul. It was freeing and

painful and I knew I would never be the same. The world I saw contained in them was far too old for someone so young. I began to understand the possibility of a soul having multiple lives in that moment. You smiled and I got butterflies in my stomach that have never flown away. From that day forward, I didn't care what role I played in your life as long as I could see you smile.

You weren't ready for me so I waited... and wow, it was worth it. The first night you kissed me I learned what weakness and safety feel like in tandem. It shook my entire world apart and scared the living hell out of me. You showed me my deepest fears and insecurities, and sparked a flame of courage and passion that burns in me eighteen years later. I'll never be able to tell you how much I wish I hadn't run from you.

I don't regret the life that I've lived, but I do regret that for a time, you weren't a part of it. I regret that I ever put your heart in any amount of pain. I regret most of all that I ever made you feel like any of it was your fault. Anam Cara, I never deserved the second or third chances you gave me, but until the end of time, I will be thankful for them. Still, all I want is to see you smile, because you have the most beautiful smile I've ever seen. I will always wage wars to keep you in my life, because I know the pain of having lost you now.

However, this letter isn't about me. It's about you and all the things that make you special. It's about the things you'll never admit to yourself. It's about the reasons I love you. Bare with me, because I know you're going to want to pretend that your emotions don't exist, but I need you to let out your closet hopeless romantic. That's the first thing I love about you. You like to pretend you're a realist, but we both know you're an optimist with a heart so deep the ocean is envious. No one will ever compare to you. Not the way you kiss, not the way you say my name, not the ease of the way we converse, not the feel of your touch on my skin. I love you because you are a blessing of a human. You are kind, generous, hysterical, and humble. You hate to boast and brag, yet anyone who knows you, knows you're worthy of those things. You are strong, intelligent, creative, and analytical. The combination of those things is so rare and consequential. You're gentle but you're passionate and you take what you want. You're so talented. If you gave yourself a tenth of the credit you deserve, you could be a Fortune 500. You deserve to believe in yourself. You believe in everyone else. You deserve to live. If there is one thing you've taught me, it's that surviving isn't living and you deserve to LIVE, Anam Cara.

Because of you, I know how to live now. I will never stop being the spitfire you admire. I will never again let the world cement my heart. I will be the girl who does cartwheels at midnight, dances in the rain, screams our song in the car with the windows down and my hair flipping through the wind. I'll be that girl because of you, but that's not why I love you. So, let me get this out. Imagine my eyes as I say these words. I love you simply for being you. No more. No less. I love you for the good parts. I love you for the difficult parts. I love your heart, your smile, the way you look when you think, when you're nervous. I love you for the mystery, and the fact that you communicate. I love the good and the bad equally. I love the angel and the demon equally. I love all of you, because you're YOU. I only have one last ask of you; love yourself the way I love you. Remember, there is no try. Only do.

T.M.A.
United States

P.S. The universe has a way of bringing us together, then tearing us apart. I am writing you this letter so no matter what happens you will always know what you mean to me.

To 2004,

The sky is the same— whether it's raining, there's sunshine, or it's just a day with gloomy grey clouds and this is exactly what I want you to remember years from now.

Dear little me, you've just finished your exams and I see you there, sad in a corner, wondering why your friends have been mean to you. Why mom hasn't listened, despite all the good things you did last year and in your glowing tears I see you. An older, maybe wiser, maybe more grey-haired— but a you— wanting to cross over all these years, reach out, and hug you.

My sweet girl, life may look sad and bleak now, but I want you to know there's a lot of good stuff and good people coming your way.

You will very soon find your kind of people who will be an answer to your prayers, you will also fall in love and be loved in return. I can't guarantee that you won't lose people you've loved like before, that is a part and parcel of life, the earwax and vomit in Bertie Bott's every-flavoured-bean bag, but you will find sweetness and warmth too. I can promise you this, the Harry Potter books will still be your best friend, and every time you turn to them you will find hope like you always do.

I really wish that at this point, someone would write to me too and say everything will be alright, but whatever form it takes, dear, it's yours— messy/patchy/bold and beautiful, your own little starry night you will one day look back at and cherish.

I want you to know that the sky will still be blue and bright, just the filter will change, and I want to be the one person who looks back in the mirror and says, *yes, you are enough, and even perfect*— for the puzzle pieces of your life are due to settle in very soon.

Keep your head high, cry if you need to— never hold it in. Give hugs out when you can and to the ones you want to. Tell the ones you love that you love them when you can in whatever form you choose to. It's okay to not feel okay on some days— your heart needs a break on those days too— but *live* and I promise, someday, you may be the person on this side writing a letter back to you.

I will always love you.

Yours,
2022
India

P.S. A letter to my younger self who didn't believe in herself and wished that someone would.

M.,

There are no coincidences in life as every step we take, has a reason. You came by to teach me, to remind me and to leave in your tornado-like path, love. You are love. You breathe it. You exhale it. You leave love under each footstep you take. You returned me to life, when I was just pretending to be alive, with a kiss. Just as quickly as you came in and left your mark, you disappeared. I have stopped asking why. I have stopped replaying every moment in my mind looking for an answer I will never find.

I have accepted that you came and left, leaving me with one of the greatest gifts I have ever received. I still find you again and again, but only in my dreams. I don't want to awaken from those dreams to find that you are not near. Your touch, your kiss, and your big smile linger in my soul as I feel you strum every chord in my body by just being next to me. Thank you for sharing your magic. Thank you for choosing me, if only for a brief time. Thank you for the happiness and sadness you left behind, which is now a motor in me, pushing me into recognizing my value and knowing that never again will I ever feel less than others.

Words of a secret poet
United States

P.S. Being at the same place, same time, and meeting can be a blessing or a curse. I am not sure yet in which category this serendipitous meeting falls. This chance meeting turned my peaceful world upside down and has been a catalyst in my life that I treasure, honor, and will never forget. I am thankful you came by. I am thankful for what we spoke about and shared. I am not sure why you ghosted me, but it was never about me. You. Be happy and may God bless your every step.

MY LOVE,
    I will never forget you.
Your blue eyes and the way they look at me
like you know exactly what I'm feeling
and we don't even have to say it,
because there aren't enough words in the English language
to express the warmth that comes only when I'm close to you.
The first breaths of morning air taste sweeter simply because
you exist in this world and now I've found you.

Words have always been my thing,
but you leave me speechless.
The way your smile lingers in your eyes after you laugh,
the way you play guitar and sing to me in Portuguese,
the way the world feels when I'm with you,
Like every street is the most beautiful thing I've ever seen
and absolutely nothing is mundane.
It's been such a wonderful summer sharing myself with you
and filling my body with pieces of you in return.
Everything you care about, I now care about,
your dreams have become my dreams,
and being wrapped in your arms has become
my favorite way to fall asleep.

It's only been one week without you,
but I can't stand this burning in my chest,
this weight of missing you.
Love and grief run the same,
so deep in your bones that once they set in,
you can't separate them from your being.
It's probably why they always seem to come hand in hand,
this extraordinary pain and this debilitating light.
The juxtaposition of having found someone
you're sure came from the same star you did millions of years ago

and not being able to spend your days in the magic of them,
because time and distance and god put oceans between you
and a million reasons why it's easier to just forget about each other.
But that's precisely the problem,
since the first night I spent without you,
after seeing your face for the first time
four months ago
you've been stuck in my mind.
The anticipation of when I will get to see you again
tugs at me in every moment.

You are so many versions of extraordinary.
You have a beautiful way of being exactly who you are,
that reminds people what they love about being alive.
I don't know what's going to happen between us,
but one thing I do know
is that you are absolutely
and completely
unforgettable.

J.E.K.H.
United States

P.S. A letter to the man I met while backpacking Europe. He made such an impact on me in such a short time, I'm sure he's the love of my life, but all the odds are against us because there is so much distance between us and uncertainty for what our futures hold and if it will align.

My (Ex) Soon-To-Be Engineer,

I am writing this letter to let go of all my remaining feelings for you. We both know that we cannot see each other and there is no way I can communicate with you without both of our partners knowing, but I am here taking the risk.

We don't have a formal closure, the last time we saw each other, I left you crying in the middle of nowhere with my stone-cold heart. I am not proud of that. Last time I tried to reach out to you, using a dummy FB account, I know you knew it was me because you also did that when you were trying to get us back.

I would like to say that I am very sorry for letting you go after two years of our relationship. It's been almost three years since that happened, and I cannot imagine what we would be right now. I cannot undo what I did and I know you will never forgive me for the pain I've caused.

I wanted to thank you for your efforts and understanding, I really appreciate all of that. But I am really sorry for being ungrateful, despite all the things you have done. I tried to be the best partner for you by that time, but I am too weak to resist against temptation. I feel like I'm a walking ticking bomb, at any time I could explode and hurt anyone around me.

I am planning to propose to that girl, yes, that girl. I wanted to enter the next stage of life. But before that, I would like to make amends with some people from the past, including you. Let's see how far this will go.

I wanted you to know that I am wishing you all the best and hoping that your dreams may come true. We may not be friends, but I wanted you to know that you are one of the greatest happenings in my life.

If ever one day, our paths will cross, I am wishing to talk to you.

See you when I see you.

YOUR ENGINEER
Philippines

L.,

It's okay love,

Sometimes we have a bad phase in our lives, sometimes it goes on for a couple of years. This is just that. I started this journey on a very self-righteous horse. I started this journey blaming the world and accusing them of all the bad, the good and the ugly, too terrified to look within me. I started by framing myself as a victim, caught in the unyielding, unforgiving thorns of the humans of the world. Too naive to realise that sometimes the monsters exist within. The monsters that are given birth, by experiences, circumstances and situations being repeated over and over again.

Somewhere along the way, I just started accepting that everyone and everything I wanted was doomed and that I didn't deserve it. I didn't deserve the happiness I had with you. I was so addicted to human suffering. And you, my boy, made me so so happy. So, I willingly went ahead and let my self-sabotaging soul take away the things I loved so dearly; my friendships. I revelled in the depression because at least I knew it was safe and I was so used to it. Just so used to it. The anxiety reached peaks and I felt more insecure (yes, a lot of it was brought on by my surroundings) but I could have handled it better. I could have snapped out of things, I could have let go or at least that's what I thought.

I was so absorbed in my own sinking despair that I didn't see how it was destroying you, the people I loved so dearly. I'm not entirely to blame, but I felt so helpless that I just didn't know what to do.

My friends and their hugs that once made me feel warm and comforted were ripped away, again. Destroyed. I was in ruins once more and not the kind you write poetry about. And I couldn't see a way out of it. I contemplated every decision until that moment and sunk into it further. I thought of death, but not actively or consciously, because there was so much I wanted to do and wanted to be. I wrote this on a particularly upsetting, but beautiful day—

> I'm a ghost of who I once was
> A wisp of air
> Trapped… but still not
> For now I'm free to roam and do
> As I please.

And it encapsulated everything so perfectly. Every day from that dark depth of a tunnel straight from hell is difficult, every day I find myself still waiting and trying to forgive myself. To forgive myself for what I put myself and everyone through, but after 2 years I've realised there are some wounds that are best left open. As a doctor, we advise certain cuts to be kept open as the body heals them faster (not all kinds of cuts and gashes, it depends on the depth and such). And much like that, I think every day will bring a different wave to either settle or carry the pain.

To make me understand that not all good is amazing and not all bad is the worst. That sometimes, to forgive yourself, you don't always have to re-live everything you went through at that painful time. You can just let it be and see how it unfolds in due time. That you can heal at your own pace, irrespective of what other people say. And no matter what happens or what has happened, I will always love you.

DOCTOR D.K.
India

P.S. It's a letter to someone I feel horribly guilty of disappointing, someone I can't move on from because I cannot forgive myself.

TO THE ONE WHO CHOSE ME,
In a time when all the world

is a beaming ray of sun,
I find your love is like a pearl,
unique is every one.
There is no love alike to yours,
no one so warm and true.
No river, mountain, sky, or shore
could near compare to you.

This beloved rose
that's grown from Spring til now,
will wither at the Summer's close
unlike your solemn vow.

You've loved me through Fall,
through Winter and Spring,
now you've made it through the Summer
and still, you're choosing me.

Much love,
Maddie
United States

Dear Diego,

I know this letter won't get to you so I'm laying it all out. There almost isn't a day that goes by that I don't think about you, trying to find ways to forgive myself, and let it go. There are people out there who still talk to their first loves. Not us, huh? My bad.

I remember our nervous smiles, outside of the high school after we graduated. When you stole your first kiss before getting on the 152 bus. I promise you weren't just a summer fling. The stars knew I was in love with you, even the universe around couldn't ignore it, no matter what people said. "If you were in love you wouldn't have done that." I didn't ignore those nervous laughs, unwilling blushes, extreme butterflies, first shot at true vulnerability. You brought the best out in me, cracked my cold exterior as no one had before. Deep down in my soul, you shifted me like never before. That was definitely love for me.

Being each other's first love was a blessing. Only we hold that title for one another. I'm the privileged one.

I'm sorry for the 30 millionth time for what I did. No one deserves that. But I will not let people curse the name of love, let it be rained on, for what

I did. I carry that weight— it's all on me.

I was 18 and didn't know who I was, why I did what I did, what I needed. But I did know I was in love with you, completely, deeply. I'm surprised my heart hasn't cracked completely open from thinking about you, especially when I wear that hoodie I stole but never gave back (which you didn't mind).

I sincerely hope I can leave this all behind with this letter. I still love you deep down, the strength it took to create this bond, too strong to break even after 7 years. You were too good for me. Be well, get that job you wanted, continue to love that girl in your profile picture, you look happy. Be well, Diego.

Yours truly,
Your first love
United States

P.S. Final words to the one that got away.

Andrew,

There was a day and time when I didn't think I would need anyone, when all I thought I'd need would be myself. Then came the day when I lost someone, and you were the only friend who came through for me. It's hard to express feelings through three-hour phone calls, or texts that sometimes go past midnight. The random goodnights that warmed my heart when I wasn't expecting them. I don't know how to thank you enough for literally just existing, so I thought I would put a note for you here and see if you find it. Now I want to share how I found you.

It was the last week I had when my grandpa was alive. I didn't know it then, but somehow someone did, some spirit somewhere. Because at the end of one of the worst trips I'd been on, at the end of one of the most golden chapters of my life, you crossed my path on my way home and I caught your smile as you walked inside your house after we said goodbye, after saying hello, for the first time.

I didn't know then that you were the first sentence within my new chapter.

I remember being nervous, and I can't believe how I ever could be nervous after what we both experienced. It was the most natural meeting I have ever had with anyone, how normal it felt for you to slip into my daily life, my little corner of the world, like a perfect puzzle piece I knew I was missing, but didn't realize it until I found it. Now it's as if, in my new chapter, you were the character to simply appear and fit perfectly into my plot.

You added light to a time that was fluttery with shadowy wings. It was so much light that it was to the point where I barely felt that shadow of death that had crept into my house. You helped me keep it at bay, helping me look forward by just talking to you. Do you know how much power you hold as a person, just by making someone survive with that simple spell? When my grandpa died, and friends somehow eluded to find me, eluded to be there for me, when friends began to disappear, when I grasped at them for support and fell through their nets, you caught me with one phone call.

That's all it took. After I messaged everyone who mattered to me (and everyone I thought who mattered as much as they did) you were the only one who called me the day I found out my first grandparent died, and that made you stick out to me. When funeral services and my first time seeing a casket get put into the ground finally reached me, you were there to embrace me, to talk with me outside that crowded church. To take me outside the wave of condolences, of questions, of meet and greets with family members I didn't even know. Of people I didn't end up remembering anyway.

Even though family comforted me, you held me up and were my rock during that trip, one I didn't expect to be on after just visiting my grandparents last June. The reason that made it okay to go and see death for the first time. Although it hurt, your presence with me made me see life despite that, a new life that was made possible afterward.

I didn't really expect to find a diamond amongst all that black sky, especially before the sun went down on it, but I found you like I found Venus glittering in twilight, just before the sky grows dark, hovering above the sunset. And just in time too, because someone was making sure we crossed paths before tragedy struck like night slowly falling and I was found without the one I wanted to help me through it. Someone knew, so he gave me you.

Your voice comforted me in those new nights of mourning, our laughter gave me something to look forward to every evening, and in the glow of my new bedroom I didn't know I would have the honor of ever talking someone to sleep over the phone and helping them sleep better. Of being there for someone in such a way that my presence would be enough to help them so much, and in such a simple way.

Of all the letters I have written to people, I'm hoping this one gets read by you, under my name, and I'm hoping it gets found. If one letter found its receiver here, in the letters I have written, I hope yours is the one that gets found, because you deserve to read this. You were my rock, you kept me afloat when not even my family probably could have done so well at it, you checked in on me, you reassured me, you listened, you were the real friend I didn't know my poor little friend circle needed so much. You made death feel more like life to me, and darkness was eased at the simple prospect of talking with you in the quietude of my grandma's empty porch. I have a lot of my life to share still, pieces I'm scared to talk about, unsure about, love about. Afraid for. But what made me feel okay about saying a few of these things was the fact I already felt I could trust you from the very beginning. I hope you can trust me too. Please know that you can.

As natural as anything could be, I think our chance of meeting was written in the books before either of us was even born, and I feel lucky to be a friend to you. No, I feel found, at last. By you. By whatever put us together.

I don't know how deep you can dive into things, but the depths of this letter will be here until you find the breath to do so.

>   Forever a friend,
>   McCartney
>   *United States*

P.S. I met Andrew right after my grandpa fell ill last summer, at the end of my last week seeing him alive. Little did I know he would play such a huge part in dealing with grief, in supporting me and helping me see life after seeing death. We grew in our friendship until Grandpa passed away that July, and Andrew was always there. This letter is very special, an appreciation for his friendship and how he literally got me through a very confusing time in life. I'm forever grateful to him and his support.

The three words I almost said,

For years the words *I love you* sat at the back of my throat waiting to come out, but it was never the right time. So, instead, I write it here in hopes that one day you might read it and realize this letter is for you. For the woman that I thought was the answer to my prayers. For the woman that my lips never kissed. For the body that my hands never explored. I always believed in angels and with you, I felt like I finally met one. Your presence was always like heaven. You had a smile like the golden hour with a laughter that was contagious and hands that folded together to pray for others. You had the voice of an angel and there was nothing more that I wanted than to have you sing me to sleep.

There was a way about you. A feeling that felt warm and a feeling that felt like home, but somewhere along the way you turned cold. We turned cold. We both lived with a darkness inside of our minds. Pushing away anyone that tried to tear down our walls, but we knew at the heart of us there was light. On paper we would be perfect together, but together our darkness would be too much for us to handle. I told myself that we were not good for each other no matter how much we believed in the same God, because that was easier than believing you just didn't see me in that way.

We were growing up. We're still growing up, but from when we were younger, my mind holds a space for you. Thoughts of you. Memories of you. Me wanting you. Thinking I needed you. We stayed chasing the wrong love, building a career, finding new friends, and creating a new way to live every day. I wonder if I'm on your mind at all or if what we had has been forgotten? A part of me wonders if I saw you again would there still be magic between us? Would the world feel like it stopped and only you and I existed? I wonder what it would feel like to be in your presence again. It feels as if the clock is always ticking with us in some way because we will always have an unspoken bond even if we're miles apart.

Some days I yearn to turn back time so I can be sitting across a table from you, drawing hearts on the sunroof of your car and using music to distract us so we can dismiss how we feel for each other. Months of spending time together quickly disappeared overnight and it leaves me wondering, did you ever really see me at all? Where did we go? Were we scared? I try to blame you over and over but I know we both vanished into thin air. I didn't know the sorrow that my heart would feel losing you to time, but I would do it all over again to go back to the night that we met.

WITH LOVE AND A WHISPERED PRAYER.
United States

P.S. For the woman that never got to hear those three words from me because fear and time kept getting in the way. For the woman that needed to know in this lifetime she was loved for nothing in return.

MY FIRST TWO SONS,

It's summer and I miss you.

The season's sun is sweet and slow and everything sticky and stone fruit and sentimental—and I imagine how it all would feel if you were here.

Do you remember our story as I do?

It was early fall when we discovered you. Now, sitting at my desk, nearly a year later, in an entirely new landscape of life set amid the season of long, lazy days, I recall the strange haze and bright joy of that time in the same sibylline way as I recall my dreams upon waking.

We didn't know it then, but in midwinter you would slip away. Under the full Snow Moon you arrived— as she pulls the tide, so to she pulled you, out of this world and onto another.

Spring came early in California, as it does. All manner of life tricked out of hibernation and the trees blossomed too soon. You did too— soft white petals, wrinkled velvet, delicate and reaching for life and light before winter's dark days had passed. We were out of tune with the seasons and you would not survive— your weightlessness like a bird's: hollow bones and downy feathers, born ready to fly.

I began weaving a cocoon after you left— a process which became an antidote to the pain of losing you, sustenance for the ache in the emptiness, salve for a mother's weary heart. Spring was all around and I spun the fibers of your brief existence into a space fit for metamorphosis.

I sat outside and let the sun sink through my skin until I could feel its warmth in the marrow of my bones, marrow I'd have given if it meant you might live, even if for just one sunrise. Does the caterpillar know the metamorphosis it will undergo when it enters its cocoon? I once thought it did. I would never again be as I once was, and as I picked up the pieces and stitched this world together, a sort of mosaic took shape. Fragmented remnants of life caught light in a new way, to reveal something far more kaleidoscopic through the lens of you.

Summer came and the chrysalis broke, unraveling at the edges as I emerged from the cocoon a butterfly— each wing a son, teaching me to fly, perhaps so I could see the beauty of this world the way you do. I suppose this might have been your plan all along.

Can I ask to see your faces again? Can I hold you just one more time, feel your impossible weightlessness as you lay upon my chest in that hospital room on a cloudless winter morning? I remember so clearly what it was like to hold your tiny, fragile bodies, newly outside the walls of my being and wrapped in a bundle of knit blankets and caps; to witness something so precious before we were ever meant to; holding your small hand like a feather between my fingers as I heard your aunt say that you have my nose and your father's mouth.

Can you whisper in my ear something that would give me a clue as to who you would have been?

Can I imagine just for a moment that you were here, perhaps one room over, fast asleep for your afternoon nap with summer's golden sun awaiting your waking, and I will open the blinds and take you out of your cribs once you stir from slumber? I think of how naptime might have been complicated by one of you waking before the other.

I imagine coming into the nursery and seeing you standing against the rails of your cribs, talking to one another in the language I learned twins will develop, a language unique to you. I want to know your language. I want to know your voices. I want to look into your eyes— even if just once— and witness that brand-new curiosity as you study my face and I study yours and our loved ones tell us who you remind them of.

What color would your eyes have been? Could they have been the kind that changes like your father's— dependent on your mood, the weather, the color of your shirt? I want to wash your new skin, untangle your fine locks, count the twenty fingers and twenty toes I would never tire of kissing. Would you have had my curls, been left-handed like your father? I want to kiss your tiny hands and tickle your little wiggling bodies and make you screech with delight.

I want to witness all your curiosities and listen to you share your world and answer all your questions, even the hard ones. I want to document all the funny things you say in a little notebook that would grow worn with time, a treasure I would one day give to you, but not before we read it together and laughed at how hilarious you both were as I reminisced about those early days, my nostalgic heart caught in the reverie of the way the years pass.

I want to watch your aunts and uncles delight in your personalities as you play with the dogs who find you a bit overwhelming at times, but care for you fiercely nonetheless. I want to see the unparalleled joy your grandparents have as they hold you, their first grandchildren, the ones who shifted their place in the order of things and made everything brighter.

I want to watch you eat your first foods and hear your first words— what would they have been? I want to show you all the beauty of this world and raise you to make it better. I want you to experience the way the sun glistens brilliantly upon the water before it sets over the ocean, then rises again each morning to shine upon the endless possibilities a day holds.

Can I be there when you witness the wind blowing through trees and hear the calming sound of leaves dancing on the breeze as the tall trees sway in that slow way that seems to make everything in this life so very simple? I want to let you stay up late just to watch the stars come out as the moon rises and describe to you what the moon looked like when you were born.

I have so many things I want to tell you before you move out but I hold my tongue— I know it will be hard to watch you stumble and fall as you find your footing in this life, but I'll watch you make your own way and be here for you always.

I want to witness the beauty you'd bring to this world, the places you'd travel, the memories you'd write, the stories you'd collect. I want to know who you would have become in this life, how your heart loved.

I wanted to give you this life and give you my heart and set you free to breathe it all deeply into your lungs before you flew away.

I'm jumping ahead. It's almost 2:00 p.m. and I know you'll be up soon, though I really know you're not in the room over, there are no cribs and the dogs are barking and it's okay because you're not napping. You're not in this house. We didn't bring you home when we left the hospital that winter day, you went home a different way.

It's late summer now, the days are growing shorter and the smell of fall is starting to settle crisp on the air as the sun rises later each morning. Nearly a year has passed since our journey with you first began, the seasons change with a nostalgia that settles deep in my bones.

I remember the air around you, the tranquility amid the tragedy, your peacefulness and the strength I witnessed through you that day— yours and my own. The leaves grow brittle in summer's twilight and dusk cloaks everything and I feel a longing for you; an ache in the place you once were that tugs now at my heart and I forget how to breathe again.

I wear your handprints in a locket around my neck and listen to the bells we hung for you dance a lovely tune as they catch the wind. I know now that grief and love can look the same and that can be beautiful too—as much so as any other brilliant facet of this fleeting human existence. Since you, life seems to radiate outward in all directions, everything richer with a depth of meaning far beyond what I could have known before you.

It's late in the day and I must bid you farewell as the last of summer's sun begins its descent below the horizon. So I tell you again like I've told you a thousand times before: I miss you. Never a day will come that you are not on my mind, in my heart, on my tongue. I will forever wear your memory like a heart upon my sleeve.

In my final breath I will remember what it was to dance with you beneath a setting sun. And there I'll stay, dancing in the fading light,

until we meet again.

Love,
The mother you made

P.S. Your uncle is planning to hang a swing down by the creek for you, a place we can go to remember you, to spend time with you, to imagine what it would have been like to hold your hand and show you the beauty held within the corners of this world. It's a hike to get there and I haven't been yet, but I hear it's the most magical place and I know you'll love it. Once he builds the swing and hangs it from the tree over the water, I'll meet you there.

Your Mother
United States

P.S. A love letter from a mother to her stillborn sons.

September 21, 2022

Dear Sunshine,

This is the first & last time I'll write your nickname in a letter. You're married now to the first girl you dated after me. I thought it would hurt more to see your wedding photos on Facebook but you were already a stranger by then. I didn't even wish you a happy birthday because I knew you wouldn't answer what you're up to. You stopped years ago.

You can be such a jackass to me, which hurt more because you were already thousands of miles away from me. I remember how you said you wouldn't read a book despite knowing how it'd be good for you. Despite knowing how much I love to read. Why choose to be cruel to someone who cares about you so much? I just wanted to be with you & instead, you make our far too little time together into a cruel joke. I hope you treat your wife a hell of a lot better than you did me. Oh God, I'm tearing up now and I thought that was long over.

Still, I truly want you and her to be happy together. To support each other and have many milestones & so much growth. To love the way I wish I got to love you. I've only seen you face to face the first day we met. How I long to know your lips, your touch, my head laying on your bare chest. Maybe it would hurt more to let you go if I knew your taste, but not ever feeling your hand in mine still lingers too long.

For a brief moment, you wanted us to work— to take flights in turns, to help me grow. And I know you were sincere. That's a gift no one has ever given me and I'm working on myself to feel the same for someone else. I think I could've helped you too— to love you when you get suicidal & hopeless. Encourage you & aid you in finding your passion. Reassure your parents that you will be safe & happy if they're gone. I know your wife will do all of this and more. At least I hope so, I don't know her.

I wonder if you think of me or read my posts that you always say were too long, haha. I hope you don't have regrets about me. I can honestly say I don't have any for you— thoughts, but no urges to turn back the clock.

May your Tomorrows hold more promise than our Yesterdays.

Eileen
United States

P.S. A letter to someone she met the night before she took a flight home thousands of miles away. To someone she's never seen in person again. He asked her if he could online date in their own area and she said yes; he ended up marrying the first and only girl he met there. This letter is a farewell to him and her bitterness and a way to finally move on.

Dance with me...

We thought the song would never end. We never thought the lake would get cold, the ground would harden, snow would replace the sand, or the sun would go into hiding. Somehow, we convinced ourselves we were inseparable, invincible and infinite for those 3 minutes and 29 seconds. It was inconceivable to think our world could end when in truth, we won't ever be able to listen to *If the World Was Ending* after tonight. Holding you so close I could see right to your soul, and you, mine. 3 minutes & 29 seconds was just long enough to know, long enough for our hearts to drop, long enough to feel that something in us will never be the same. Dance with me.

You're a pastor's boy, and I'm a wild card. You are pure, whole, and radiate light. I am a tainted mess, already ruined by a life of trauma. While you walk confidently with carefree joy, I am trying to catch glimpses of sunlight in the breaths between the waves of darkness that seem determined to drown me. We are the exact opposite of everything, yet we found ourselves rooted in one another's arms; which was nothing short of a miracle, even for love, the most incomprehensible & seemingly miraculous force of all. We were completely oblivious to all the sparkling potential we held, but something about us felt right; like when you sip coffee at the perfect temperature— an occasional moment of magic. Dance with me.

Because when this song ends, we may never see each other again. When the dark sky turns light, we will pack our bags, double check our bunkbeds & corners of the cabin. We will go on one last walk around the campgrounds, taking in the morning breeze, the air still heavy from last night's rainfall. As though the sky were mourning us too, cleansing the ground for the next pair of ill-fated lovers. We will hug the new friends we've made tightly, promising to text & write & call. But as for us, we will only make brief eye contact before my taxi door gets slammed shut and you board the bus. Just long enough to, long enough for our hearts to drop, long enough to be the only thing on our minds through the breathless dash across airport terminals, luggage check-ins, & security scans to catch separate flights. Dance with me.

Until we're strapped in our seats, defying gravity way above the clouds, it is only then will we realize that we haven't been able to breathe properly since last night, because all we can think about is how we promised to never think about each other ever again. To never think about the way your eyes saw right through to my soul. To never think about the melodious tune of your voice & how the eloquent flow of your words made me feel sane. The way your lips held mine, the way our hips aligned. Your hands on me & all over me. To never think about how we didn't have a reason to say goodbye in the forever of 3 minutes & 29 seconds. Dance with me.

You'll go on to be a doctor & I might find my way someday, sitting on a patio a world away, sipping morning cold brew coffee at a French café. Be safe, be true, & I'll think of you. I'll think of you and look down at the scar on my foot, the one I haven't thought about in a decade. The one you gave me when you bumped into me & dropped your switchblade. I'll swear in that moment I could see your eyes; the instant of reminiscence will be just long enough for me to know, long enough for my heart to drop, long enough to remember everything. How different life is now, yet nothing has changed. You've always been, & you are still my favorite scar. Dance with me.

After all these years, have you ever felt more alive than we did that night under the starlit sky? What I would do to go back to the place where we shined so bright, where our fears were irrelevant, where we were undeniably larger than life. There is no guarantee that our paths will cross again, or that our souls will ever be able to see the light. So, hold me like you mean forever, like the world itself is ending, & dance with me.

C. Le

P.S. I've written another unsent letter, & I think this is the last one…

An Afterthought

Thank you, my darling, for reading. For holding these letters in your hands and for listening to their honesty, hopefulness, and heartache. I'd like to think they have offered you some solace, understanding, or even a sense of togetherness. I hope, maybe, a particular letter has reached you in a way nothing else has, as if it was written just for you (because maybe it was.)

As this book comes to an end, I have one last unsent love letter left to share. This is a final letter written by C. Le, intended as a goodbye. It seemed fitting to be our goodbye to you.

Before you go, I invite you to turn the page again, and write your own unsent love letter. Become a part of this collection. Let your words be kept company by so many others. I promise, your unsent love letter will be safe here.

May you close this book with a sense of release. May you view the world with a new perspective on what others around you may be going through and carry with you the idea that kindness is essential. And above all— may you place this book on your shelf with a deep knowing that you are not alone.

Rachel Clift

April 2021

To the person who feels like home,

If love is all you needed... but darling, love isn't all you need. If it was, if only it was. God, I wish it was.

If love was enough, I would be halfway across the world dancing with you in fields of marigolds, putting a flower in your hair, running across moonlit beaches, & strolling through narrow streets with our fingers interlocked.

I would be cooking your favourite meal, waiting for you to come home from the farmer's market. Home. Where the afternoon sunlight streams through the windows, smiling on oak floors, white furniture, & messy sheets. I would be twirling honey, glowing in the sunlight, and looking exactly like your eyes. The golden nectar dripping slowly over lemon tea. In the back, the whistle of a kettle and its steam, like white flowers in full bloom, disappearing as quickly as it fills the space. I would get butterflies as I hear you come through the door, the rustle of paper bags, & the familiar sound of your keys. I would feel liquid gold running through my veins. Spreading a smile I can't resist— the kind that comes from the inside.

I would be on my toes, calves flexed as you pull me in close. Our eyes widening, realizing that we fit perfectly into each other every time like it's the first time.

Smiling. Laughing. Deeply. In love with you. With one arm wrapped around your neck and the other around your waist, like my mind has been wrapped around you ever since you left.

You left me holding all this love. And I wonder if it's worse than never knowing love at all. Maybe. Because I miss you still. And I'll miss you every single day. But then I think of you, and all I am with you is home. And all I can see is sunlight. I can taste the honey infused lemon tea. I can hear the crinkle of paper bags. I can feel liquid gold spreading through my veins. And I can promise my hands that they'll get to hold you again.

Maybe we can't go back to who we were, and though we no longer exist in the same world, I will always miss the adventures we would've gone on and all the love we would've shared, and I will always dream of a future with you. One where love would've lasted to the end of time and the first time we kissed would've been a toast to the beginning of life. In a world where love is all you needed, I would be on my way to you. I am on my way to you, and all I know is that I can't wait to meet you there.

C. Le

WRITE YOUR OWN UNSENT LOVE LETTER HERE

Acknowledgements

In the year it took to bring this anthology to life, hours of dedication poured into the creation of it. Thank you to each and every person who helped me in the process of publishing this collection. My family was a constant voice of encouragement and support. T.L.C., Sarah Jeannine, and C. Le assisted with copy editing the manuscript. Laura, Angela, Morgana, Leigh, Vanessa, Nicholas, Danica, Lauren, Sarah, and Olivia offered insight and reassurance during the long nights and many obstacles. C. Le coined the term *unsent love letter* and sent the first one to me through the post in 2020, inspiring this project. This book would not exist without her. The 200+ anonymous writers featured in this book retain all credit and copyright to their own individual letter(s). I have published their letters by the written permission of each author. Thank you for trusting me with your words.

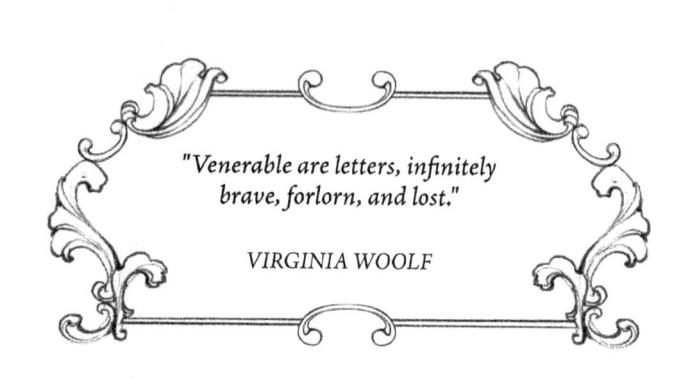

"Venerable are letters, infinitely brave, forlorn, and lost."

VIRGINIA WOOLF

CPSIA information can be obtained
at www.ICGtesting.com
Printed in the USA
LVHW112026050123
736471LV00004B/756